Deviant

Jeremy Bamber and the White House Farm Murders

Paul Harrison

Vertical Editions
www.verticaleditions.com

First published in the United Kingdom in 2015 by Vertical Editions, Unit 4a, Snaygill Industrial Estate, Skipton, North Yorkshire BD23 2QR

www.verticaleditions.com

ISBN 978-1-904091-92-9

A CIP catalogue record for this book is available from the British Library

Cover design by HBA, York

Printed and bound by Jellyfish Solutions Ltd, Swanmore

Dedicated to my two wonderful children, Paula and Mark, who I have greatly missed. Your Dad is back!

Contents

The Furies – the Three Goddesses of Vengeance:

Tisiphone (avenger of murder), Megaera (the jealous) and Alecto (constant anger)

They are the daughters of the night

Without mercy, the Furies would punish all crime

They would strike the offenders with madness

The worst of all crimes were patricide or matricide

First and foremost the Furies would punish this crime above all others

Horrible to look at, the Furies had snakes for hair and blood dripping from their eyes

Prologue

This isn't simply another book on the White House Farm murders of 1985, nor is it just a record of my personal opinions, or a stick to attack the Criminal Justice System with. This is the story of the White House Farm murders compiled mainly in the words of those involved: detectives, friends and Jeremy Bamber himself. Not my words but their own, discussed during many private interviews and in letters and telephone calls. I attended the trial of Jeremy Bamber as nothing more than an interested young police officer and crime historian. I wasn't from Essex and didn't police Essex. I lived there for over a decade, though in truth I didn't feel at home there as my strong northern accent and passion for Leeds United didn't sit well with some of the Essex football community. But despite having opposing football allegiances we always managed to shake hands and stand a drink at the bar until the next time.

Looking back, I have traversed a horrific journey in bringing this work to completion and undoubtedly I've upset many people along the way. Never in all my crime writing career have I encountered so much nastiness and offensive behaviour from a small group of individuals – cyber bullies who willingly associate themselves with this case and use it to satiate and pursue their own personal vendetta against the system and people who dare speak out in opposition to their beliefs. I've encountered an officer in the Essex Police Data Protection Unit who made unfounded assumptions about me, a barrister made false accusations against me, I have been maligned by the Jeremy Bamber Campaign team for being what they term a 'betrayer' and so excommunicated, I have endured character assassination and had deliberate lies published on the internet about me.

Some of what has been said comes from the keyboards of convicted (time served) criminals who clearly have a grudge to bear against the Criminal Justice System because they were caught out by it. I've also seen instances of people who gave testimony and evidence or voiced an opinion on the case being harassed and intimidated by Bamber disciples, and in one instance a single mother was so frightened by a Bamber supporter that she claims she had to move house. In addition I have received countless threatening letters and emails and one threatening my life and telling me that Jeremy is watching me! There was a period of time when I feared for my own safety and that of my family, so harsh and personal were the threats. The police response when I discussed the situation with them wasn't great or supportive, 'you play in the bear pit, you deal with the consequences of the bear pit' in other words, you write about murderers so you deal with the dirt that associates itself with their crimes ... nice! To gain some protection I went public with the threats in a national newspaper which effectively forced the culprit to stop, and no further threats were received thereafter. On one internet forum I've been proclaimed dead and on the same forum of not existing at all! So it's with some satisfaction that this journey has ended with the publication of the book – even though it has not been a pleasurable book to write.

An altogether seedier element of society seems to have attached itself to this crime, more so than any other case I have researched or investigated. I hasten to add that not all those involved are of such a dubious moral standing, there are some excellent researchers and sensible debaters among these groups. People whose research I would rely on and whose opinion I respect. It's been hell, but throughout I remained resilient in my aim to publish my research and findings despite the deliberate obstructions that were thrown at me.

In this book I examine what has been claimed to be potentially the most incompetent murder investigation ever carried out by a professional British police force since policing records began. Essex Police, like so many forces, have a chequered past when their handling of some criminal investigations come under scrutiny. As will be shown in this work, the initial stages of a criminal investigation are all important – make a mess of the initial crime scene and investigators are forever chasing their own tails in an attempt to put things right.

One can be forgiven for believing that by the mid-1980s the police would have mastered the art of catching criminals, particularly murderers. I will let the reader cast judgment on the professionalism of the Essex Police Force during what can only be described as one of the vilest murders ever committed in Essex. In Tolleshunt D'Arcy, an entire family was slain; shot dead at point-blank range by a cowardly executioner in the dead of night where most of the victims offered no resistance having retired to the sanctuary of their beds much earlier. Two of the victims were sleeping children. Whichever way the details are conjured to appear, it was a heartless, cold blooded act driven by pure greed. It's 30 years since the crime occurred, yet it remains one of the worst murders to have been committed in the United Kingdom. Those who choose to recall the crimes still recoil in horror when one mentions the name Jeremy Bamber. His name is recognised as that of a pariah who not only bled his family of their finances but their lives also. More damningly, many refer to him as 'the child murderer', the ultimate symbol of all that is evil. The term evil is not used lightly in criminal court proceedings, yet it was a detail eloquently highlighted by the trial judge during his summing up when he referred to Jeremy Bamber as 'evil beyond belief'. The crimes were bad enough, but the act itself defies all rational reasoning. The killer was never certified insane, nor was he unfit to stand trial; he was from the outset, devious and manipulative, issues I firmly believe remain with him to this day.

I know from my own police experience that when a suspect is convicted of a serious crime in a court of law and is 'sent down' for life, there is a huge sense of relief among investigators, prosecutors and police officers, especially so when the crime involves child victims. I know that in 1986, Essex Police felt elated that Bamber had been dispatched to prison and was never likely to again enjoy any freedom that could permit him to hurt another living soul. 'It was a job well done,' one of the officers involved in the investigation told me. But was it really?

It's no secret that the investigation that led to the conviction of Jeremy Bamber has forever been regarded as a farce, 'a circus played out in the big top' as another retired officer described it. A circus it was and so it remains, with doubt, suspicion, conspiracy and subterfuge being an integral part of each ongoing performance. It should be said that neither the circus nor the accompanying farce are the sole property of the police or authorities. These bodies are bit-part players in every act, which is enthusiastically re-enacted on public internet forums by a tiny group of fanatics and followers of Jeremy Bamber who mostly believe his claims to innocence and his subsequent wrongful imprisonment. Others simply follow and thrive upon the countless dubious tales of conspiracy, mass governmental cover-ups and police corruption. Many condemn those who disagree with their often bizarre and puerile claims and theories. These fanatics are little more than disciples of the man who, to my mind, orchestrates and controls almost every aspect of the case – circus ringmaster extraordinaire Jeremy Bamber! Unfortunately for him, his disciples are damaging and undermining both his claims and the genuine work of his campaign team.

So, the tragedy continues to be played out and the circus ringmaster continues to manipulate every act from within a secure prison with the goal being to gain his freedom. It may come as a surprise that despite being incarcerated, Bamber still has the ability to carefully orchestrate the flow of information that appears in the media or public domain about him. Not many prisoners – let alone mass murderers – can claim to have their own internet blog, their own website, and even two forums that are largely dedicated to the crimes. Furthermore, Bamber has his own campaign team which, through clever propaganda, protects and defends his character at all costs. It certainly achieves one thing, it keeps the name of Jeremy Bamber in the public domain despite many people viewing it as a contemptuous waste of public funds, allowing case reviews and appeals to take place that bring no new evidence to the table. Sadly, as enthusiastic and loyal as his campaign team are, to date they have not been able to produce one piece of evidence that proves Jeremy Bamber's innocence. 30 years on it has to be asked whether such evidence to support that belief actually exists. Most recently Bamber himself said he was innocent but couldn't prove it, I would suggest that he never will, not because such evidence has been buried or hidden by the authorities, but because it doesn't physically exist and it never has. Jeremy Bamber alone knows the truth of what happened at White House Farm in August 1985, yet he can never reveal it since it would finally expose him as the killer and ultimately, through his protracted claims of innocence, a deceitful fraud too.

So why write this book you may ask? My own research into this case dates back to 1985 and my personal attendance as a spectator at the 1986 trial in Chelmsford. My interest wasn't a sanguinary one, it was aroused because then I was a serving policeman, and like countless police officers across England and Wales I found myself deployed on Campaign for Nuclear Disarmament (CND) demonstration duties at such far flung (from my northern home) locations as RAF Greenham Common and RAF Molesworth. Together, as a team of police officers, we patrolled dozens of miles of perimeter fence, thus preventing incursions by demonstrators. I found it mind numbingly boring, but both me and my canine best friend – I was a dog handler at the time – did all we could to keep ourselves focused on the task in hand. I was very much aware that my police dog 'Jaffa' missed nothing – certainly no criminal was likely to get past him or bypass his attention!

It was a particularly unpleasant environment in which to work as protecting weapons of mass destruction was never my idea of what policing was about. It felt as though we had become the enemy of the people and we were protecting politicians and governments and not fighting crime in communities. Every so often when on our foot patrols, we would meet up with other police officers and stop and chat around wood-filled oil drums that had been given a fresh lease of life and transformed into braziers. It was during such times that I began to question the genuineness of the Criminal Justice System, as day after day and night after night with little else to occupy our minds, we would openly talk of how good or bad individual forces and officers were and how weak leadership at the top and the poor policing methods adopted by some forces were far too prevalent. This led to my professional intrigue being aroused by the investigation into the murders at White House Farm and thus I committed years of private research into the case, and all of the proceedings that followed. I hasten to add that at no point did I have any personal interest in Jeremy Bamber, or proving his innocence. Over the years I've seen enough culpable criminals in the dock claiming they are not guilty, I know that Bamber is another of a long line of criminals who won't accept responsibility for their actions, these people believe the crime was always the fault of someone else, and you guessed it, he claims he was a victim too!

To be brutally honest, genuine miscarriages of justice are few and far between. In most instances, release from a custodial sentence comes by virtue of police and prosecution failures or the mishandling of evidence. That's the way it is, the police are not perfect. From my own professional experience, police officers are like everyone else in society, they gossip, they make mistakes and a few lie, cheat and deceive their colleagues, and yes it can be historically proven that some have 'fit people up'. That is certainly not to say that all police officers are bad, the vast majority are inherently honest and professional. Unfortunately, gone are the days when policing was a vocation, today it's a well paid occupation which is too often interfered with by political masters.

Policing in the 1980s wasn't what it is today, back then there was still a need for dedicated hard work, a genuine desire to help people, and a scheming mind to bring criminals to justice. My own career spanned three decades from the late 1970s so I was a copper of the era in question. I know how it worked, I understood the police mentality and being a police officer then you had to earn respect, not expect it like the modern day contemporaries. Detectives were driven by catching criminals, they had expert minds and tried to understand how the criminal mind worked by getting among them, talking to them and gaining respect.

Police officers often say they can smell a criminal a mile away; essentially it's true, though the distance may be an exaggeration. Unless you've lived it, there is no way of adequately describing the smell of fear or guilt on a person as it's a tangible thing, every bit as obvious as the demeanour and behaviour of a person who is not speaking the truth. Add to that crime scene evidence and as an investigating police officer you often find that the case falls into place. That is what happened in the case of Jeremy Bamber, and despite all claims to the contrary, not one police officer of the era that I know has ever claimed to me a belief that Jeremy Bamber is innocent. This is a detail that was reinforced during my attendance at Bamber's trial. I felt no suspicion or doubt that the evidence presented by the prosecution was anything but truthful and honest. Indeed, the one aspect of the trial that did stand out for me was the arrogance and almost nonchalant attitude of Bamber himself, this wasn't the demeanour of a man stunned by incredulous shock at his dire circumstances, or of a man who believed his innocence would ultimately be proven to the world. I remember noting down at the time that Bamber, throughout the trial and during his own evidence, seemed ruthless and without remorse or sympathy for his slaughtered family. I said at the time his emotional state was so cold that it was likely ice water coursed through his veins and not human blood.

It has been no mean feat carrying out further research into the case, speaking with people connected with the police investigation and others who were called as witnesses despite seemingly appearing to be disconnected from the crime. There was a period of about twelve months when I sensed that some form of impropriety may have taken place and the Criminal Justice System had erred. This belief was fuelled by Bamber himself and the astoundingly obstructive attitude of Essex Police which seriously unnerved me, and still does. Parts of the Essex force deliberately adopted an unhelpful attitude to my formal requests for the most basic information relating to the investigation. Thus I was forced to dig deeper into the case by alternative means and, by virtue, closely examine Essex Police themselves. My research was objective, I did not set out to find fault with Essex Police, however their failures are numerous and have continued in serious crime investigations since, many of which are well documented and easily found on the internet.

The real story behind the crimes of Jeremy Bamber doesn't rely on him or what he claims to be the truth. As an incarcerated prisoner, he's got very little else to do but to dig around the case paperwork looking for loopholes in the police and prosecution files. He is a shrewd character who considers the relevance of each of his claims. He repeats the same mantra, protesting his innocence, to all who listen. This doesn't in any way show that he is free of guilt, in fact it may be that after such a prolonged and sustained episode of denial he has now convinced himself of his innocence.

To progress anywhere in the case I needed to learn more about the police investigation and what did and did not happen. I spoke to dozens of police officers during my research. Many were reluctant to openly speak out, mainly because they feared this would make them outcasts of the police family. Also the threat of losing a healthy police pension by expressing opinions against the system remains a very real one and hangs over many retired officers like the Sword of Damocles. Police officers were not alone in their concerns about expressing a view or private knowledge of the case. The first thing that struck me during my own investigation was just how many people were reluctant to come forward because of the fear of reprisals! For a time I wondered what reprisals there could possibly be. The killer, Jeremy Bamber, is incarcerated in prison and in the current climate unlikely ever to be released. What I had not considered at the time was the obsession some have with supporting Bamber that arouses real hatred for those who defy their own beliefs!

I have researched every 'Bamber is innocent' claim, and to be truthful most have a boring monotony about them. In all the years since the crime, nothing of any legal relevance emerges from anything his disciples produce – decades of propaganda through misleading press releases, cleverly worded blogs and manipulated documents, even official appeals – there is no real substance to any of it. One legal professional likened the continuing campaign to 'a broken record stuck on the same track'. This seems so true.

My physical research for this book has taken me around the globe and back. I've followed leads in such far-off locations as New Zealand, where my aim was to speak with Brett Collins, Bamber's friend at the time of the murders. Countless messages were left for him. Eventually I received a return call and thereafter we spoke many times about the case. Fearing I was something to do with Jeremy, or I was the police or the press, Collins refused to meet and it became apparent that fear of reprisal was very real to him. He had in-depth and extremely private knowledge of the case and Bamber. Crucially, he told me he had completely altered his stance and opinion of Jeremy Bamber and now believes him to be guilty, explaining that at the time he dismissed such thoughts because his friend was convincing in the lies he had told him about the murders and he felt a misguided loyalty to him. Collins said that after the murders Bamber would boast how clever he was and how rich he was going to be. He also said that Bamber was selfish and emotionally cold hearted and spoke of the animosity he held for his parents and family. He repeated that Sheila, Bamber's sister, wasn't innocent either but had been wholly deceived by Jeremy. To my surprise it was recently claimed, again on an internet forum, that Brett Collins had passed away. I generally dismiss such unsubstantiated gossip yet curiously the person with whom I spoke said he was extremely ill and suffering from poor health!

Whatever one may morally think of Collins within the Bamber scenario, his implication in the commission of the crime is by association only. Other contacts have happened by chance, such as prisoners who at one time have been incarcerated alongside Bamber. Many of these felons know him well and have discussed their private and innermost perception of the mass murderer and child killer. Some of what they have said is eye-opening to say the least. I should add that not one of those who have contacted me believe him innocent, Jeremy Bamber has countless detractors and very few real allies.

I appreciate that the word of convicted criminals isn't as reliable as some would wish, however it should be borne in mind that such people know the system inside out. Indeed, in the very real world of criminal investigations, the majority of quality police intelligence comes from trusted sources within the convicted criminal fraternity. Not one person within this book has asked for any payment or reward for information and no inducement has been offered or paid to any informant.

I have made every effort to speak with as many parties – official and otherwise – involved in the original investigations and the later proceedings. In my opinion, the manner in which the police operated during this investigation was far from professional and there existed so much internal subterfuge and an obvious lack of leadership that I can see why the force would want to bury this from further public scrutiny. The silence therefore is more likely to be the system protecting itself from far greater criticism than it already has suffered. The allegation that it, Essex Police, is hiding evidence that proves Jeremy Bamber innocent is without any foundation, and for the Criminal Justice System I believe it's a matter of maintaining police integrity at all costs. There is no belief whatsoever that they are keeping an innocent man in jail.

I was disappointed that surviving relatives of the Bamber family failed to respond to any of the letters I sent to them requesting an audience. Whether this was a deliberate act to convey a 'not interested' message I cannot say. I do, however, genuinely understand why they would not wish to regurgitate memories from such a morbid past and therefore be suspicious of a retired police officer writing a book on the case. My aim is not, and never has been, to cause the living relatives further grief. I recognise the appalling treatment they receive from many of the Bamber disciples and totally sympathise with them, and in some small way I hope that by exposing such vile and offensive activity here it helps stop it and allows the family to move on in any way they can.

I did receive a communication from a so-called 'family spokesperson'. This felt rather superficial, creating an illusion of the family being surrounded by an active team of protectors which, after this length of time, is both irrational and bizarre. I initially wondered why such protection would be necessary. Yet when I consider how I was publicly maligned by the disciples of Bamber, I can easily understand why anyone would be reticent to speak openly about the case.

Several years ago I spoke at length with two of the lead investigating officers in the case, Stan Jones and Bob Miller. I had actually met Bob many years before but had lost contact with him. Both men were retired from the force and were generous with not only their time but in their candid recollections and opinions. I threw everything at them during our meetings, sometimes they flinched because of the need for political correctness, but not once did they refuse an answer or fail to comprehensively explain anything in a way that was clearly truthful and, to the best of their knowledge, honest. There were no allegiances, both officers knew I was interrogating them and I asked more searching questions than any QC asked at trial. Believe me, I worked them hard and offered no room for doubt, and neither man had any knowledge of the questions I would ask, nor had they the opportunity to research or jointly discuss anything.

Likewise Peter Simpson, an altogether more influential retired senior officer, was more than helpful with his own recollections to my questions. I am pleased to be able to place in the public domain for the first time ever the recollections of all of these officers, sadly they are no longer with us and I wish to place on record my respect for their truthfulness – they are of the highest integrity. Perhaps now the condemning criticism these officers have endured since the trial can be finally laid to rest. Without their kind assistance such finer intimate detail of the police investigation would be forever lost. The transcripts of the interviews have been demanded by several parties but they remain solely my property, and prior to this book were not ever in the public domain. Needless to say, they may not be reproduced anywhere without my written permission. To Stan Jones, Bob Miller and Peter Simpson, a huge and genuine thank you.

I confess that some people have been omitted from my acknowledgements but this should not be viewed with cynicism. The fact is some people don't want to be named or involved, and therefore I have respected that but have objectively used the detail they openly provided.

Throughout my research I have tried to offer a balanced perspective to the reader, I have attempted to incorporate equally all parties, and to give everyone of note a voice. I have sought every grain of truth and consolidated the real evidence that matters, continually assessing the relevance of everything. With a wealth of contradictory detail and plain untruths already in the public domain, it has been an onerous task achieving this and pulling it together. I knew it was going to be a difficult and tiring journey, but both emotionally and physically this book and research has taken its toll, and the death threats, nuisance telephone calls, poisonous lies and general deceitful attitude of some have proved an additional barrier that at times was difficult to handle. For months I worked from sunrise to sunset, poring over thousands of statements, documents and official reports, indeed it could be cogently argued that I should have been living and sharing a more constructive life without the grief this case created in my own world. That said I'm glad that I ignored the countless threats and persevered to finally put into print the truth about this police investigation and the case. Yes, it's a surprising and difficult end, yet it completes years of conjecture.

I could never have finished this book without the kind assistance of many others. My sincere appreciation goes to many former police officers, particularly the late Stan Jones and Bob Miller, who played a huge part in the investigation and took time to speak with me and discuss their candid opinions on many of the individuals involved. I also want to mention the late ACC Peter Simpson for sharing his memories and those of the late Ed Lawson QC, a chance encounter and discussion with him at the Royal Courts of Justice in 2002 revived and reinvigorated my interest in the case. Ed was a true gentleman and one of the finest barristers to grace the court system of England and Wales. He once told me that despite his place in the Bamber defence team, he became subsequently convinced of Jeremy Bamber's involvement in the crime, but not necessarily as a lone killer!

A message of thank you goes to Professor David Wilson, with whom I shared coffee, a podium, a public talk, and later a very hectic book signing session in Stirling, Scotland. A sensible and truly honest and open psychologist and criminologist whose beliefs, despite at times being contrary to my own, I genuinely respect. A mention too for the staff of the Essex Police Museum, Chelmsford, especially for the information and documents sent to me regarding Detective Chief Inspector 'Taff' Jones, I do hope the donation sufficed!

Sadly, the Essex Police's Freedom of Information office warrants a mention for their completely negative manner as they were deliberately obstructive to my requests and unnecessarily rude. One such example pertains to the Essex Police policy on document retention. I simply asked to be pointed in the right direction to locate this public document. My request was rudely dismissed and subsequent formal complaint completely ignored. As public servants these people have a remarkably unhelpful attitude, the worst I have encountered throughout my career in the world of criminal justice and the documenting of it.

Thanks must also go to Colin, Dawn, Brett, Matthew, Archie, Liz, Fred, Beverly and Chris. Also to Ronald DeFeo, Stephen Bentley, Graham McDonald, Tony Bennett, Peter Healey, and not forgetting the talented researcher Caroline Rowland for providing additional detail on the case. A mention must go to David Chakrabati for his knowledgeable opinion and messages of support, and to Ben Borland, Editor of the *Scottish Sunday Express*, who I spent many enjoyable hours with discussing unsolved murders and the mysteries that attach themselves to such crimes – the Alistair Wilson murder and the prostitute murders of Glasgow are actively being researched and pursued for a future Scottish murder compendium. I shouldn't forget to mention the Essex brats, you know who you are.

Again, my absolute appreciation goes to my excellent publisher Karl Waddicor at Vertical Editions, who achieves a superb job in creating high quality books and supporting my crime writing and Leeds United (football) projects. Karl endured some horrible delays in my trying to complete my research for this book. I can only apologise and thank him again for being so understanding and patient.

Last, and certainly not least, I want to thank my three wonderful German Shepherds, Angel, George and the incredible Sherlock. This motley crew helped maintain my focus on the important things in life away from Bamber research. Such things as walks, feeding time, play and loads of cuddles were the outstanding reality checks I needed. A mention too for Mia and Tom, you are the best little helpers in the world, and to Ben Poulter, the best electrician on the planet. Adoring thanks go to my wife Mandy, you above all others know what levels of energy it took to get this far with this difficult book, thank you again for everything.

Paul Harrison, May 2015

1

Background to a Murder

Yes, we are saying we got it wrong, but that is with hindsight. It would be a very wise man who would sit here today, one year later, and suggest that we would investigate things any differently. There will be no investigation into police methods as a result of the (Bamber) case, though we will look at ways of improving internal procedure.

These are the comments in 1986 of Ron William Stone, outgoing Deputy Chief Constable of Essex Constabulary, and Chief Superintendent Jim Dickinson, then head of the Essex Constabulary Criminal Investigation Department. They were made to the gathered press in the immediate aftermath of the trial and conviction of Jeremy Bamber for the murder of five members of his family. Whichever way these officers tried to decorate the statement, the police investigation wasn't a good one. Dickinson stated that there would be no investigation into police methods as a result of the case, such an arrogant statement that showed how far removed the force was from public opinion and adopting a professional attitude. The truth of the matter is that no one, not even the trial judge who, as part of the fabric of the Criminal Justice System invariably sits on the side of the police, could accept the unsatisfactory conduct displayed in parts of the police investigation. The comments did not escape the attention of then Home Secretary Douglas Hurd who instantly ordered a 'thorough' inquiry into the way Essex Police handled the investigation. So what was it that caused the investigation to be so criticised and how was it allowed to happen?

Many parts of rural Essex can be described as divine country locations where the stress and struggles of city life can be forgotten. Tolleshunt D'Arcy is one such place, lying in calm and peaceful countryside offering wonderful isolation for those wishing to get away from it all. That's how it was in 1985 and to an extent it remains so today, though its peaceful harmony has forever been disrupted courtesy of the crimes of Jeremy Bamber.

It all began in Tolleshunt D'Arcy on the night of Tuesday 6 August 1985. A night that was damp and decidedly colder than normal. At around 3.00am a belt of cloud cover had formed, occasionally obscuring clear moonlight, as the temperature dropped to around 11 degrees. In Pages Lane – named after a farming family who had worked the land there since the 19th century – White House Farm stood in broody silence, a few lights from its windows illuminating parts of the surrounding farmyard but elsewhere there was absolute darkness.

The farm itself can lay claim to a somewhat chequered and morbid past, for accidental deaths and even suicide have occurred in this place. It is said that between the wars a farmer hanged himself in a barn there, and in early November 1950 in a more documented case, the then tenant retired farmer Frank Page who was 77-years old, attempted to drown himself in a water tank at the farm. Page had apparently suffered a nervous breakdown in June 1950 and had threatened to kill himself through drowning several times. At around 3.00am his sister, Minnie Page, went to check on Frank but found his room empty and his bed cold. Seeking the help of local people, a thorough search of the farm and surrounding area was carried out. The body of Frank Page was found in water within a three foot deep tank. Two tractor wheels had been moved next to the tank and had been used by Frank as a step to climb in. The local pathologist, Dr Alfred E N Prentice, was of the opinion that Frank had undoubtedly intended to kill himself but had died of a heart attack after his body hit the cold water contained in the tank. There was evidence of chronic heart disease. He was buried at the church in Tolleshunt D'Arcy on 15 November 1950.

Yet no one could have foreseen the vile tragedy that was to occur in early August 1985, a crime that decimated a family and brought the reputation of a police force into question. By 3.45am, the tranquillity of Pages Lane would be destroyed with the arrival of a number of unannounced visitors to White House

Farm. Officers from Essex Police had been alerted to a potentially violent situation at the farm via a telephone call received from Jeremy Bamber, a relative of the farm occupants. Within hours, this peaceful home became a hive of police and media activity as news of a major incident, a murder scene, emerged. It was to become one of the most serious incidents the county of Essex has suffered.

At around 7.30am a number of police officers forced their way into the farm house. The scene that greeted the first to enter (Messrs Woodcock, Manners, Delgado, Collins, Hall and Alexander-Smart) was harrowing and a truly sickening one. No murder scene is pleasant nor is it something that one can readily rationalise or mentally accept, yet the horrors that greeted those first few officers is one they are unlikely to ever forget. Shockingly, in three different rooms, five people lay dead, two of them pensioners, another two were sleeping children shot at point blank range as they lay peacefully in their beds. The fifth body was that of a young woman, the mother of the dead children. All were seemingly dispatched from this world by a solitary crazed killer, a ruthless individual who in a cruel and merciless act destroyed an entire family.

Jeremy Bamber is the man convicted of the murders and over the years since he has been described as evil personified. In 1986 after a trial that lasted for eighteen days, he was jailed for life. It is a fact that Bamber was found guilty after a trial in a court of law by a jury that consisted of his peers. Had the conviction been straightforward I would not be writing this book.

Since being charged with the crime, Jeremy Bamber has refused to confess to the authorities or admit his guilt, and three decades later he continues to vehemently express his innocence. As a result, the case continues to make newspaper column inches as the media seizes every opportunity to recount the tragic circumstances that still stun a nation. For years, Bamber and his relatively small band of campaigners have produced what in truth can only be regarded as mainly irrelevant minute detail that they claim proves his innocence. They blame the system for not allowing him the opportunity of a further High Court appeal. Suspiciously, many of the matters raised by Bamber were not used as part of his trial defence, they are details identified retrospectively during the decades since his conviction and consist mainly of administrational affairs that realistically prove nothing and are solely about interpretation. When such claims have been investigated, and many have done so over the years including the authorities, there is no supporting evidence to back up these so-called assertions.

The overwhelming allegation which Bamber and his disciples rely upon is that he was framed for the murders, initially by his family, then through police and judicial corruption. To believe that injustice on such a scale could occur and be maintained, one must accept that the family influenced a senior police officer who in turn influenced hundreds of police officers and civilian employees to make up evidence, commit perjury and generally conspire to keep the entire matter a secret since that time. Putting it simply, it didn't happen. I appreciate that possible comparisons will be made to the Hillsborough tragedy of how the police can conspire en-mass to determine an outcome. However, rumours of how senior officers manipulated the details about the football disaster have been circulating in police circles for many years. Yet in the case of Jeremy Bamber, no such suggestions existed at the time, nor have they since other than the propaganda promoted through Bamber's own supporters. I have had no assistance whatsoever from Essex Police during this book, and at times they have been deliberately obstructive. I was aware that they may be a force with secrets and that suspicion was a motivator as I became committed to thoroughly researching their behaviour in serious criminal investigations. They were heavily criticised for the manner in which they handled the White House Farm murder investigation, but no sinister secret has surfaced or exists about this case.

To my surprise and benefit, I have found that a willingness to talk between police officers continues after one leaves the service. I genuinely believe that of all the researchers, writers and authors who have delved into this case, my ex-profession has procured me deeper access into policing matters and issues of the time. Because I had been a copper with three decades of policing behind me, there was an appreciation that I had an operational understanding of how the police service really operates, and with that comes a bond and trust. If there was any suggestion that Bamber had been fitted up and evidence concocted or manipulated, then something would have surfaced during my research. I was constantly looking for some comment or piece of evidence that might show corruption or impropriety, nothing ever did. That isn't to say the police come out of this with much credit for there existed subterfuge among some ranks that clearly affected how the investigation was handled and managed. That fault lies primarily with poor leadership in parts of the force from high ranking officers through to supervisory positions lower down the chain of command. This wasn't a loyal and united group of officers working together, it appeared at times disparate and disembodied and clearly some were undermining the leadership of the senior investigating officer. None of which affected the outcome of the investigation, rather it was unsettling for those working within that cocoon, and unprofessional in some of its more public dealings.

Whatever, the fact that the case remains the subject of such conjecture continues to cast a shadow over this peaceful area of rural Essex countryside. Every year since, dozens of ghoulish sightseers flock to the main crime scene sites in Tolleshunt D'Arcy and Goldhanger, all desperate to satiate their sanguinary desires, eager to get a glimpse of the area and perhaps an encounter with those left behind. It's a sad fact of life that such is the interest in the case that such visitors often forget the emotional trauma the tragedy left permanently upon relatives that remain. These are the people who, on a daily basis, are left to deal with the aftermath of the murders and I feel the utmost sympathy for each of them. Principle among these must be Colin Caffell, the father of the two innocent children who died in the slaughter. To his credit, Colin has dealt with not only the loss of his children but also with the unwanted publicity and media attention the crimes brought to his door. For me, he has done so with a great deal of dignity and I have nothing but respect for Colin and his integrity as a father and human being.

Historically it's unusual for society to seriously consider the lasting and negative effect murder has on a victim's family, and in some instances, the killer's family too. When these relationships are inexplicably intertwined it becomes all the more difficult. Grieving relatives need closure, the jailing of the offender isn't solely the key to being able to move on, there exists a need for answers, a need to understand how and why the tragedy happened, or if they could have prevented it. In the case of Jeremy Bamber we know a successful prosecution was achieved and, according to the law, the right killer was imprisoned. Yet despite such facts Bamber, although locked securely behind bars, has been able to form alliances with sources in the outside world and manipulate them into supporting his claims. As a result, a propaganda machine the likes of which no other convicted child killer has previously benefited from, has been spawned. From this, the deceased victims and the remaining family members have been unacceptably targeted and accused of all things, including providing false testimony.

For the family and friends touched and undoubtedly scarred by the crime, there remains great difficulty in moving on with their own lives post conviction. I am reliably told of one family member, a leading prosecution witness, who regularly reads and checks Bamber related internet discussions, reviewing each and every topic and the current public perception that surrounds the case. It's morally wrong that they should be subjected to such inappropriate accusations, and whilst I agree with the right for freedom of speech, I see no benefit in unnecessary and unfounded systematic public maligning of these people on the internet or elsewhere.

It's a little considered point that personal attachment to a murder investigation creates a certain vulnerability to family life as it comes under the scrutiny of the police and the media, every move is questioned, every comment analysed. To have one's personal life subjectively assessed in public destroys privacy and ensures that moving on is virtually impossible. Historically, families who have suffered such ordeals or atrocities tend to move away from the immediate district of the crime and attempt to build a new life in a place where they aren't known or reminded daily of the trauma. In this case some of the relatives connected have moved into White House Farm (the murder house), thereby living in a permanent reminder of what happened there – the carnage in the kitchen, and the savagery in the bedrooms. That said, people grieve in different ways and if the family feel comfortable in that environment then it is not my place, nor that of anyone else, to question where they choose to live. It's surely time the relatives were left alone and allowed to lead their own lives as few families could withstand the persistent critical and cynical bile that is spewed out about them.

Elsewhere, a number of people associated with the murders, almost immorally in my opinion, have generously profited and made a great deal of money from the crimes. One key witness at the trial had so little moral integrity or respect for the grieving relatives, or murdered family, that she sold a story to the press and was happy to be interviewed about many months of intimacy with Bamber just minutes after the trial ended. This individual then posed in a partially undressed state, revealing a somewhat less than flattering pose for press photographers. The resultant image was then printed as part of an exclusive in the *News of the World* newspaper. As if this tactless act wasn't sufficiently bad or in poor taste, the said individual then sold a kiss-and-tell story discussing amongst other things her past sex life with the man jailed. Few rational people see such behaviour as acceptable or morally correct. It is of real concern that the witness was portrayed at trial as being innocent, naïve, and wholly under Jeremy Bamber's spell and control. Whilst that may be the case she was certainly capable of making her own decisions before, during and after the crimes and I disagree that she too was a victim of Bamber's manipulation.

As can be seen without delving further into the investigation at this stage, there were questionable activities that require explanation. The behaviour and actions of some of those involved appear dubious at best, but I hope this work will assist in providing answers and giving some closure to those who seek it.

Over the years I have interviewed and received letters from murderers and serial killers from across the globe. Most ask me to visit or write and to consider writing their story. Few have a story worth telling, they are vile manipulators keen on self glorification only. So it was with much confidence that I knew there was little or nothing Jeremy Bamber could communicate to me that could shock or surprise me. We first started communicating in 2012 and it was then that I decided I would accept an offer to write the story supported by his first-hand testimony, official documents and with the help of his campaign team. My trust in him was and remains non-existent, though I felt it only correct to give him a voice and the opportunity to answer direct my questions. He was shrewd and cleverly avoided the more relevant issues that he recognised as potentially critical to his defence. This is normal practice for guilty criminals, they wish to be seen as being helpful and open, striking up a friendly rapport, yet all the time they are scheming and like an illusionist with a slight of hand, calmly skirting around key matters. Experience shows that an innocent party will directly answer every query, making no attempt to deviate from the topic or change the focus, or indeed ask for more time to respond as Jeremy Bamber did with me.

My cynicism was aroused that Bamber was toying with me and trying to manipulate my research when he volunteered, without any provocation, that he felt it would be of no benefit in me viewing crime scene or post mortem images of the murdered children, since these images were as such irrelevant to my investigation and research. This struck me as odd, I had never once mentioned images of any description, and since he knew I was an ex-police officer, and through my profession had seen and attended countless post-mortems and violent scenes of death, it felt as though he was trying to manage and control what I saw. The message he tried to portray was of someone showing consideration for my feelings, but why should he do that? In reality it is in fact a trait among child killers that they don't like to discuss the brutality of their crimes on a defenceless child. Bamber, from the outset, was setting his own parameters and letting me know he didn't want to discuss the murder of the children. Child killers attempt to disassociate from any or all direct or visual evidence of their acts, they know it is difficult, if not impossible, to justify the consequences of their crimes against a child since such acts arouse public revulsion, and for someone like Bamber who seeks public support and sympathy, it puts him at a distinct disadvantage.

Conversely his strategy permitted him to seemingly believe it acceptable for me to see the crime scene images of the other (adult) victims, and whilst these people may not be children they were his closest family. This displays a total lack of sensitivity and personal empathy with the victims who he continues to use to his advantage even in death. It was a devious act employed by the killer and provided an early insight into what I was dealing with.

I should make it clear that I generally believe that people are in prison for a good reason, that they have committed a serious crime and have been found guilty. As I said previously, my interest in the case was initially aroused in 1985 not because I felt Jeremy Bamber was innocent, but because of the internal subterfuge surrounding the police investigation. Many of the rumours circulating on the police grapevine at the time suggested that a police officer had been forced off the inquiry, his career effectively destroyed by external Masonic influences.

I know only too well how the brotherhood can influence all manner of decisions within the police service. I was outspoken of it during my own career in the service and despite being invited to join, and being advised how much easier life could be as part of the brethren, I declined. I'm not suggesting Masonic foul play interfered with the case as it didn't, however, within the code of conduct in the police family it's accepted that Masonic influence has additional elements of support that does curry favour.

This brings me onto a police related myth that has been spawned from the case, and over the years has actually been used by some as supporting evidence to show that Jeremy Bamber is a victim of a miscarriage of justice. It is the term 'Doing a Bamber' which is alleged to have been used as police terminology nationally as slang for improper (dodgy) police investigations. However, this phrase never existed in police circles, and of the officers known to me both in Essex and nationally, not one had heard of it previously until mentioned by me during interviews. It is yet another detail which has been purposely invented to show a level of unscrupulousness in Essex Police, if not throughout the police service in general. In reality, whilst many police officers may have cringed at the way Essex Police appeared to mismanage themselves during their inquiries, there was never any real sense of criminal injustice felt among rank and file officers throughout the land. It is well documented that police forces everywhere can and do make wrong judgment calls in a criminal investigation, and yes, innocent people do occasionally go to prison as a result of such appalling and unacceptable behaviour. Yet, no matter where I have searched in this case, no such belief that Bamber was 'innocent' or 'fitted up' can be found or has ever been attached to the Bamber case by police officers, nor can I find the existence of any such doubts throughout the entire Criminal Justice System. If it existed in any form I would have exposed it here. And, as difficult as this may be for the Bamber disciples to believe, like many other aspects of Bamber's defence, it's a fabrication, a true nonsense.

The trial, as many tend to be, was true theatre, a room filled with colourful actors, some more believable than others, the reality being that none were overwhelmingly so. There was very little drama other than a few definite facts that were expounded between parties and the lack of clarity to some of the issues discussed permeated the entire trial. For over a fortnight, Chelmsford Crown Court became home to three temporary and unwanted visitors in the form of conjecture, subterfuge and illusion. The trial Judge Mr Justice Drake, a man who himself had courted judicial controversy, effectively told the jury in his summing up to consider who was the most believable speaker of untruths in his court, and he gave them just two alternatives: Julie Mugford or Jeremy Bamber. So it proved that Bamber, in the eyes of the jury, was the least convincing performer.

At the time I believed the prosecution case to be weak, however there was nothing produced at trial that showed Bamber to be innocent. That evidence has been examined ever since as armchair barristers and wannabe detectives from the Bamber team tear it apart, and some do it exceedingly well. Their verdict is resolute, the evidence is apparently tainted and questionable, therefore flawed, so Bamber is innocent! I don't for one moment believe the evidence to be flawed, however the manner in which it has been misrepresented ever since creates an illusion that foul play by the legal authorities did occur.

It is my opinion that so much subterfuge existed amongst the different factions involved, that the dreadful reality of the crime became lost inside an invisible vault that housed equally mistrust, jealousy, animosity, disharmony and misunderstanding. From everything I have learned from those who knew and from my own interaction with him and his supporters, Jeremy Bamber displays a hard, selfish streak, driven by a desire for money, material possessions and the social trappings he believes all of these things can bring. Today, he sees his freedom as the key to the vault that would allow him to acquire such things. However, it should never be forgotten that members of a family were cruelly murdered due to the avarice and personal greed of one man.

It was Jeremy Bamber himself who granted me so-called access to the wealth of official documents that he and his team had possession of. The internet yielded some detail but the provenance of much of what is alluded to about Bamber through that medium must be regarded as suspect. Deliberate lies are concocted and openly posted online with some positively wild and libellous claims being asserted, such is the strange and complex personality types of some who have voluntarily attached themselves to the case. None of which helps Bamber's cause in addressing any potential miscarriage of justice, in fact these people do little but damage any such argument. Such is the world into which the White House Farm murders has been inexplicably drawn, the fate of the victims and the tragic family loss are all but forgotten within the pretend world in which these people survive and operate. The loss of innocent human life should never be so crassly and coarsely diluted.

2

British Justice – Essex Style

'It is fortunate for this community that I am not a criminal.'
Sherlock Holmes – The Adventure of the Bruce-Partington Plans

Since this case is often discussed as being a potential miscarriage of justice, it would be remiss not to mention other cases where justice has come under the public spotlight and its honesty and fairness questioned. When I began writing this book it had not been my intention to question the failings of Essex Police, or the integrity of any sole or collective body or individual working within the Criminal Justice System. Unfortunately, details of such failings were continually thrown up during my research, with many people being vociferous in their opinion of how inept policing was, and in some instances, still is. Can we truly accept what many would have us believe, that the police and the judicial system get it wrong with alarming frequency?

Many will have heard of the high profile campaign to clear killer James Hanratty who, according to his supporters including the late John Lennon, was overwhelmingly innocent. DNA tests were demanded by his defenders and as a result of these being carried out, it was proved that DNA matching that of Hanratty was found in critical areas of the crime scene, thus all claims of his innocence were destroyed. There followed unsubstantiated claims that the samples had been contaminated! It seems that no matter what evidence there is to prove his guilt, it will never be sufficient. Does anyone consider the after effect such denials have on the surviving victim or their families?

More recently, convicted murderer the late Simon Hall, vehemently proclaimed his innocence for over a decade. An entire movement, including academics, researched and backed his claims. Members of Parliament and the BBC television *Rough Justice* programme were vocal about this miscarriage of justice and so forced it into the public domain. Two separate applications to the Criminal Cases Review Commission were submitted to no avail. Simon Hall eventually confessed to the murder and tragically, several months later, took his own life. He deceived and hurt many through his lies, undoubtedly causing serious collateral damage in his claim that miscarriages of justice occur all too often. The family of his elderly victim said of his confession, 'During the last 10 years the publicity surrounding the appeals has been very distressing for our family, making moving on impossible.' One must feel sympathy for his own family too, they supported and believed in him throughout. An utter tragedy indeed.

That's two randomly selected cases and despite claims to the contrary, in both instances the system has got it right. However, the Criminal Justice System is deceptive. It remains fundamentally flawed in that the suspect, despite being innocent until proven guilty, actually has no voice once the system moves beyond arrest. Today it is regarded as far superior to what it was back in the 1980s when it relied on the integrity of police officers and sound police procedures. Forensic science was almost unheard of, the first DNA conviction in a British court didn't happen until two years after the carnage at White House Farm. These were times when scenes of crime officers held responsibility for crime scene analysis and investigation – fingerprint powder and a camera being the most used tools. To a large extent, instinct was the major power in the investigating officer's armoury. In good cops, if exercised properly, it was an excellent tool, in poor cops it could be as dangerous as any weapon if abused or misinterpreted.

The Criminal Justice System isn't solely about the police, it's about judges, the courts, juries and all importantly, individuals and fairness of trial which should ultimately aid the journey in the correct course for the truth and justice. The system would have us believe it is flawless, and that all who work in it are paragons of virtue. For over four decades I worked in that system and I can categorically state that the Criminal Justice System is not squeaky clean. Skeletons are secreted and exist in many cupboards, those hiding places are heavily protected and closely guarded. It's a complete misnomer that because someone has 'breeding' or they speak well, or work within the Criminal Justice System in some capacity or hold a seemingly powerful position in it, that they must be honest or beyond doubt. Without doubt, many believe themselves untouchable, however, like everyone, they do err and when they do they shouldn't be protected. It's well documented that judges do break the law and I know that from experience. What they don't do is allow openly corrupt practice to take place in their court room.

Following my police career, as a clerk to a High Court Judge I got to know the judiciary very well, both professionally and personally. I didn't always agree with how they addressed matters in court as at times it felt heavily biased when they instructed the jury on certain aspects of a case or on a point of law. Yet on other occasions I felt they were utterly brilliant in how they handled an entire trial.

There has been some suggestion that Mr Justice Drake at the Bamber trial was less than impartial in his summing up, which is solely down to personal opinion, but from a legal aspect he put the crucial elements of the case into plain and clear language for the jury to consider. No one came out of the trial with any real credit – not the police, not all the witnesses, and certainly not Bamber. The Judge is said to have held private discussions in his chambers with both QCs and once again that matter has been seized upon to add credibility to the 'lets frame Bamber' conspiracy theory. Such meetings do take place, but there exists no conspiracy and no sinister motive, they are extremely formal affairs with no niceties being shared. They are not for the purpose of sharing tea and biscuits or to discuss potential outcomes or second guess anything. Such discussions are brief and based upon points of law and trial management alone. It will be reiterated many times during this book that the trial of Jeremy Bamber was not unique, it was made confusing because of the number of conflicting tales being told, not least by the accused himself who has continued to create confusion in an attempt to divert from the facts.

The judiciary and the police would have us believe that innocent people don't get punished for crimes they do not commit or have no knowledge of. There are few police officers who do not believe that all suspects, by the very nature of being associated with a crime, are guilty. Once committed to a course of action it takes a lot for a police officer to admit they got it wrong. They rarely do because of the professional stigma such a misguided guess would have on their own career. As for the Judiciary, their perception of wrongful conviction is aptly summed up by the words of Baron Denning. Denning, who as Master of the Rolls (Lord Chief Justice of England and Wales) in the highest Judicial position in the land from 1962 to 1982, a man whose position was to oversee and ensure fair justice said:

> Hanging ought to be retained for murder most foul. We shouldn't have all these campaigns to get the Birmingham Six released if they'd been hanged. They'd have been forgotten, and the whole community would be satisfied ... It is better that some innocent men remain in jail than that the integrity of the English judicial system be impugned ...

Despite the obvious impropriety of this statement, an admission that the judicial system does get it wrong but should itself be beyond criticism or punishment, is fundamentally immoral. So arrogant and blinkered was Denning that two years later, in 1990 he said:

> They'd probably have hanged the right men (Guildford Four). Just not proved the case against them, that's all.

Denning's quotes are based on the ideals of the judicial system, a select group of individuals (Judges) operate and control this, the statutes under which the law operates have been passed down since time immemorial. Their's is an insular and inward facing system, reliant upon the police and prosecution or defence counsel to produce evidence to prove or disprove the guilt of an individual brought before them. In a utopian world the police would deliver hard solid evidence to the court, facts that proved beyond doubt a person's guilt. Sadly utopia is but a fictional place, and it most certainly does not exist within the British Criminal Justice System.

In both of the instances mentioned by Denning, the Guildford

Four and the Birmingham Six, the so-called offenders went on to be released from prison as legally proven innocent men and women. In the case of the Guildford Four a damning formal statement made by one of the Counsel involved in the hearing said:

> New evidence of great significance has come to light after a police inquiry. It has thrown such doubt on the honesty and integrity of a number of Surrey police officers investigating this case ... the Crown is now unable to say that the convictions of any of the four were safe or satisfactory.

In the case of the Birmingham Six, scientific tests proved that statements made by the accused men had been altered by the Police and that forensic tests carried out at the time, originally claimed to prove that two of the men had been handling explosives, could have produced exactly the same results if they had been handling cigarettes! The scientist who claimed to have found traces of nitro-glycerine on their hands was retired on the grounds of 'limited efficiency'. Not one police officer involved in such outrageous and nefarious activities has ever been successfully prosecuted. Evidence surely that the system can deliberately be abused by legal decision makers. It is easy to claim 'that was then, but this is now' however police impropriety does happen today. A freedom of information request placed in 2013 revealed that in the West Midlands Police Force alone, during a two year period, a total of 111 police officers and staff resigned whilst under investigation. The ranks of the officers concerned included one Chief Superintendent, three Inspectors, 11 Sergeants and three Detective Constables! A quite shocking modern day detail and perhaps a revelation to some.

Closer to home in Essex there is a comprehensive history of failings too. In 1965, Frank Williamson (Chief Constable of Carlisle, and later of Cumberland, Westmorland), was called in to carry out an inquiry into the Chief Constable of Southend, Essex, Mr William McConnach, for fraudulent activity. McConnach had been in position since 1953. The subsequent inquiry into his crimes by Williamson was viewed by the Home Office as a model investigation, conducted with ruthless efficiency and a lack of sentimentality, there was no cover-up. McConnach was subsequently tried at the Old Bailey for stealing as a servant of the Crown, and for obtaining money by false pretences. On 22 November 1965, McConnach was sentenced to two years imprisonment. He was found guilty on 17 of the 19 fraud charges. Ten of these related to money illegally obtained through abuse of his position i.e. stolen from Southend Corporation with intent to defraud. Nine of the charges related to him fraudulently applying for official money received virtue of his employment and for his own purpose. Judge Mr Justice Waller stated that by 1964 McConnach had been using public funds on a wide scale solely to subsidise his drinking. He went on to mention the public image and reputation of the police in Essex, saying, 'The disclosures of the trial will have tarnished it, and tarnished it beyond Southend.'

Moving into November 1972, Muriel Patience was shot and killed during a failed robbery at The Barn Restaurant in Braintree, Essex. A description of the suspects was gleaned from descriptions provided by the victim's husband and daughter, Bob and Beverley Patience. A suspect was identified in George Ince, a man well known in the East End. Ince had been suspected by police of being involved in the Mountnessing bullion robbery and had gone underground, but when rumour surfaced that he was in the frame for the murder at The Barn he gave himself up to police. He had a cast iron alibi which clearly made him innocent of all such allegations. Essex Police would have none of it and believed him to be guilty. In November Ince was placed in an identification parade and was identified by Beverley Patience, her father meanwhile identified a different man. The Police had influenced the outcome by breaching legal procedural guidelines, and had shown Ince's photograph to Beverley immediately before the parade, influencing her judgment. The trial of George Ince opened at Chelmsford Crown Court on 2 May 1973. After short deliberations of three-and-a-half hours, the jury were advised by the Judge that a majority verdict of 10 votes would be accepted, however they were unable to reach a verdict. George Ince stood trial again four days later. During the second trial his defence was heard. It was revealed that on the evening of the murder he had been with a Mrs Grey at an address which wasn't revealed in open court and had to be to written down. Mrs Grey was the wife of Charlie Kray, brother of the notorious Kray twins. Ince was found not guilty by the jury and he left the court shouting abuse at detectives. In February 1974 two other men were tried and found guilty of this crime. As a result of the breach of guidelines, George Ince received written apologies from the husband of the murder victim, Bob Patience, and the prosecuting counsel. A year later in 1975, the Chief Constable of Essex disciplined several senior detectives and also wrote to Ince. The results of an enquiry were presented to the Director of Public Prosecutions but it was decided that there were insufficient grounds for criminal charges to be brought against any detectives. It was nothing but a sham.

The matter was raised in the Houses of Parliament by Ian Mikardo, MP, and Hansard records:

> … I read the list of offences which have now been admitted by the Chief Constable as having been carried out by his officers I begin to wonder whether the same standards are being applied to police malefactors as to all other malefactors.
>
> I shall quote from a long list only five examples. The first concerns the fated identification. On this subject the Minister of State, Home Office, Lord Harris, wrote to me saying: 'Mr Ince's photograph was in fact first shown to Miss Patience' – she was one of the principal witnesses – 'as one of twelve, on 10th November. Subsequently, however, both she and her father and brother were shown single photographs of Mr Ince, which was wholly contrary to force instructions. Miss Patience had seen six single photographs of him in the nine days before she came face to face with him at Colchester and identified him. There were also breaches of force instructions when sets of photographs including one of Mr Ince were shown to Mr Robert and Mr David Patience: after they had failed to pick him out from the set as a whole, his photograph was specifically drawn to their attention.' If anybody but the police behaved in that sort of way what would be said? However, the Director says, 'There ain't anything wrong with that in law.'
>
> The second example is that the Chief Constable himself admits that his officers failed to inquire into Ince's alibi. At his second trial he managed to bring forward an unshakable alibi and unshakable evidence to prove that he was nowhere near the scene of the crime when it occurred. That evidence had been given to the police, and they failed to check it. The Chief Constable says that they failed to

check it. One begins to wonder whether they look upon it as their function to get a conviction at all costs of the chap they pick on or to try to find out the truth, to find out what really happened.

Thirdly, there was another identification parade. In respect of this Lord Harris said: 'Commander Howells' – the investigating officer – 'has been unable to ascertain with any certainty exactly what happened at every stage of this parade; this in itself is a criticism of the police officers present and of Chief Inspector Gorham, the officer in charge of the parade.' There were a chief inspector and other officers present, but none of them was able to tell the investigating officer what really happened.

Lord Harris continues: 'It is clear, however, that on at least two occasions the officer in the case – who, if present at all, should have been there merely as an observer – interfered with the conduct of the parade.' Nothing could be clearer evidence that the officers concerned were determined to get the result they wanted out of the parade.

Fourthly, it is not contested that the police introduced forensic evidence – examples of fibre – without any attempt to check its authenticity.

Finally, photographs of Ince were taken without his knowledge or approval at Bethnal Green police station in my constituency. He did not know that they were being taken secretly. Lord Harris admits: 'the handing over of these photographs to the Essex Police was a clear breach of Metropolitan Police instructions.' It is obvious from all this that the police did not see it as their duty to arrive at the truth. That is what I thought that they were there for, to do their best to help the court to find the truth of the matter. They were out to get a conviction by fair means or foul, whether justified or not.

After all that condemnation by an investigating officer, the greater part of which has been accepted as valid by the Chief Constable, the Chief Constable took disciplinary action against only one of the officers. The officers have got off both judicial action initiated by the Director of Public Prosecutions and disciplinary action. The Chief Constable puts forward a fantastic reason. He says in effect, 'I shall not take disciplinary action against them now, if only because it is so long since the offences were committed.'

None of the above makes pleasant reading if one is seeking good policing practices. There exists another suspect incident linked to the Ince case, a constable from Ongar Police Station claimed to have 'seen it all' (the crime) yet he failed to report it or make any such statement at the time. Instead, it was fully seven months later when he was called to identify George Ince from photographs that were allegedly made available on the day of the parade. The officer, despite his spurious claims, failed to identify Ince from any of the photographs, yet these same images had undoubtedly been on display in almost every police station across Essex for many months. This truly is cringeworthy policing! Corruption is a dirty word in police parlance yet it did occur, and in some forces it still may. In 1989 and 1990 there were three serious investigations into Essex Police involving allegations of bribery. Neither the Police Complaints Authority nor Essex Police would release the relevant information on these investigations.

As we progress into more recent times, another Freedom of Information request revealed that between 1 October 2012 and 30 September 2013, some 852 complaints were 'finalised' by the Essex force alone. A staggering 9.5% of these were upheld. Three police officers were arrested and bailed after allegations of possession of indecent images of children, harassment and sexual offences, and sexual assault. One of these was later charged with eight offences. Another police officer attempted to kiss a female detainee and another, who attended a domestic dispute, later contacted a woman involved after accessing police records and by using online social media and sent her a sexual text and picture messages. A spokesperson for Essex Police did their best to resurrect something from such a disaster saying: 'The vast majority of officers and staff are professional and act with honesty and integrity.' The 'vast majority' isn't actually good enough, surely the public should be able to rely upon the integrity of all officers and staff?

Also in 2012, eight police staff, including a police officer, resigned over investigations into breaches of the Data Protection Act and alleged abuse of information held on police computers. In 2011, a further three Essex Police officers resigned over similar allegations. Further, in 2009, the Independent Police Complaints Commission looked into the Essex Police investigation of the death of Stuart Lubbock. The death occurred at entertainer Michael Barrymore's home in 2001. The final report was damning of the police investigation and talked of its 'failings'. In 2012, the IPCC looked into the investigation of the 2007 death of Lee Balkwell who was crushed in a concrete mixer on an Essex farm, it concluded that it was 'seriously flawed'. Another 2012 investigation by the Commission looked at the 2011 murder of Christine Chambers who was murdered by her ex-partner, again the final report highlighted 'failings' by the Essex force. Sadly, it is all too easy to see an ongoing theme as the investigations detailed above are but a few such instances which the force must acknowledge as failures, and not simply lock them away and hope they will be forgotten.

3

What We Know

'I confess that I cannot recall any case within my experience
which looked at the first glance so simple, and yet which presented
such difficulties.'

Sherlock Holmes – The Man With the Twisted Lip

To determine what did happen at White House Farm and how
five people were slaughtered, we must first deconstruct the case
and review it from not only the documented evidence but from
police testimony also. Throughout this work I have attempted to
assert a balanced view. It's impossible to ignore that Bamber has
been found guilty of the murder at trial in a court of law, but if
a miscarriage of justice has genuinely occurred and he is proven
to be an entirely innocent man then it is correct that he should be
released. As I say, my aim was not to prove his innocence but to
examine the details as we now know them – the actual facts and
not the supposition of internet theorists. It goes without saying
that if the evidence dictates something to the contrary and further
condemns Bamber's role, and so proves that no miscarriage
of justice has occurred, then that too must be put in relevant
perspective.

It is worth mentioning at this juncture that the prosecution
case has not progressed since the 1986 trial, there being no need
to provide fresh evidence to show Bamber's guilt other than the
known facts which were reiterated and reviewed at appeal. It is
also important to note that no concrete evidence that definitively
proves him innocent has yet been produced, neither are there any
new witnesses or anything that provides him with a definite alibi
or shows that he did not commit, or have any involvement, in the
murders. In essence, all we have to support Bamber's defence are

his own words, claims and police/court testimony. It has been claimed by Bamber supporters that the witnesses involved in the original investigation were not correctly interviewed or asked the appropriate questions that would, or could, show his innocence. It is their belief, through Bamber himself, that it was a heavily biased and corrupt investigation.

First we must understand a little of the family background and history. Nevill Bamber was born in 1924 and went to Christ's Hospital Boarding School in Horsham, West Sussex. He later joined the Royal Air Force, flying a number of missions to North Africa during World War II hostilities. On cessation of the war he attended an agricultural college and there met with an individual called Robert Boutflour. Both men began to court sisters June and Pamela Speakman. Nevill and June married, with Nevill soon being offered a farming plantation in Rhodesia which he seriously considered as an option since both of his sisters lived there. It was not until the intervention of June's father, Leslie Speakman, that the matter was dropped. Nevill's father-in-law offered him the tenancy of White House Farm, and so the couple elected to remain in the United Kingdom where Nevill progressed to become a successful farmer and a local Justice of the Peace. It came as something of an unnecessary confirmation that he had made the right decision to stay in Essex when news followed that both of Nevill's sisters had died in tragic circumstances in Africa. Nevill has been described to me by those who knew him as a dignified man of strong moral character who treated everyone, no matter what their social standing, with respect and decency. He enjoyed various sports including tennis and was socially interactive within the local community and church. His relationship with his wife June was a close one and his immediate family meant everything to him.

June Bamber was raised on Vaulty Manor Farm (now owned by relatives Ann and Peter Eaton) and attended Colchester Grammar School then secretarial college, gaining qualifications from which she often found local office work. On the outbreak of World War II she joined the Nursing Yeomanry and for a time served in Calcutta. After the war she met and married Nevill Bamber and the pair moved into a cottage in Wash Lane near Vaulty

Manor Farm. As a housewife June was a keen gardener and often donated flowers to many of the local initiatives she helped with, including Meals on Wheels. She was also an active member of the church and the Women's Institute. Deeply religious she was to become a church warden later in her life. The couple moved into White House Farm and looked to raise a family of their own. Unable to have children naturally, Nevill and June adopted two babies, Sheila and Jeremy, through the church adoption process. As a family they seemed happy and content. In the late 1970s June suffered mental health issues and received treatment for this illness for a time during 1982 under a specialist at St Andrews Hospital in Northampton. June suffered moments when her mental health illness affected her, but on a general day-to-day basis she was able to manage this, her religious faith keeping her focused and strong.

Sheila, the older of the two adopted children, was born on 18 July 1957, and adopted when she was just eight weeks old. She later attended Maldon Court School where she was regarded as a talented writer with excellent descriptive skills. A confident and beautiful young woman, she attended Moira House School in Eastbourne. Here, her confident bearing and manner was often misinterpreted as a kind of arrogance and she found herself expelled from the school, the full reasons are not known but one woman who knew her at the time, Carol Black, believes she had earned a reputation among teaching staff as being cheeky and awkward to handle:

> Sheila was a popular girl, the students wanted to be her friend because she seemed to have everything, she was pretty, intelligent and good to be around. There was always a queue of boys in the area who were desperate to be her boyfriend. I know it sounds silly, but many of the students believed some of the teaching staff were actually jealous of her. She always seemed to be singled out as being a bit of a problem for certain members of staff. It may have been unethical but I do think this was one of the reasons why she was expelled, they were the adults, they were teachers and shouldn't have been jealous of a child, but I do think some were, they punished her because she was smart and attractive beyond her years, for one so young.

From here, Sheila attended Old Hall Boarding School in Hethersett, Norfolk where she flourished, being attentive to her scholastic studies, and earned an excellent reputation in class and socially. During holidays, Sheila would return home to the farm and help out with farming chores. After attending secretarial college in Swiss Cottage, London, she went on to work as a hairdresser at Robert Fielding's in London but, according to Jeremy, was sacked after a few months. However, she continued in her efforts to follow a career in that world and she was briefly employed by a number of different salons but never truly settled at any one. Through this period she also gained work with a modelling agency. It wasn't long before Sheila met and developed a relationship with Colin Caffell and at the age of just 17 she fell pregnant but lost the child before birth. Around this time her relationship with her adopted mother June began to fall apart.

Sheila's wayward spirit was often too much for June Bamber and matters came to a head when she came upon Sheila in a compromising position with a man on the farm. Sheila was to later tell a specialist that June would call her abusive names such as 'Devil Child'. The name calling was to have a profoundly negative impact on her state of mind. It's unacceptable to call one of your children such a rotten thing, or to say it to anyone come to that. June wasn't averse, through her religious piety, at condemning Sheila for anything beyond the comprehension of her own beliefs. However, it must come into consideration that her own state of mind did perhaps cause her to use inappropriate language towards her family, and that she did not appreciate the damage she was doing to her daughter. It certainly created periods of ill feeling from Sheila towards her and caused a fracture in their relationship.

Sheila always felt her closest relationship was with her father Nevill, who was the voice of all reason and a calming rational influence in an often quarrelsome family. He was a man who commanded respect locally and unlike June, he did not overtly try to force his religious beliefs on Sheila. It was more often than not Nevill who resolved disputes within the family group, generally maintaining a status quo through common sense and reasoning. Whenever Sheila or June flew off the handle it was always Nevill who sorted it out and kept everyone happy. He was, however, a hard working and a socially and professionally busy man, and therefore had limitations on his time, and in particular the time he could spend with his now adult daughter. Through domestic circumstances, it appears to have been June who physically spent more time 'around' Sheila as an adult as opposed to time 'with' Sheila. The pair certainly don't seem to have had a smooth relationship, and when one considers the various issues both had, then it is little wonder they often disagreed. That is not to say they did not get on, just that the relationship was at times fractious.

At the age of 20, in May 1977, Sheila married Colin Caffell. A further two miscarriages were endured and there was a later abortion before she eventually fell pregnant with the twins. There were complications and so she spent several months in the Royal Free Hospital, Hampstead. Eventually, on 22 June 1979, the twins, Daniel and Nicholas, were born. There had been significant issues within the marriage to Colin as Sheila began to suffer more and more psychotic episodes which gradually grew worse in their ferocity. During some of these she would often throw things at her husband. Gradually Sheila's mental health began to deteriorate to a point where she clearly needed external help and on her 21st birthday, during a row with Colin, she put her hand through a plate glass window causing a wound that required stitches. Eventually the couple split and finally divorced in 1982. It was around this time that Jeremy Bamber claimed to witness Sheila using forcible violence towards the twins, putting this down to the pressure of raising the boys and her mounting debts. Sheila moved into a flat in Morshead Mansions, Maida Vale, London with the twins. Colin, then based in Kilburn, helped with raising the boys and would readily look after them. He was as devoted and caring for them as any father could be.

Sheila meanwhile went off the rails. Her modelling career all but over, she was forced to live off state benefits and also took low paid 'less than glamorous' employment in various locations across London. Her ongoing illness and needs saw the involvement of Camden Social Services who provided day foster care for the twins, with a number of different foster parents being used. It was a less than acceptable situation and did little to help Sheila's state of mind. The friendships she engaged in were not the kind she could ever have envisaged having, she started drinking heavily and had a serious drug habit. There are even suggestions that she enjoyed the company of older men, who, it was said, were the kind interested in younger women for all the wrong reasons!

Over the months that followed her mental condition began to overwhelm her and she was to show more frequent signs of violent behaviour, often banging her head against walls, screaming abuse and generally being unnecessarily erratic. Neighbours called her the woman with mad staring eyes as the drugs took a greater hold of her conscious mind. She began to exhibit extreme signs of violence, so much so that on one occasion she became manic and uncontrollable resulting in a boyfriend, fearing for his own safety, calling her family for assistance. In 1983, the twins went to stay with their father as Sheila was referred as an inpatient to St Andrews Hospital, Northampton where she was under the care of Dr Hugh Ferguson, the same practitioner who had previously treated her mother June. There follows a harrowing tale as Sheila's mental state was diagnosed, she had schizoaffective disorder. In his patient medical notes Dr Ferguson states that Sheila held a belief that the devil had given her the power to project evil onto others and that she could make her sons have sex with her and cause violence with her. She referred to the twins as 'the devil's children', the very term her adoptive mother had used about her. Sheila also believed that at times she was capable of murdering them or of getting them to kill others. She would often speak of suicide yet amazingly Ferguson did not believe this to be a real or valid threat and authorised her discharge after just six weeks in September 1983. He continued to treat her as an outpatient and prescribed trifluoperazine, an anti-psychotic drug.

Sheila would often ring her father during episodes and tell him she was the Virgin Mary, Joan of Arc or the leader of CND. Nevill always provided a caring and listening ear and never judged or condemned his daughter for her behaviour. It must have been difficult for him to see both women in his life suffer so much from mental health problems. He kept her illness as private as he could from the rest of the family. As a Justice of the Peace he understood how mental health issues can affect how people sometimes act, and he recognised the stigma that attaches itself to such illness. No doubt he hoped that she would one day settle down and lead as normal a life as she could.

Sheila was still struggling in 1985 and was readmitted to St Andrews Hospital before again being released, this time being prescribed with haloperidol. Sheila remained unwell when on 4 August she arrived at White House Farm for a week's stay as part of the recuperation process. At this time the dosage of haloperidol she had originally been prescribed had been significantly reduced to 50 per cent by her local doctor. She had also been warned of the dangers of taking drugs alongside prescribed medication, but it was good advice which went ignored as she continued to smoke cannabis. Despite the resultant episodes, Sheila was described by those who saw her at the farm shortly before the murders as seemingly happy, the only person whose opinion differed on her apparent frame of mind was her adoptive brother Jeremy who said she was quiet.

Jeremy Bamber was adopted by the family as a six week old baby having been born in 1961 of an illicit affair between Sergeant Leslie Marsham of the Royal Army Medical Corps and Juliet Wheeler at St Mary Abbotts Hospital, Kensington, London. His natural father rose to the rank of General in the army, and both parents later worked at Buckingham Palace. His genetic father was to say of him after conviction:

> It was traumatic when we had to hand him over. He went to lovely people who looked after him and gave him the best start in life. He abused them. He's a murderer. It's well proven. He's as guilty as hell. Most murderers complain to the bitter end they never did it. We had no part in his upbringing whatsoever. I don't know and don't wish to know whether he is our child or not. He has ruined our lives. He is a horrible man.

Not the greatest or kindest testimonial a father has ever given a son. As a youngster he too attended Maldon Court School, Sheila being in her last year there when he started. On leaving Maldon Court, he was extremely fortunate to attend the renowned educational establishment, Gresham College. He was no academic genius and left the college with no qualifications, though later at sixth form college, gained seven GCSEs. A confident and often amiable young man he was never short of friends from both sexes. Wanting his son to gain valuable life experience, in 1979 Nevill subsidised Jeremy on a trip travelling round Australia where he found short-term work and took a scuba diving course. From Australia he moved onto New Zealand where he made friends and developed a drug habit while also dealing in drugs and smuggling heroin. It has been further alleged that during this same period he had a propensity for stealing things, though the provenance of this claim remains unsubstantiated.

On returning to England he lived in Colchester for about six months, three of them with then girlfriend, Sue Ford. In March 1984, influenced by his father, he was moved into rent free accommodation at 9 Head Street, Goldhanger and was given salaried employment at White House Farm. In addition his parents provided him with an eight per cent share of a family company, the Osea Road Camp Sites Ltd, and free use of a family car. No young man could have wanted better or more supportive parents. Yet there are witnesses who say he had issues with his parents and felt aggrieved that he didn't get more financially from them. There is much to support these claims, not least that Jeremy broke into the family business, Osea Road Camp Sites Ltd, and stole money from it. When found out he claimed he wanted to make a point about poor security measures. Is this the action of a fine son who genuinely cares and respects his family and would do all he could to protect and help them, or is it the actions of a spoilt young man, used to getting his own way and wanting more and more irrespective of who it hurts?

So, hours before the murders occur, we have an adopted son and daughter in the house, both with parental issues. One is driven by greed and money, the other is suffering a mental breakdown and is being made to feel bad about herself and made aware of her maternal weaknesses by her own mother.

According to the police statement made by Jeremy Bamber, on 7 August 1985 at 7.30am he went to the farm as usual, first visiting the farm house to discuss the work for the day with his father, he then left and returned to the house at around 9.00am to do some work and again speak with his father. On entering the kitchen he saw Sheila, the twins, and his mother having breakfast at the table. Throughout the day he worked in the fields and periodically visited the farmhouse. In the afternoon at around 4.00pm he saw Sheila as she walked down the lane to the rape field where he was working, she was with the twins. The pair had a ten minute chat and she returned to the house leaving him to his work in the fields.

Bamber claims that he next returned to the house between 8.00pm and 9.00pm and remained there for about 30 minutes. Both of his parents and Sheila were having supper, the twins had apparently gone to bed. He had something to eat and was aware of the conversation taking place in the kitchen. It was about future plans for the children and what further treatment Sheila needed to have, though effectively it was his parents' opinion of what was needed and not Sheila's. There was a mention of foster parents and other potential solutions that might help her cope better. Bamber claims he picked up his .22 semi-automatic rifle from the study and loaded the magazine in the kitchen after tipping a box of ammunition out onto the side close to the kitchen telephone. He was in rush as he had seen two rabbits outside that he wanted to shoot, so loaded between eight and 10 rounds into the magazine and exited the house leaving the rest of the ammunition out on the side. All this with the family seemingly sat talking around the table and no one commenting on his actions. He was outside for about five minutes before returning back to the house, making the weapon safe, removing the loaded ammunition, and placing the rifle on a small bench, covering it with a small blanket that was used for this purpose.

Nevill, June and Sheila were still talking in the kitchen. He didn't speak to them but went directly outside to take a trailer to the combine. Crucially he didn't feel it necessary to clear up after himself in the house and return the loose ammunition to its box, yet deemed it important to clear up his work outside. It's known that Nevill didn't agree with leaving unsecured firearms and ammunition about the house, so for Bamber to do so was contrary to Nevill's sensible rules.

He then returned to the house at about 9.30pm when he again spoke to his father who remained seated around the table with June and Sheila. He claimed there was no sign of any tension and they all seemed happy. Bamber said he discussed farm work with his father before leaving for the night and returning to his Goldhanger home at approximately 9.45pm. Once there he watched some television and went to bed. At about 3.10am he was awakened by the telephone ringing. It was a call from his father, whereupon Nevill told him something like 'Sheila's gone crazy, she has got the gun.' The line then went dead. He tried to call back but instead got the engaged tone. He then telephoned Chelmsford police to inform them of the call he had allegedly received. Rather than go to the aid of his family, he then decided to call his girlfriend, Julie Mugford, in London. He said it was about 3.25am when he made this call and he wanted to tell her that something appeared wrong.

In his handwritten communications to me dated 26 July 2012, and in answer to my asking him about the family's movements and activities the day before the crime, he states the following:

> It's best to stay with known facts first. Late afternoon I stop the tractor and trailer in the lane and say hello to Sheila and the boys, they seem happy enough, off on a walk to Primrose Wood I think. I don't stop for long as I have to unload my trailer full of rape seed. We said not much more than hello and goodbye, see you later. If I'd not been busy I'd have had Nicholas and Daniel in the cab for a trip to the barn and back in my Tonka Toy tractor – it had four-wheel-drive and four huge wheels and it was new, lovely it was. The boys had been with me earlier in the day when I'd let them steer and pull the throttle lever and get all the lights going – I know how I loved all that at six or seven–years-old, so I'm sure they loved it too.
>
> I continued to cart the rape seed from the combine to the barn – it was not too time consuming as I'd only a few hundred yards to go from the barn to where the combine was working. It was when I returned with a load in the early evening that I saw rabbits between the Dutch barn and the bridleway. There's some grass on the side of the ditch which always grows lush. My plan was to sneak up on them, as that near corner of the field at the end of the Dutch barn always got nibbled to death by rabbits – they had to go.

I tipped my load of rape seed, checked the bins etc were all okay, then nipped over to the house to get the rifle. Just so Dad knew it was me if he heard shots, I came into the kitchen and loaded the magazine by tipping the shells out onto the side by the phone. As I filled it, I told Dad what I was going to try and do, Dad said good as these rabbits were costing us money. On this occasion not much else was said, though Mum asked me to pop in for a sandwich either prior to my going out or when I came back. The rifle did not have the telescopic sight attached or the moderator (silencer) when I took it from the cupboard. It had good sights on it anyway and the moderator is only useful when shooting long distances. By the time I got myself round to the Dutch barn with the loaded rifle the bunnies had gone. Sometimes I'd simply have taken a few pot shots at a tree or a can or brick or whatever, just 'cos it's good practice and it saves unloading the magazine. But I didn't fire a shot, so I went back to the house, I took out the magazine and put it on the settle and propped the gun in the angle between the settle and the wall. I know some of the police mistook what I said as they say I told them I put the gun on the kitchen table on my return to the house – I put the magazine on the kitchen settle and the gun against it. I went back to the barn, picked up a load of rape seed, tipped it in the barn and came back to the kitchen for a drink and sandwich. I told Dad the rabbits had gone, and joined in the table's conversation – how to help Sheila.

Mum, Dad and I all struggled to understand what Sheila and the boys needed. Lots of options were mentioned by Mum and Dad, including Sheila having my house and us doing up the house on Gardeners Farm – I'd have loved that as a winter project. The biggest concern though was Mum didn't like Colin having Daniel and Nicholas almost full-time. He was too much of a hippy for Mum, and so child care to support Sheila so she could keep the custody of the boys was important. We'd used foster carers many times before when they lived in Hampstead and Mum and Dad were exploring this issue. It wasn't the only option but the boys' wellbeing was important and foster care had been really successful before. Sheila didn't say much and I didn't pick up any anger or frustration from her, just that she appeared distant. I wasn't there long – a sandwich and a drink and a few more loads – then I closed the barn up, took the tractor back to the field. By now it was around 9.15 and when I got back Dad and Mum were still at the kitchen table. Dad was happy to collect the tractor and trailer for me, I said goodnight and went home around 9.30. I never thought to replace the rifle in the cupboard, it never occurred to me – it wasn't a lockable gun cupboard. And that spot by the settle wasn't unusual as a staging post. I watched some TV, rang Julie, which I did most nights, she'd been smoking cannabis with friends and drinking, we spoke for a bit and said our goodnights – nothing out of the ordinary at all.

There are some very obvious differences in his recollection of events, particularly where he returned and placed the gun after apparently going outside to shoot rabbits. We now have the rifle in three different locations and no real explanation why he didn't put it away. He knew that the twins were in the house, his own father had never been one to leave rifles and ammunition accessible, yet on this night he recklessly ignored his father's standards, feeling it acceptable to leave it out, complete with a loaded magazine and further ammunition at the ready. This is the same father we are told he respected and looked up to.

From everything I have learnt about Nevill Bamber, I find it hard to believe that he would simply ignore the presence of a firearm or leave the ammunition on open display in an area that was frequently used by the twins. So he either acted in a very different manner to how he ordinarily did and wasn't bothered about the situation, or the rifle wasn't there when he retired to bed. We know from Bamber's own testimony that Nevill was made aware of the firearm being loaded and the ammunition being out on the side, therefore if Bamber is telling the truth we must believe Nevill changed the habit of a lifetime and simply left it out.

Taking all of this into consideration, I don't believe the firearm had been taken out of the gun cupboard prior to Nevill retiring to bed, nor had the ammunition been dumped on the side as it was so out of character for him to ignore this, and of course, being an upstanding member of the community, he would know it was illegal and dangerous to do so. This is further confirmed when we consider the testimony of another key witness, Barbara Wilson, the farm secretary. At 9.30pm, Wilson had called White House Farm and spoken with Nevill. She said he wasn't his usual cheerful self and she believed she had interrupted an argument of some sort as Nevill was abrupt, impatient and very short. More recently Wilson has claimed:

> For some weeks he looked really drawn and ill. He seemed to stop and seemed as though he had the worries of the world on his shoulders. I thought he might have cancer ... He said he hadn't got anything like that but he had got great problems. I asked him to elaborate and he said that he thought he might die. I said, 'What makes you think that?' He said there might be a serious shooting accident. Knowing what had been going on, I thought that he knew that Jeremy was going to perhaps shoot him There seemed to be an awful lot of bickering. Sometimes when Jeremy came up they would have a hectic row ... Whenever Jeremy was around the atmosphere was so different. He would provoke his mother June by riding his bike round and round her in circles, trying to hit her.

It should be noted that Barbara Wilson also declared that Nevill had previously stated: 'I must never turn my back on that young man' meaning his son, Jeremy Bamber! She said that Bamber once left a bag of live rats in June's car, and would torment his magistrate father by wearing make-up in public.

When one puts Nevill's comments into context of the evidence we do know, it makes it even more unlikely that he would leave rifles and ammunition laying around the farm house, and so calls into question Jeremy Bamber's own testimony on this issue.

Also phoning the house that night was June's sister, Pamela Boutflour. She had rung at about 10.00pm. The phone was initially answered by Sheila Caffell who, Pamela felt, seemed quiet. She afterwards spoke with her sister June and noted nothing unusual in her tone or in their conversation that would cause her concern. According to Bamber, after he left there remained just three adults in the house, one of which he believed was a deranged killer capable of wiping out the entire family.

4

The Final Countdown

'My horror at his crimes was lost in my admiration at his skill.'
Sherlock Holmes – The Final Problem

We are wholly reliant on the testimony of Jeremy Bamber about what followed that morning when the murders occurred, this again is taken from his communications with me:

Around 3.10 to 3.15am I'm awoken by the phone ringing, it could have been 3.20, I didn't remember what time it was except I registered it was the middle of the night. It was Dad asking me to come over and quickly. I asked why, he said that Sheila had one of the guns and she was acting crazy. I told him I'd be straight over and the phone disconnected and went dead before I could ask him if he wanted me to do anything else, ring the doctor or whatever. I tried ringing him back at least twice, probably three times on my last number redial. It was engaged so Dad was ringing someone else. I didn't ring the police straight away, I went and got dressed. I was tired and, at that point, I wasn't overly concerned. I'd dealt with Sheila's nutty episodes with Dad and we always managed to calm her down. Dad didn't make it sound like panic stations but I was thinking that we could probably do with a policeman to disarm – not sirens blazing, 999, scaring the life out of everyone – just the calming influence of our local patrol bobbies. None of our local police stations are manned at night. I did not phone Witham, someone made that up and it became something I am supposed to have said, the only thing I said was when asked why I phoned Chelmsford I said I knew Tollesbury, Witham, Maldon etc don't man their police stations at night. I looked up Chelmsford in the phone book, I spoke to PC West which he times at 3.26am. Told him what Dad had said and asked if a car would pick me up or should I meet them at the house. He said he had already sent the car during our conversation, but it was sent by West after Dad's call to him. My guess is that Dad was on the phone to PC West when I tried to ring him back.

Dad certainly was not injured when he spoke to me. I think that having phoned me and the police that Dad went upstairs to calm Sheila down and it was at that point Dad got wounded. I'm puzzled by Dad's actions. I think I'd have run out of the front door, perhaps Dad was heading for a gun or to use the phone again. We don't know if Dad went upstairs again or up to his office – the offices upstairs were never examined by SOCO – but Dad had guns and ammunition in his upstairs offices and I don't believe for a minute that SOCO didn't examine every room in the house ... why would the police not even go into these rooms? Seems inconceivable to me. The only explanation is that there were things in these rooms helpful to the defence case but I don't know what!

After I'd phoned PC West, and it was no more than four or five minutes, I was worried that I'd done the wrong thing. Looking back that seems so selfish but I wasn't worried about Dad, I was sure he could handle things – of course as we found out later he couldn't, but I had no idea of this – all I had was Dad's short call. I know that I was stressed in case I'd let Dad down by getting the cops. I had no idea either that he'd phoned them himself, so that's when I rang Julie, I thought she'd be up as she'd said she was smoking drugs and drinking. I never really thought anything other than I want to be reassured that I had done the right thing. Julie was smashed on drink and drugs and just told me in response to go to bed. I should have known I'd get no sense out of her and there wasn't time to ring anyone else so I drove over to the farm ... I got out and spoke to two officers, told them the house was about half-a-mile down Pages Lane – we'd park by the cottages. We got in our cars and drove to the cottages, parked and spoke again. They asked me to say what I knew, the radio car was used by PC Saxby to inform Malcolm Bonnet (Control Room Operator) about the guns in the house, I gave him a list that Sergeant Bews got me to write. We then made a reconnoitre of the house.

In a further letter to me discussing his arrival at the scene Bamber informed me:

We spoke for a minute or two about what Dad had said to me. They asked about what guns were in the house and I gave them a list. PC Saxby then radioed this to HQ. PS Bews and PC Myall then set off to recce the house. I stayed with PC Saxby, happy to give him all the information whilst they took a look at the house. 30 metres down the track they turned around and returned to the radio car, they wanted me to come with them which I did. We walked round to the house, stopped by the wall and looked at the house (back door side). The lights were on in the bedroom, bathroom and kitchen – we didn't see anything out of place. We headed along the track next to the pond and around to the front of the house, observing from behind the garden hedge that borders with the field, PS Bews to my right, PC Myall to my left. Mum and Dad's bedroom light was on, we could see the naked bulb was on from where we were standing. PC Myall said he was sure someone was standing by the master bedroom door, PS Bews said he thought so too, at which point this person moved towards the bedroom window – there's no doubt that we could see someone in the master bedroom. PS Bews suddenly ducked down behind the hedge telling us to get down too. All three of us confirmed that we'd seen someone, though I couldn't tell who it was other than an adult. PS Bews said he'd been a firearms officer but lost his nerve so stopped doing it.

Because I've been thinking a lot about this incident over the past weeks for you, I have recalled other snippets of info from my memory that happened. PS Bews said that he thought the person he had seen had something in their hands, PC Myall hadn't noticed that and nor had I. But PS Bews used what he'd seen as a reason not to approach the house saying no way was he getting shot and, 'We'll call out the firearms guys', at which point he raced off running back to the radio car. PC Myall and I chased after him. Nothing else of note happened and so that is all PS Bews could have said to HQ in his situation report to justify calling out a firearms unit. 15 minutes later he returned to look at the house with PC Myall. He checked the bedroom window and concluded we'd seen a shadow or a trick of the light. But with the bedroom light on, the glass doesn't reflect, it only reflects if it's darker inside than out. So during those 15 minutes between visits to the house, the bedroom light had been turned off. This is the only way he could have seen reflections. And Paul, I'm pretty certain we'd seen someone walk towards the window in the master bedroom. We all of us thought so at the time but we might be wrong, however, someone pulled the curtains closed, someone turned the lights on, off, on, off and on in the house, so this someone was probably who we all saw.

I was sitting in a police car with PC Saxby outside the cottages at 7.30am when PS Bews told me that my family were all dead. The police got me to write out and sign a note giving them permission to destroy bloodstained carpets, bedding etc, they had me sign this whilst I was still at White House Farm and it was purely on their request that they could destroy things ... If I'd asked them to do so, how stupid would that look? And, they'd not pay any attention to such a request if they had any doubt about it being anything but murder then suicide by Sheila. It was totally down to the police requesting that I write such a note less than an hour after I'd been told such tragic news about my family.

The telephone call Bamber claims to have received from his father is a crucial aspect of his claim of innocence. It must therefore be considered in some detail. Primarily we must look at the content of the call made to Bamber and his claim that afterwards Nevill rang the police. He states about the initial telephone call he received:

> ... It was Dad asking me to come over and quickly. I asked why, he said that Sheila had one of the guns and she was acting crazy. I told him I'd be straight over and the phone disconnected and went dead before I could ask him if he wanted me to do anything else, ring the doctor or whatever. I tried ringing him back at least twice, probably three times on my last number redial. It was engaged so Dad was ringing someone else ... I wasn't overly concerned. I'd dealt with Sheila's nutty episodes with Dad and we always managed to calm her down. Dad didn't make it sound like panic stations ...

We must look at this testimony sensibly and with a reasoned mind. By his own admission Bamber states it was the middle of the night when he took the call from Nevill, an unusual time to receive a telephone call from anyone, let alone one's parents. Nevill asks him to 'come over, and quickly', he also mentioned that Sheila had a gun and was acting crazy. Bamber also refers to Sheila's nutty episodes. To most people, the inclusion of all those issues in one brief telephone call would cause alarm bells to ring and signify a dangerous situation. Bamber says he wasn't overly concerned by what Nevill had said during the conversation and that he didn't make it sound like panic stations. Nor was he concerned by the fact that the call was abruptly disconnected! None of this makes any sense and the action he took defies what he says. For example, why, if it wasn't a panic station situation, did he believe that Nevill was calling the police when he had tried to call him back, and why, if he wasn't overly concerned, did he use the redial function twice, perhaps three times, to try to regain contact with the farm? If the call was ever made it is clear that Nevill needed help quickly. According to Jeremy Bamber he didn't provide that, instead he got dressed and then called the police after finding the number in the telephone book. His justification for not calling 999 is that his father might have wanted to keep it low key and would not want an over-reaction. Even then before making his way to the scene, he took the time to call his girlfriend, Julie Mugford, who by his own confession he knew to be high as a kite on drugs and alcohol and he never expected to get any sense out of her, so why did he do it? His answer to that is because he needed reassurance that he was doing the right thing in involving the police. There is also some debate whether he called Mugford before or after he made the call to the police. He initially said he called her before the police but couldn't recall what was discussed, he then changed this detail saying he called her after he rang the police. Later, under police questioning, he was asked the same question about the timing of the call and replied, 'no comment'.

This wasn't a game, five members of Bamber's family were dead, surely he would want to do everything he could to help the police identify the killer? So why, if he was innocent, would he make 'no comment' answers to something that he had commented upon prior to his arrest? He had been more than free with his opinions to the police before being arrested, yet after this he suddenly stopped being so helpful. A brief look at the questions and answers identifies that he used negative (no comment) and one word responses to many of the questions. It is usual for a suspect under questioning who does not wish to implicate themselves further to give no comment answers, it's generally a time gaining ploy, or because the questions being put to them in interview are being asked for the first time and they genuinely cannot answer. The question about the telephone call was being put to Bamber because he himself created it as the scenario as part of his own alibi. One of the first officers on the scene that morning was the highly respected Detective Inspector Bob Miller who told me in a private discussion:

We were first told of the situation at the farm when the son of Nevill Bamber (Jeremy) had rung the police station to say that he had received a call a short time earlier from his father stating: 'Please come over your sister has gone crazy and has got the gun'. He also said that the phone conversation was cut short before he could ask anything further. He had tried calling his father back but it was engaged. As much detail as was required to dispatch a police unit was obtained and Bamber was told by the police control room to make his way over to the farm and to liaise/speak with police officers at the scene. That is the only record that exists, there is no record or log of a call being made to us by Nevill Bamber, the only call we received was from Jeremy Bamber. The staff in the control room stated immediately that the call had come from the son. No other calls had been received about the situation.

If Nevill Bamber had called us, as Bamber claims, he would surely have rung the emergency 999 number and not casually phoned the local police and conveyed a message similar in content to that communicated by his son Jeremy Bamber. In addition to that, we know from medical reports that due to the horrific injuries he sustained during that attack, it would have been impossible, and I use the word impossible to prevent his condition being misinterpreted, for him to use his jaw correctly and to calmly speak on the telephone. Nothing about the call adds up, it didn't happen, the call to us never existed, it's been fabricated by Bamber, and yes, he's tried to decipher and manipulate the notes recorded in the logs to prove that Nevill did call us, a deliberate misinterpretation.

The injuries sustained by Nevill also prove that it was impossible for him to have made the call to Jeremy Bamber, that's a further lie. Ask yourself this, why would Nevill call his son and endanger his life by getting him to come to what was a locked and secure farm house, where a gun-toting maniac is randomly shooting the family dead? If such an opportunity had arisen during the carnage, then Nevill, who we know was the protective alpha male of the family, would have called the police and ambulance to try to save his family. This was a life and death situation, it was the middle of the night, he could not be certain that Jeremy would answer or how long it would take him to answer. The telephone company weren't able to confirm that either of the calls allegedly made by Nevill (to Bamber or the Police) were ever made.

Ultimately, where the telephone calls are concerned, Bamber effectively backed himself into a corner by claiming he had received a call from his father. In doing so he reduces the number of suspects to just two – him or Sheila. If Nevill didn't make the telephone call to him, there was no way Bamber could have known about the murders unless he was involved. Forget all the other evidence, the bloodstained sound moderator (that had been on the murder weapon but removed and hidden in a cupboard), Julie Mugford's testimony, Sheila's mental health or psychotic state, this was the key piece of evidence that came from his own mouth, it was either Bamber or Sheila. It was proved well beyond reasonable doubt that Sheila could not have killed herself, therefore it leaves one option and one suspect: Jeremy Bamber.

5

The Police

'It is a capital mistake to theorise before you have all the evidence. It biases the judgment.'

Sherlock Holmes – A Study In Scarlet

As I said earlier in this work, my position as a crime writing ex-policeman has I believe provided me with a little more exclusivity in my research, especially among fellow retired officers. This chapter contains the dialogue from interviews held with Peter Simpson, Bob Miller and Stan Jones and for the first time in print, a unique insight into the late DCI Jones, courtesy of his official record of service and from the recollections of officers who served alongside him, including the said Messrs Simpson, Miller and Jones. All the interviews were held individually, there was absolutely no conspiring or discussions held. The individuals concerned were aware I was researching the case for a potential book and that my questions were likely to be searching.

Despite being put on the spot countless times, not one of them gave a 'no comment' or one word answer. They were helpful, insightful, genuine and truthful in their response, even when I was levelling criticism at their conduct, they responded as best they could.

Detective Inspector Robert (Bob) Miller

In an exclusive one-to-one interview with me in 2010, retired Detective Inspector Bob Miller agreed to answer every question I put to him about the case. He not only gave an insight into the methodology of DCI Jones, but also a very thorough overview of how difficult and political the police investigation was, with more than an element of Masonic influence affecting the course of the investigation and the destruction of one man's career.

It was a difficult investigation for everyone, and it's not been made any easier with all the wayward speculation that's been happening. Personally I feel sorry for the family and friends more than anyone, what they have had to put up with over the years, people telling lies about them and analysing everything they say and do, it can't be easy. The best of it is some of those who are inventing and throwing that bile are hardly in a position to do so, there are ulterior motives behind the rationale of many of them, not many are genuine campaigners, why would anybody with in depth knowledge of the case subsidise the spurious claims of a banged-up convict unless in the long term they saw something in it for them?

You've asked me to talk about the police investigation and my own part in it. I'm not actually certain what else there is to say that hasn't already been said. I'm agreeing to do this because you're an ex-copper, you know what it's all about and you can put things into better perspective maybe? Stan (Jones) said you gave him a really tough time, so go ahead, do your worst on me. I've nothing to hide, there is nothing to hide about this case. There's been accusations made that I was influential in getting a colleague removed from the case, it's not true. Nor is it true that the officer, Taff Jones, was wholly convinced of Jeremy Bamber's innocence. He wasn't. Truth is he was methodical, and in this case he was working through every detail in order to trap Bamber. Blaming Sheila was too obvious and there existed too many anomalies for it to be so clear cut.

Let's be honest, there isn't a detective on this planet who doesn't enjoy investigating a murder. It wasn't something we thought a great deal about in our part of Essex, so when the call comes in about some sort of domestic incident involving firearms, the old alarm bells start ringing straight away. Initially, because of the detail Jeremy Bamber had given to Chris Bews at the scene, it was thought there was likely to be an armed suspect inside the house. A stand-off of sorts was likely, bearing in mind we didn't know anyone was dead at the time, it was all about ascertaining who was inside, what was going on for the situation to arise, and any additional detail we could obtain that might help us peacefully resolve it. We were told that the son of Mr Bamber had rung the police station to say that he had received a call a short time earlier from his father stating: 'Please come over, your sister has gone crazy and has got the gun'. Bamber said the phone conversation was cut off before he could ask anything further. He tried calling back but it was engaged. He was told to get over to the farm and to liaise with police officers at the scene.

Chris Bews and Steve Myall asked Bamber to accompany them on foot round the exterior of the property from a safe distance and quizzed him about relevant detail relating to the occupants. He did this so that the information could be passed onto the firearms team for a sort of risk assessment. Bamber told them about the firearms and ammunition that was available inside the house, which was a real concern. He said something along the lines that his sister was a nutter. All in all it was a pretty bleak picture he painted. Bearing in mind what he said was all we had to go on, he was the person we had to rely on, so at the time what he was claiming we had to accept as fact.

The first officers on the scene were obviously a bit nervous, after all, a potential siege situation isn't something uniformed officers in Essex have to commonly deal with. It was a dangerous situation they were in. The thought that someone inside the property may have a rifle trained on them, and be ready to use it against them, is worrying enough. So their senses were on extra alert. At one point Steve Myall thought he saw movement from inside the house through an upstairs window, Bamber seized on this suggestion and claimed he saw it too, but ask yourself why he didn't mention it to us in his first statement. He didn't say anything, yet now he says it must have been someone! On closer examination, both officers (Bews and Myall) dismissed it as nothing but a trick of light, but realising their vulnerability they felt it correct to retreat to a safe place. So satisfied were they that it was a trick of light they didn't make it into a significant matter for the firearms officers.

The firearms team took a quick briefing from Chris Bews then asked further questions of Bamber. It all takes time – calling officers out, getting them briefed and into position, and then providing updates for the control room to log everything, alerting other emergency services – with facts that come from a single source. It's a race against time because the safety of those inside is important too. Bamber claimed that the firearms team, before entering the house, were in conversation with someone inside the property. He's manipulated that information and forced it out of context. The person he alludes to was actually him, he knew the layout inside the farmhouse, he had lived there, he knew the occupants personally, and based on that information officers at the scene were correct in saying he was from inside the farmhouse. There was never any communication by the police with anyone physically inside the house prior to entry being made. I want to make that clear. The only thing that could be heard inside the farmhouse at the time was the sound of a dog barking. I know some of the entries in the incident log are ambiguous, however, there was a lot of radio traffic being broadcast to the control room and general police duties still had to be carried out across the region. Clerical mistakes were made, but operationally on the ground we were gathering as much information and intelligence as possible.

Moments before the firearms team entered the farm there was a call from one of the officers who had snatched a look through the window and called in that he could see one dead female in the kitchen. Seconds later on entry it was called in that the body of a dead male had been located in the kitchen. Anyone viewing the corpse in situ would see that, at a glance, it could be misinterpreted as a female because of the long hair (it was Nevill Bamber who usually combed his hair back) that had fallen forward covering the face. The log entry says something along the lines of: 'bodies of one male and one female in kitchen'. It was a clerical error. Again this has been actively pursued by Bamber as evidence that he claims shows Sheila Caffell to have been alive (unconscious, having failed in an attempt to shoot herself) in the kitchen when the police entered. The noise the police made apparently awakening her, she runs upstairs to the main bedroom then shoots herself again. An absolutely incorrect assertion by him as it can be seen from images and blood flow that Sheila was shot where she was found in the bedroom.

Of course, the information being processed in the control room could never truly reflect the horror of the situation or the crime scene itself. It was ghastly and one that I will never forget. Stan Jones probably won't ever admit it, but we both filled up with tears when we saw the bodies of the two children, it was sickening. The person that did that to those sleeping little ones was an absolute animal. It was clear from the wounds and injuries that some of the people in that house were obviously dead, we didn't need a doctor to pronounce life extinct, albeit officially that had to be done. We were aware from the information provided by Bamber to police officers at the scene, and to PC West, that Sheila had been identified as having got hold of a gun and was allegedly going berserk. So when her body was found laid beside the bed in the master bedroom, her condition would have to be assessed to make sure the scene was absolutely safe. No one to the best of my knowledge deliberately interfered with the crime scene on entry, or during the investigation, and I didn't photograph the bodies or the inside of the house, so cannot speak on Scenes of Crime behalf. It is clear that in some of the images of Sheila the rifle has been moved, as has her arm, however, this could have been for a number of official reasons, the doctor may have had to move it to examine her. The one thing I do know and can confirm is that the resting positions of the victims remained intact, and no evidence was tampered with, as has been suggested.

It was a chaotic scene and there were police officers badly affected by the carnage they saw. Stan was one of the worst, as was Taff Jones, they were both ashen in colour when they came outside from viewing the scene. I remember Taff telling Stan to speak with Bamber who had aroused a hell of a lot of sympathy from officers by his emotive comments. Stan was told to get as much information from Bamber as possible and to be professional but distant. Something was troubling Taff, I'm not certain what it was but I don't think he was at all convinced by the crime scene. Nor was I as it actually felt contrived, something didn't fit. It was Taff who first asked the question how the victims had been contained and controlled, then individually massacred by such a slightly built young woman. He had an amazingly inquisitive mind and sometimes you felt he was testing your powers of observation. What had puzzled Taff struck me as odd too, pandemonium must have reigned for the minutes it took to execute them all as while the shooting was taking place, surely the other adults in the house would have been alerted – unless more than one killer was responsible?

It was shortly after this that word began to circulate that the officers who had been speaking with Jeremy Bamber felt he was putting on something of a show. Stan (Jones) pulled me to one side and told me he had a bad feeling about him and how he had an arrogant attitude and everything he was saying seemed to be measured and carefully controlled, which is unusual in someone who has just lost their entire family in the most frightful circumstances. It wasn't the grief filled son, brother, uncle that many of his supporters and writers portray, no, he was hell bent on telling us how crazy his sister was. He was devious in that he tried to focus our minds on her problems, and that's not only cunning but downright evil. You have got to agree Paul, most people learning of a tragedy like this would have been in a real mess – confused, angry, anxious even – not Bamber, he was absolutely collected in his thoughts.

Another thing that he can't justify is why, when we asked at the scene about the various points of access and exit of the farm house, he said nothing about the insecure windows he often used to climb in and out. He was asked that question specifically because we obviously didn't want the killer escaping out of a window. If he had nothing to hide he would surely have said something and told us. He realised that we would find doors locked with keys on the inside, and that left no other means of getting out of the house, which of course intimates that the killer must still have been within the property so pointing the finger at Sheila. He knew it would incriminate him to mention that he could climb in and out of windows, so kept quiet until he could cover that weakness in his plan. Which, of course, he did by entering the house a short time after being arrested (but not charged) by the downstairs bathroom window, and leaving a note on farm secretary Barbara Wilson's desk, telling her he had done so because he had left his house keys in London and he needed some papers for his trip to St Tropez! How bloody insidious is that? Making it appear an innocent act and with no sinister motive in him entering the property via that method. That was another matter that didn't quite feel right, after the carnage he was quick to move on, the holidays and the socialising, a young man grieving, or a manipulative killer without a conscience?

At the time I gave Taff the heads up at the crime scene, I informed him some officers thought Bamber's response to everything and the situation didn't seem right, he told me that there was no textbook manner for people to grieve or accept such a situation and that we needed to look at what was before us, we could look at Bamber later. Taff wasn't stupid, nor was he someone you could easily fool, he sensed something wasn't right but then other matters overtook the investigation that genuinely upset him. What he saw as interference into the investigation by some of the relatives really did wind him up. I think it was this that caused delays in his own investigation. He was a thorough detective and knew it wasn't always easy to nail an offender, I think he always believed that Bamber would incriminate himself but he never had time to pursue that. It's such a pity he's not around to tell us his opinion because I know he would agree that we got the killer. All the made up propaganda about him believing Bamber innocent and wanting to give evidence on behalf of the defence is absolute lunacy, he never once said or implied such a thing. It's more garbage created by the Bamber supporters to give credence to the 'Bamber was fitted up' theory.

I have to admit there were issues between Taff and Stan Jones, in the job we call it a clash of personalities, but they really did used to rile each other with their barbed and flippant remarks and comments about one another. Stan could be good with people, victims, offenders and witnesses, and he seemed to get the best out of them and win over their trust. He was one of the few officers I know who could be the good cop or the bad cop in an interview. I like to think he saw me as supportive in his career, a good advisor if you like, I got on well with Stan but we too had our moments, that's the way it was with us with no hard feelings afterwards. I'm not so sure it was so forgiving between him and Taff. In hindsight I do think he should have explained to Taff how the relatives felt his opinion of the case was blinkered and shown more loyalty to the boss. Stan always said that he had no option but to pass on the complaint made by Robert Boutflour, if he hadn't he was potentially jeopardising his own career. He wasn't the sort to deliberately go behind anyone's back, but him and Taff weren't similar, and in this instance he felt Taff was convinced it was all Sheila's doing and he wasn't listening to anyone else's opinion, or that of several other officers including myself. Stan wasn't aware of Taff's innermost thoughts, only a few were. I think what upset some officers was Taff going off to play golf, it was early days of the investigation, none of us knew it was pre-booked annual leave, but saying that, some officers would cancel their leave to work on such an investigation!

I reminded Bob of police officers' universal love of overtime and the money it brought in, I therefore felt his last comment improper, he apologised and agreed with me.

I was called upon to give evidence at the inquest which took place a week after the murders. By now we held real suspicions about Jeremy Bamber's part in the crime. You know the situation when you just don't have the whole story because lies have been told and things don't tie up, well it was like that. The whole scenario just didn't sit right with any of us. I had a gut feeling that Bamber wasn't telling us the truth and it wasn't down to anything anyone else had said to me, it was my instinct. When he was spoken to after the event he had a 'couldn't give a damn' attitude, and there was obviously more to his story than he was telling us. But you can't stand up at an inquest and say to the coroner that you are concerned that someone is telling lies, they want answers and closure. I told them that we were satisfied it was a murder-suicide pact, and that the wound on Sheila was by her own hand.

I know what you are going to say, there were two wounds on Sheila, I wasn't being clever, or deceiving anyone, nor was I telling deliberate lies, I was referring to the non-fatal wound. At that stage of the investigation we held a belief that this was probably self inflicted. It really was too much to suggest that Sheila shot herself twice, so we wondered had someone else shot her. The house, to all intents and purposes, was secure, the weapon used in the slaughter still lay on top of Sheila's body, so we could be expected to believe that she fired a shot into her head – which we know was non-fatal – then composed and repositioned herself to shoot herself a second time to make sure it was fatal. It was a complicated scenario, I know that such things can happen and there are documented cases to show it, but this tragedy definitely wasn't one such instance. The lack of heavy blood staining on Sheila's nightdress showed that she hadn't wandered around. Experts said that she had been in a seated position when both shots were fired, the second shot, the fatal one, would have caused her to fall back. So Sheila was dead, shot through the neck twice while sat on the floor. Her left arm was bent and had fallen back to a position where her hand was close to her head, the right arm still rested on the rifle. It was an unusual position for the rifle to remain in, laid across the body, and since the body must have fallen back and hit the floor with a jolt it just didn't seem right.

Of course there was no sound moderator or sights attached to the rifle when police arrived at the scene, so we were expected to believe that this young woman, whilst in a psychotic state and after committing this carnage – the murder of her family including the children she adored – then calmly removed the sights and sound moderator from a rifle she wasn't ever proven to be able to confidently handle, let alone dismantle, and then has the where-with-all to place the sound moderator in a box and put it back in the gun cupboard which is downstairs, before returning upstairs to sit down and shoot herself in a room that wasn't hers! It gets more unreasonable by the minute to be honest. In my experience you don't get many people who can so proficiently dispatch a family during what must have been frantic and emotionally terrifying scenes – some were moving targets and all shots hit the intended target – then she sits down and fluffs her own suicide and has to shoot herself twice before she kills herself! It doesn't make sense and these were some of the discussions that took place.

I will always remember one of the final things Taff said whilst he was on the case, he asked if we believed there was any one individual who had more to gain from the deaths than the collective body of the family. It was like he was intimating that he knew Jeremy Bamber was guilty, but at that time proving such was difficult. As you know, Taff was removed from the case and to a certain extent I think it was his own fault. He didn't like the outside interference or that which was coming down from above, and he had an inkling that Stan, as one of the team, wasn't being straight with him. I think he lost focus because he felt undermined and accepted that the four murder, one suicide theory, was initially for him the most reasonable option. I know he had concerns about the house being locked and secure, and if another party was involved how such a killer could get in and out, he had a notion that someone may have innocently given the killer (Bamber) access then locked the door once he was inside. The fact that Taff was investigating these things shows he wasn't absolutely convinced that Sheila Caffell was a crazed rifle wielding killer!

Another matter that didn't tally was why she killed herself next to the bed in her parent's room. Surely she would have wanted to be with her children in death, not laid in the same room as a woman she had very serious issues with? It didn't make sense, and yes we can pontificate about her seeing the children as devils, or possessed, or whatever else has been claimed, but it doesn't take a genius to recognise that she did actually love her children, and despite her illness she did her best with them. As with all children accidents can happen, I don't know of a child yet who hasn't had an accident and hurt themselves. So to say that Sheila wasn't a caring mother is wrong, it's inaccurate, all the evidence shows the contrary.

It's a fact that we only have Jeremy Bamber's word that she showed any violence towards the twins. Is he a trustworthy and credible witness? Quite frankly no he isn't. So you can see how our suspicions arose. The entire scenario as described by Bamber just didn't work out and serious doubts existed in our minds from the outset. We have never wavered in our belief that Jeremy Bamber was and remains guilty. I believe the evidence today is, if anything, stronger than it was at his trial in 1986. He, along with numerous supporters and his campaign team, has spent almost 30 years looking at police documents and trying to find mistakes in them. Can he find anything that shows he didn't do it? No, he can't, and that's not because it's locked away in a secret locker at Essex Police HQ, it's because he actually did it, he's guilty of murder.

I read somewhere he's passed a number of lie detector tests. That means nothing at all, and the examples you provide prove how dangerous those things can actually be. We are talking about real life killers here, not the ridiculous antics of those on the Jeremy Kyle show or on television crime programmes.

The examples Bob Miller refers to is documented evidence that proves polygraph tests are not accurate and improper reading of the results can be dangerous, in truth they prove nothing. For example, Charles Cullen (The Angel of Death) was working as a nurse and murdered up to 40 people over a 10-year period through lethal injection. After the death of his first victim in 1988, he was identified as a suspect and volunteered to take a polygraph test to prove his innocence. He passed the test and went on to kill a further 39 times at least. Experts believe he may be responsible for up to 400 deaths/acts of murder. Additionally, in 1984, Gary Leon Ridgway (The Green River Killer) had been given a polygraph test and passed it, four murders had occurred at that time. Ridgway went on to kill many more times before finally being caught and confessing and plea bargaining to murdering 49 women – the real figure is potentially double that – in the Seattle area over two decades. The failure of the polygraph cost dozens of lives and destroyed those families. There is a wealth of material available that questions the validity of such tests.

Elsewhere, a quick search of the internet produces pages of information on how to cheat or trick your way through a polygraph test! The American Psychological Association, the world's largest association of psychologists, has carried out much in the way of thorough research into polygraph testing, with damning conclusions: 'Although the idea of a lie detector may be comforting, the most practical advice is to remain sceptical about any conclusion wrung from a polygraph.' So for Jeremy Bamber, or any other killer proclaiming their innocence and using the validity of passing a polygraph test as real or conclusive evidence, the test holds no significance, it is not a scientific method of proving one's innocence. It may make a news story but, other than in the minds of those who want to believe it is conclusive proof, it holds no credibility.

> I think he (Bamber) would earn some public respect by admitting his guilt than by playing these stupid games and wasting taxpayers' money. How many times does he mention freedom and his inheritance in these media releases he has produced? You hit the nail on the head when you called it the Bamber propaganda machine. It's truly sickening to think what the remaining family are going through every time he gets column inches spouting his innocence, and the so-called police conspiracy to frame him. What makes him think he's so special to warrant such a thing? He was a nothing, he wasn't even on our radar, a small-time crook who stole from his own family, they make him out to be this paragon of virtue, a quiet respectful young man who has suffered. Ask his so-called friends, Julie or Brett, what they really think of him, or the many other people he has used for his own devices over the years. Kind and generous words? I guarantee there will be few. He is a cold-hearted, ruthless child killer, and he deserves to stay where he is until his life is over and he no longer poses a threat to the public. Just my opinion of course Paul.

Detective Chief Inspector Thomas Emyr (Taff) Jones

I had known since pre-trial that one of the principle and key individuals involved in the case was not the killer or any witness, but a police officer. This is an officer who never gave evidence at trial, yet his understanding of the crime is crucial. The man receives few plaudits but much criticism for his part in the initial investigation as it is inaccurately claimed by some that he held beliefs that Bamber was innocent! The officer in question is Detective Chief Inspector Thomas Emyr 'Taff' Jones. For a full 33 days, Taff and his team worked a case they apparently believed was a murder and suicide. He was eventually removed from the investigation by a senior officer and sadly passed away before the case ever came to court, thus his professional opinion was never officially heard.

We have to examine whether the claims of Bamber's supporters that this officer believed Jeremy Bamber innocent, are accurate. Once again we only have the pro-Bamber supporters' word for this, along with some anecdotal detail that he intended to give evidence on behalf of the defence at trial, because he felt so strongly about Bamber's innocence.

A vastly experienced officer, Taff Jones rarely got it wrong, yet here we are asked to believe, mainly by relatives' claims and those of junior and vastly less experienced officers, that when investigating this crime – a serious multiple murder investigation – he got everything totally wrong. It is a fact that some retired officers, inappropriately in my opinion, infer that Taff was something of a hothead and a bully. Such claims commonly surfaced after he passed away. I can confirm here for the first time that there is not one blemish or accusation of misconduct on Taff Jones' career record. Yes he was tough, driven and would stand his ground if he believed he was right, but he was no bully.

Taff Jones was a proud and dedicated family man and a police officer who went out of his way to help and support his colleagues and the public. As far as crime clear-up rates are concerned, he was an incredible thief taker, and many said he could spot a lie the moment it was uttered. The inferred investigative failures that have been attributed to him by some police officers involved in the Bamber case, officers who some might say want to distract from their own failings, is nothing short of misinformation. Taff deserves much more credit and respect than he has been shown. We now know that a small group of police officers appear to have been actively working against the operational direction of Taff Jones. It could be portrayed as him being undermined as there was certainly an element of subterfuge taking place within a tiny element of the investigating team.

DCI Jones was widely regarded as an outstanding and experienced police officer, a supportive man-manager, a strong leader and generally a good and fair man all round. Like many honest men he spoke his mind, didn't court favour or accept sycophantic praise, and all importantly, didn't suffer fools gladly. Taff expected from his colleagues honesty, integrity and loyalty which he provided to his team in abundant quantities. It's a sad indictment that Taff has, to my mind, been deliberately made a scapegoat for the Essex Police. Some claim that Taff was easily manipulated by a cunning Jeremy Bamber and had got the investigation wrong. There follows self-glorification by certain officers who claim from the outset they knew Bamber's guilt, therefore they had got it right!

Throughout my research I have heard from ex-Essex Police officers who themselves visited the crime scene at White House Farm, most saying that some detective officers were running around like headless chickens while one described them as clueless. It must be considered that relatively few of these detectives had ever seen a murder victim in the flesh, let alone carnage of the magnitude found inside White House Farm that morning. As a result, it seems that some struggled to know what to do and what was expected of them! Some were asking when DCI Jones was expected on scene, they knew he was an experienced officer and a good delegator and decision maker and they wanted and needed him to direct the operation and take responsibility. Almost all said that from a police perspective it was a circus, almost farcical, a chaotic scene that was spiralling into a state of panic as across Essex and beyond rumour and gossip began to spread of the tragedy.

It was a unanimous opinion throughout the force that DCI Jones was an officer regarded by virtually all who knew him as a thorough detective and a fair copper and a good bloke to have on your side. Jones had an undeniable skill and ability to solve crimes. His career record shows a dedicated, conscientious and brave man that paid attention to detail. Here for the first time in print are the details of the official Police 'Record of Service' for DCI Taff Jones, courtesy of the staff at Essex Police museum.

Thomas Emyr 'Taff' Jones was born in Llandudno, Caernarvon, Wales on Wednesday, 21 June 1939. After a grammar school education he went on to join the army and was a serving soldier with the Welsh Guards between January 1957 and 1960, attaining the rank of Lance Sergeant. On 21 January 1960 at the age of 20, he was sworn in before two Justices of the Peace (A.S. Raven and F.R. Holt) at Chelmsford, Essex and formally joined Essex County Constabulary as a probationer Police Constable. Standing at almost five feet 11 inches, and of strong athletic build, he very much looked the part of a police officer. Within twelve months of joining the Essex County Constabulary, he married his girlfriend Maureen, and together the couple settled down and were to have three children from the relationship.

Known as 'Taff' to his friends and colleagues, his police career saw him serve across much of South Essex region, starting at Colchester, then Harlow before moving to CID Fraud Squad and later to Chelmsford CID. He was promoted to Sergeant in December 1967 and remained with the department for a little over nine years before attaining promotion to Detective Inspector on the Stolen Vehicle Squad. He later moved to Basildon CID and had spells working for the Regional Crime Squad at Brentwood and Harlow before returning to CID at Chelmsford.

Taff Jones had a wealth of experience across all areas of police work, not only had he natural leadership and investigative skills, he was highly respected by all who knew and worked with him. A qualified firearms officer, he also had a mass of experience and was qualified in surveillance and operational techniques, he was also trained in an advanced course of criminal investigations. Throughout his career Taff consistently produced impeccable standards of work which is proven by the 11 commendations he received over a 23-year period.

In 1962 he was officially commended by the then Deputy Chief Constable of Essex County Police for arresting a hardened criminal who had violently assaulted him during the arrest, as a result a further nine criminal offences were cleared up.

In 1966 he was commended by Justices at Harlow for the painstaking work and commitment he had shown investigating a series of crimes, and the subsequent arrest and conviction of two men for these.

The following year, 1967, he received a further commendation from Justices at Harlow for his perspicacity resulting in the conviction of a serial thief. In 1968 he received further commendations from Justices at Chelmsford, and from his own Chief Constable, for the level of investigation and enquiry into a series of crimes (larceny, receiving and store breaking) where three men were successfully convicted. Later in 1968 he was commended by the Chief Constable for the painstaking investigation and successful conviction in a case of conspiracy to cheat and defraud.

A further Chief Constable's commendation was received in 1972, again for his outstanding and painstaking work in detecting a serious criminal who had committed numerous offences.

In 1976 he showed his bravery and integrity as he was again commended by his Chief Constable for the manner in which he had dealt with an affray in Witham the previous year.

In 1981, the Chief Constable formally commended him for his professional ability and diligence over long periods, which resulted in the conviction of eighteen men for offences of theft and handling.

In April 1985 he received a High Court Judges' commendation from Aylesbury Crown Court for his investigative work in the conviction of four men for widespread offences of fraud. A further Crown Court commendation was received from the High Court Judge at Chelmsford Crown Court in 1985 for his investigations and diligence that resulted in the arrest and conviction of David Pearce and Marion West for blackmail.

As can be seen from the above record, Taff Jones was an exemplary officer in every way imaginable, even his sickness (attendance) record shows that throughout a police career which spanned 26 years and 111 days, he had just 45 days absence. There is no recorded sick absence from 1982 to the date of his sad and untimely death on 11 May 1986. His death in itself was remarkable, since it was caused by a freak accident at his home when he fell from a step ladder. A sad end to fine life.

It's blatantly evident that over the years Taff has been blamed for all manner of things related to this case and, without physically being there, it's difficult to understand how he has been made a scapegoat for the failings of other officers who for whatever reason didn't take the correct course of action. Instead the area became what has been aptly described as a circus and news of the tragedy spread like wildfire across Essex.

Stuart Phillips was a freelance journalist in the area and in 1986 he told me his recollection of how news of the massacre broke:

I first heard about the murders at the farm when I overheard a conversation in a paper shop in Chelmsford. The two men were chatting away and one said that a local bobby had been telling him that something major had happened at White House Farm in Tolleshunt D'Arcy. It was a siege and there were guns involved. I called Chelmsford Police Station but got no information, so made my way to the place. Other press were gathered at the top of what I now know to be Pages Lane. There were quite a few police and onlookers in the area too. It seemed to be common knowledge that a nutter had gone berserk inside the farm, the identity of that person hadn't been confirmed at that time, it was between 7.30am and 8.00am. Then there was a defined buzz that ran through the crowd as detail circulated that five people had been shot dead within the house. Someone local who knew the people that lived there said it's likely to be the Bamber boy that's done it, he can be a nasty piece of work when he wants to that one. It was a man who made the comment, he would be late fifties or early sixties I would think, a scruffy looking farm worker sort of chap.

At that time there was no mention of Sheila Caffell as a suspect, or victim, I think that must be because she had been visiting the farm and obviously not everyone knew that. I tried to sell the story based on what the man said as a scoop before it all broke further but nobody wanted it and later, when Sheila had been named, nobody in the press would touch it because it seemed inherently wrong. Police and other officials were coming and going all the time, it was bloody busy. I often wonder if the chap who made the comment about Jeremy Bamber being a nasty piece of work, before more detail of the story broke, was ever spoken to by the police. I know it was only an opinion, but he must have known more about Bamber to say such a thing!

Anecdotal it may be, however, it shows that someone who must have known the family felt suspicious about Jeremy Bamber before any serious detail of the murders emerged. It's clear from this information that the location was busy since Stuart mentioned it to me. We can never know, with any degree of accuracy or certainty, who actually visited the scene. The official record compiled by the police was not concise, nor in my opinion, reliable. Realistically, official statements should have been recorded from everyone entering the house or visiting the crime scene outlining their reasons for being there, it's plainly obvious that the more individuals who visit the scene, the greater the likelihood is that it may be accidentally compromised.

The crime scene by any standards was extremely busy. On 7 August 1985, according to police records, an official total of 73 police officers visited the farm. When civilians are included, the total rises to 87. From that number, 62 individuals are recorded as entering the intimate crime scene i.e. inside the house. That's 62 people within what must be regarded as a restricted area. It's a ridiculous number of official bodies to have on scene and to be expected to manage. None of this, I hasten to add, was the fault of DCI Jones.

Few of the rooms within the crime scene were so large and clinical in their appearance that movement in and out could be easily achieved. This was a working farmhouse and a family home, it wasn't particularly well designed or clutter free, each of the rooms housed furniture and household goods, thus making it awkward not to disturb evidence. Putting it bluntly, until the arrival of Taff Jones at approximately 8.55am this was anything but a controlled environment!

Police incompetence at securing the crime scene, which it undoubtedly was, doesn't make or prove Jeremy Bamber's innocence, nor does it take into account Taff Jones' apparent belief that Sheila Caffell was responsible for the murders of four members of her family before committing suicide. Listening to other officers who knew him, there is no doubt that Taff was looking at the bigger picture, he was investigating an entire scenario based on the evidence available at the crime scene and from the antecedents and movement of every individual involved. It has always been believed that Taff Jones was convinced it was a case of murder then suicide inflicted by Sheila Caffell, however, my own investigation shows something altogether different. There exists a genuine belief among many officers that Taff Jones did hold some suspicion about Jeremy Bamber and his role in the crime. He did not, it seems, believe him wholly innocent. Other officers have since told me that Taff spoke privately of taking a 'softly softly' approach to catching Bamber out with his lies, and taking the time to allow him to say too much and virtually convict himself.

Unfortunately, officers did unofficially attend the scene.

Having spoken to some who claim to have done so, it is clear it was through the best of intentions, and in some instances nothing more than curiosity. It becomes evident that White House Farm had more police officers in its grounds and was busier than anywhere else in Essex that morning. Police officers are human beings and like all of us they are inquisitive. It had been a quiet night of policing across the region, so the unfolding tragedy in Tolleshunt D'Arcy aroused interest from officers on night duty across that part of Essex. One officer now retired and requesting anonymity told me:

> That morning, when the initial firearms incident went live, the police radio went absolutely crazy. There were calls going into the control room from officers across the county, everyone was offering their assistance, the airwaves were the noisiest I can ever remember throughout all my years of service. At the time, almost every police officer on duty wanted to attend and to sweep the area to try to catch whoever had carried out the killings. I'll be honest, the control room staff did well to cope with the amount of detail coming in from everywhere. There were too many inconsequential messages being broadcast by officers wanting to get involved. If you've ever been in a police control room when a major incident is taking place then you'll know it's a hive of activity and there's a good deal of noise – telephones ringing, management and senior officer requesting minute by minute updates, members of the public calling in – and on top of that, the general day-to-day policing of the county continues, crime doesn't stop because of one incident, it all has to be dealt with and managed.
>
> There were officers posted at the top of Pages Lane preventing public access but police officers were arriving all the time. It's accurate to say that police officers were not trampling all over the house, so the actual murder scene was as secure as it could be. It just felt as though no one was actually taking control, not that the senior hierarchy are of much use at a scene like that, but it just felt as though junior officers needed some direction. As you well know, police officers do need to be told what their role and responsibility is at a serious crime scene, and such leadership was absent in the initial stages until after the firearms team had arrived.
>
> Once the CID turned out, things seemed to get much calmer, and I remember there being suspicion about Jeremy Bamber at that early stage, with uniform officers saying he was 'unreal' in

his attitude and crying crocodile tears. He seemed self-centred and talked about what he was likely to gain from the death of his family – a Porsche sports car was mentioned as I recall. The officers there felt he knew what the outcome of the police search was going to be well before the firearms team entered the house. I spoke to him several times after the morning of the murders, and to say he was cocky and overtly confident would be an understatement. To me, the man lacked genuine integrity in the way he spoke of the deaths and in wanting to have a family dog put down. The daftest thing I heard later was that he made the suggestion that the dog might have accidentally fired the second shot into Sheila, how bizarre is that?

The other person I felt particularly suspicious of was his girlfriend, Julie Mugford. She was hiding something, and whenever I met her she couldn't look me straight in the eye. I was never interviewing her or anything like that, just talking to her as a normal police officer going about his duties. The performance that both she and Jeremy Bamber gave at the funeral was completely out of place with the occasion and people who knew them were shocked by his appearance and said they – him in particular – were putting on an act. I thought he looked different and it was said that Julie put make up on him to give the appearance of the doting and devastated son. She desperately clung onto his arm but rarely looked into his face which was a bit strange too. The rest of the family looked empty and lost, devastated, and in a state of disbelief, but not Bamber or Mugford. I'm not suggesting she had a part in the murder, but we know she was aware it might happen and said he (Bamber) had been planning it and talking about killing his family for a time before it happened, yet she didn't do anything to prevent it or immediately report what she knew afterwards. It's quite astonishing her conduct.

Once news of the murders was revealed, White House Farm was under a different kind of siege, this time it was an official and safe one as police officers descended on the area. With so many patrol cars and officers about, it would have become an impossible task to accurately coordinate every movement. Indeed from all we know, it's clear that some loss of management control did occur, not that this affected what had happened during the commission of the crime, but it certainly created confusion among the ranks and made life that bit more difficult for those protecting the scene.

No police investigation ever translates into true textbook format, and this one was no different. And while it's easy to make judgements with the benefit of hindsight, it's vital that a sense of order is managed from the outset and radio transmissions kept concise and to a minimum, or at the very least switched to a separate police radio channel. By contrast, the policing situation at White House Farm before the arrival of Taff Jones, was anything but calm or controlled, no doubt fuelled by a genuine keenness to assist and catch the perpetrator.

As we know, initially the mentally ill Sheila Caffell was named as the perpetrator of this ghastly act. The police, through information provided by the only living witness, were misled to believe that she took the lives of her family then her own. The motive for the crime was casually produced by Bamber as he told officers that after an evening meal family discussion regarding her ability to properly care for her children, Nevill and June Bamber believed the children would benefit from foster care and that Sheila needed long term treatment for her ongoing mental health issues. This apparently left Sheila quietly seething, and through the night she apparently went on the killing spree. It was a harrowing scenario created solely by Bamber, and one which the press instantly seized upon. There followed countless images of the beautiful and innocent looking young model and mother, Sheila Caffell, covering the front pages of the national press. The murders, despite being so horrific, aroused a wave of public sympathy for all concerned. With there being no surviving witnesses, and from all the evidence available at the crime scene and family antecedents provided by Jeremy Bamber, the original police hypothesis seemed acceptable and correct.

Just over five weeks later that perception altered dramatically when it was revealed that there may be more to the crime than Sheila Caffell's mental breakdown. A family inheritance of a then estimated £423,000 was cited as being influential in the modus operandi of the killings, and today remains central to all arguments about the case. Further, it was now stated that the murdered family's surviving heir, 24-year old son Jeremy Nevill Bamber, would be the one benefactor who would handsomely profit from the deaths. Police suspicion grew about the part

Bamber played and, aided by the pointed finger of accusation, it was learned that he had a vested interest in the matter and was not on the greatest of terms with either parent.

So it was that some relatives of the dead family felt uneasy about the claims levelled at Sheila Caffell. They expressed their private concerns believing that she was incapable of committing such acts, in their opinion it was more likely to have been Jeremy. From the outset, DCI Jones dismissed such allegations as weak and improper, since they came from individuals who, at that time, could be regarded as suspects themselves. One officer explained to me how 'Taff' had told one relative, Robert Boutflour: 'Show me the evidence, show me the proof and I will act. Until that time, you are as much a suspect as the man you accuse. Everyone is a suspect until we state otherwise. My team will investigate every angle, not just what you want us to.'

It wasn't what Robert Boutflour wanted, nor expected to hear. Disturbed by the official shun, he elected to take matters into his own hands and with the aid of some of his family set about actively pursuing his own investigation to prove Jeremy Bamber guilty, effectively undermining and ultimately discrediting the police investigation up to that point. It became a race against time and decisively a battle of power and personalities, with DCI Jones instead of being seen as an ally, emerging alongside Jeremy Bamber as a nemesis to Robert Boutflour.

The relatives were convinced of Jeremy Bamber's guilt and were dogged in their determination to prove their case. It became evident to DCI Jones that Bamber wasn't a popular figure among certain living members of the family, nor of some of the staff employed on the farm. Indeed, as recently as 2013, some have publicly revealed suspicions about him and his behaviour in the months leading up to the tragedy. For reason known only to themselves, they chose not to voice such concerns for 28 years! As a result, the content and implications of their official statements that were volunteered to the police at the time, and during subsequent inquiries, has changed not to support Bamber but to portray him in an even more sinister and damning light.

Determined to have his own way and not to be dismissed, Robert Boutflour made a call to DS Stan Jones on or around 6

September 1985, the call was to Witham Police Station. Boutflour asked for an update on the investigation. It wasn't the first time such a call had been made to the detective, he had frequently discussed non-sensitive proceedings as part of the investigation. This is where DS Jones can truly be faulted, since he carried out such discussions without the expressed permission of the Senior Investigation Officer, DCI Jones.

Ultimately Boutflour reported to DS Jones his concerns about the Senior Investigating Officer. DS Jones was himself three ranks junior and a good deal less experienced than his DCI, so advised the complaining Boutflour to speak with the Assistant Chief Constable of Essex Police, Peter Simpson, who was in overall charge of the investigation. Simpson later said that the most stressful time of his career was, 'The Bamber inquiry, when for more than a week the media pressure was incessant, and the investigation went through several complex changes.' (*The Law*, Sept 1993).

So it was that Robert Boutflour was invited to speak with Simpson, and with much enthusiasm expounded his personal opinion about how and why the murders at White House Farm had occurred. He expressed concerns about the manner in which the police were investigating the crime, and fastidiously maintained a portrayal of Jeremy Bamber's guilt and Sheila's absolute innocence.

It would take a brave and extremely assured person to categorically state that the main police suspect in any investigation was innocent, especially when there existed at that time no substantial evidence to support such an accusation, bearing in mind Boutflour was declaring that the police had it all wrong, and it was Jeremy who killed everyone and not Sheila. A dramatic claim indeed.

Most police officers could be forgiven for being wary and sceptical of accepting such a view as definite fact, not so Peter Simpson. He had heard of the suspicions held by some of the investigating team and was open to looking into all claims. Incredibly, he responded positively to Boutflour's claim and despite the integrity of his senior investigating officer being called into question, not to mention that of his force, by persons who clearly held a major material interest in the outcome of the case let alone an emotional and physical association with the tragedy, he was submissive to Boutflour's insistence. Simpson ordered a secret review of the case. In doing so, he undermined all of Taff Jones' credibility. This was regarded as an act of betrayal by some officers. Here we have one of the most senior police officers in the Essex force seemingly complying with a member of the public against an officer in charge of a murder investigation.

There exists no record of DCI Jones being informed or advised of what was taking place, or that a formal complaint had been made about him, initially to a junior officer who was under his command, by Robert Boutflour. There is no easy way of saying this but the junior officer took it upon himself to escalate the complaint, potentially causing trouble for his superior, by directing that complaint to a more senior level, that of Assistant Chief Constable. No matter how anyone tries to address this detail, a loyal, respectful, and close team this clearly was not!

The camaraderie and togetherness one expects and generally finds in a tight-knit team of loyal investigators working together on a tough case was clearly absent. I quote an Essex Police statement made in the January 1999 edition of *The Law*, it relates to Essex Police officers supporting each other. 'Gradually a team culture was established and the officers, working together and supporting each other's needs, created a formidable Police unit working in the countryside.' Such an ethic clearly didn't exist in 1985, not in that team of detectives anyway.

To be fair to Robert Boutflour, he had tried to convey his private suspicions on several occasions to Taff Jones, who in turn assessed the allegations and the reasons for making them before forming his own judgment, which was based solely on the crime scene, plus the actions, records and searches made by police officers at White House Farm. His views were not based on mere supposition. DCI Jones recognised that some of the relatives were clearly upset about all manner of things, principally some were worried about their own futures and financial security, a position which was very likely to alter as a result of the murders. As can be seen, from the outset of the investigation there are different factions within the police, all had one main goal, to find the killer, but with different objectives causing them to work against one another. Then we have a killer freely spinning lies and creating illusion, confusion and mayhem – deceit reigned in this picturesque part of rural Essex!

In any criminal investigation, especially a case of murder, everyone with an association to the victim(s) is treated as a suspect. It's extremely rare for a member of the public with any association to the crime to have influence over an Assistant Chief Constable, let alone have sufficient authority to convince him that the appointed senior investigating officer in that murder inquiry should be replaced – in this instance, replaced by someone less experienced! Putting it plainly, it's unimaginable, therefore making it a brave decision for Simpson to make. If this was a work of fiction and we were discussing a police investigation that went seriously astray, it would make for unbelievable reading and readers would dismiss it as utter fantasy. Yet here we have a senior detective of the finest stock who is publicly and professionally humiliated, his career fundamentally ended, because of concerns and suspicions of a member of the public who himself had links to the crime!

The pressure on Simpson to ensure his decision was a correct one that was to dramatically change the course of a criminal investigation, increased tenfold once it had been actioned. In making such a decision, his own credibility and future career was in jeopardy, he depended on it being the right thing to do. A more sinister and complex working environment is hard to imagine, Taff Jones had colleagues working against him across all ranks.

It is now clear from information provided by Stan Jones himself that he held closed door discussions with Simpson at the time, and backed the claims of Robert Boutflour, which he believed to be accurate. Whilst I am critical of the ethics used to achieve this directional change, it was ultimately based upon genuine belief. It saddens me as an ex-police officer that such circumstances did occur. It does, however, reveal an insight into the executive managerial machinations of the Essex force of that era. Simpson, who had joined Essex Police on promotion four years earlier, can rightly claim that his decision was proved to be the correct one, his reputation remained respectable and untarnished. Peter

Simpson retired from the force in October 1993 and sadly passed away in 2008.

I didn't know Taff Jones, nor did I ever meet him, though I am experienced enough, and have been around long enough to know when a police officer is revered and held in the highest regard by those peers and colleagues who genuinely knew him. During a very early part of my research into this work it became evident that Taff was one such police officer. People spoke of him with great respect. I have talked to a number of his colleagues who worked alongside him and for him, they were open in chatting to an ex-police officer about a great detective. Unfortunately that openness disappeared once they knew my aim was to write this book. Suddenly no one wished to be named in the work, they feared reprisals, not physical harm but the all consuming worry of losing ones pension. This is a concern that hangs over police officers like the sword of Damocles, especially when it comes to speaking out against the establishment or former employer. Yet without hesitation, almost all I spoke to provided glowing eulogies and testimonies to Taff's brilliance as a detective, and of him being a good, honest human being. There were those who claimed his removal from the White House Farm murder investigation was influenced by Masonic connections, the brotherhood working to support its brethren before all others. Almost all viewed his removal as the ultimate insult to his integrity and professionalism. I know of not one police officer who could think of a worse scenario or a more detrimental professional insult than to be removed from any investigation, let alone as senior investigating officer in a murder inquiry!

One officer who knew Taff extremely well, told me:

> It really hurt Taff being kicked off the investigation, it shocked just about everyone on the force, except those involved of course. Taff was a legend, his thief-taking skills and man-management of his team and of criminals were respected by just about everyone. Taff could spot a criminal a mile off, he knew when someone was spinning a yarn, or when witnesses weren't to be trusted. He always called it as he saw it, and so far as I can remember, he never got it wrong. Taff always took time to explain his judgment calls and decisions and would explain his rationale in doing so. I

know dozens of officers of all ranks who went to him for advice on investigations and interviewing witnesses and suspects. Taff was a one-off. I remember him telling a few of us of a time when he attended a burglary, it was a wealthy businessman who made the call to the police and, to all intents and purposes, the man was the victim. Taff smelt a rat in the tale the man told, and within five minutes he had him banged up, the so-called nicked property was found hidden in the house grounds, and later, during the formal interview, he confessed to fencing some serious value stolen goods. As a result, there was a mass crime clear up as dozens of crimes were solved. That's how Taff was, he had the old fashioned copper instinct and you can't buy that.

The decision to take him off the case was shocking, it didn't seem right at all, he genuinely believed that he never called the investigation or the outcome wrong, he reiterated that he knew Sheila Caffell played an important role in the murders but she couldn't have acted alone in committing the crime. Whichever way you look at the act, it was a sad event, a massacre, and as well as the adult victims, two little children were murdered. Taff was a real family man, the hurting of children affects coppers too, most of us are parents and we are human, it causes real pain when a child is the victim of any violent crime and we tend to go that extra mile to make sure we catch the right perpetrator. It hurt him that someone could do that to two innocent sleeping children, the evidence pointed to Sheila but I remember him voicing concerns about her suicide and the positioning of her body. I recall him advising a few of us that this was a case of softly-softly, catchee monkey.

Everyone was a suspect to Taff, until such a time that he could factually eliminate them from the inquiry. It was known that Taff held suspicions that more than one killer was involved and the case wouldn't have a quick or obvious solution, meaning he knew there was some aspect or detail that had yet to reveal itself. I know he held suspicions about a number of things in the case, details that he never openly talked about. He never liked external interference from senior officers, or detective officers, who were without all the facts and details, and he definitely did not like the influence of anyone whose overarching motives could be regarded as suspicious.

No matter what anyone says, I know that Taff wouldn't take the word of anyone at face value. He has been made to look like he was easily gullible and manipulated by Jeremy Bamber, he wouldn't even accept another copper's word without supporting evidence.

In the department (CID) back then there existed many sycophants, junior detectives who would agree with the opinions of other officers to get on their right side. Looking back, I think Stan Jones was saying one thing and doing another behind the boss's back. That's bloody bad behaviour in anyone's book, but then Taff didn't always tell Stan everything either, so I expect it works both ways. I think it boils down to respect really, or the lack of it.

Taff didn't suffer fools gladly, he couldn't do with gossip or with back-stabbing and he would bollock anyone who he caught gossiping or who he thought had a loose or careless tongue. Whenever he had someone like that allocated to one of his teams, he would give them a chance to integrate and deliver. If they didn't or couldn't, he moved them from his team and on to something less challenging. He was that kind of person, fair, honest, open minded and impartial as a copper and a great man to know, he gave his all to Essex Police. When he passed away, there were dozens of officers in the force who believed that we had lost one of our best ever detectives, that's how highly he was rated, so you can see why it came as something of shock to most of us when he was taken off the White House Farm murder investigation.

I admit Stan Jones wasn't one of his greatest admirers, he seemed intimidated by Taff's confident manner and approach. They weren't enemies but they weren't good friends either, it could never be inferred that Stan was his right-hand man. During the early part of the investigation, Taff passed the interfering family over to Stan and told him to listen to what they had to say, but not to get too involved (personally) with any of the relatives, he told him that he expected his officers to be professional but distant, and not to readily acquiesce. Stan took this as a criticism I think. After that, it was obvious he was not of a mind to defend or respect Taff.

To be honest, police officers aren't good at keeping animosity private, it became the worst kept secret in the force that Stan was influential in getting Taff removed from the inquiry. Don't get me wrong, Stan was a decent enough copper and a good bloke as well, but he wasn't a patch on Taff Jones. From a personal perspective, I'd back Taff's judgment against any other detective of that era, and that isn't exclusive to Essex, but from any police force in the land.

I also know he didn't like or trust Jeremy Bamber. He regarded his testimony as unreliable, and as a witness he believed Bamber was holding something back, he called him a good liar. It's true, Bamber was an expert manipulator, but Taff wasn't the gullible sort. When the Boutflours started to force control of the investigation he spoke out against them, his suspicion and inquiring mind is the main reason why he told the family to back off, and to stop trying to influence him and the route of the investigation. As I understand it, Robert Boutflour was persistently telling him that Jeremy Bamber was the killer and that no one else was involved, therefore Sheila was totally innocent. When Taff asked for supporting evidence, none was forthcoming, it was simply their personal opinion. As a person, he wasn't the sort to listen to gossip, he dealt in hard fact and irrefutable evidence that could pass every test and courtroom examination.

He had something of a reputation for scrutinising a crime scene, many thought him to be a bit anal about it really, as every scrap of evidence was examined in detail and evaluated on its merit, very little got by him. He practiced what he called the 'A B C D E F' guide to the commencement of a criminal investigation, and inspection of the crime scene. This being: Accept nothing. Believe nobody. Check everything. Double-check everything again. Examine every detail. Focus suspicion on voluntary information by family or friends who try to influence. That was Taff for you, he was cynical yet very thorough. Anyone who believes that Taff did not suspect Jeremy Bamber has got it very wrong.

As bad as it seems, it's commonly accepted that he was thrown to the dogs over the Bamber case, and his career and life ruined by job officialdom. I don't think there was a copper in the land who didn't know because it was all down to the influence of powerful local connections. The Masonic brethren played a part, and we know the power those sort yield, these were dangerous forces to engage against. The influence of the brotherhood forced our hierarchy to sufficiently change the entire course of the inquiry. There may well have been some honest reasoning behind it, it was all kept quiet at the time, a need to know basis only. Whether that was to save Taff from any embarrassment or to disguise what his fellows had done to him we never did find out.

I do know that Taff never accepted it, he continued to express his concern that he believed he had been well and truly shafted by people who he was forced to refer to as colleagues. I remember talking to another detective around the time of his funeral. He said he knew that Taff believed Jeremy Bamber was involved in the murders, and that he had considered whether it was Sheila and him who had been accomplices in the crime! He didn't get chance to act or prove it, because it was all taken out of his hands, but it's said that he told someone else that he would prove Jeremy

Bamber's guilt and that whilst Sheila was also involved, he was the one actually responsible for the massacre because with Sheila's ill health and her poor state of mind, she was easily manipulated by Bamber.

We can never know the truth of what went on during the 'behind closed door' discussions that were held – conversations and meetings that eventually saw Taff completely removed from the investigation. I have no doubt in my mind that Taff Jones was made a scapegoat in this investigation, ultimately thrown to the wolves by his colleagues. One thing that is clear from my research is that Taff Jones too, was an innocent victim of the White House Farm murders!

Detective Sergeant Stanley Brian Jones

It has been claimed that a number of junior officers involved in the investigation felt very differently about what had happened. One of these was Detective Sergeant Stanley Brian Jones, who later gained promotion to Detective Inspector and who believed that Jeremy Bamber was not as honest as he appeared to be and that he was hiding something. Stan Jones initially based this assumption on the manner in which Bamber dealt with the grieving process. Not the most accurate way to gauge a person's guilt, yet Jones believed it was inconsistent and not the way a close relative would act on being made aware of such a tragedy.

One offered example of this suspicious activity was that Jeremy Bamber apparently ate a 'hearty' breakfast which consisted of bacon, toast and coffee just hours after news of the murders and death of his family had been broken to him. To me that is quite a ridiculous judgment to come from the mouth of a police officer. I say this because I remember as a then serving police sergeant, whilst on duty I received news of the sudden and unexpected death of an extremely close family relative, my brother. In this instance the news was broken to me by a senior officer tasked with conveying details of the death. I had police officers around me, none of whom I regarded as friends, so would not confide personal matters to any of them. Obviously the news came as a shock and devastated me, it felt as though I had been hit by a steam train. My brother and I were extremely close. My mind was in turmoil, yet I didn't cry or break down, I did though retch and was physically sick. I suppressed my emotions until I felt able and comfortable to release them, that was to be when I was on my own. Furthermore, within a couple of hours of receiving the news, I was eating and enjoying a 'proper' English breakfast in the police canteen – rashers of bacon, eggs, sausages, mushrooms, black pudding, fried bread, toast and coffee. Throughout, I was chatting and discussing everyday matters to my colleagues. Does that behaviour make my actions suspicious, or cause concerns about my character, alternately did it make me capable of mass murder? Of course it didn't, it's absolute nonsense.

Subsequently, Jeremy Bamber's suspicious breakfast consuming activity turns out to have been at the bequest of the police, who were to later admit that they sent out for a breakfast. Indeed, Stan Jones also confirmed that he and Jeremy Bamber drank some whisky around the same time. The whisky drinking wasn't suspicious, yet the eating of a breakfast was? The gut instinct police officers often perceive about an individual's guilt on this occasion appears to have been misinterpreted and confused with a natural appetite.

Taff Jones meanwhile was an old school detective, he worked with 'conclusive' and 'real' evidence, it is little wonder he so readily dismissed what was little more than the fanciful misinterpretations of Stan Jones. It is well known in the world of psychological profiling that if one desperately wishes to see something dark or sinister within a person's mannerisms or behaviour, then that behaviour will, no matter how meaningless, appear suspicious. In this case Stan Jones believed it indicated a guilty mind, and so communicated that suspicion to his own peer group who in turn felt the eating of a hearty breakfast to be rather sinister!

In 2010 I managed to interview the then retired police officer Stan Jones. I was somewhat surprised and pleased that he agreed to meet with me and discuss the case. We met at a hotel in Chelmsford and I asked him many pertinent questions. Despite it having no relevance on my research, I found him to be a likable and straightforward man, and to his credit, he never once shirked a response or tried to side-step anything I put to him. It goes without saying, Stan Jones was totally committed to his belief that Jeremy Bamber was guilty of murder, and that Essex Police were innocent of any manipulation of evidence, or of the facts. I admit I found him likeable and thoroughly believable and didn't once get the feeling that he was deliberately making anything up. I initially asked him to give an overview of the police case, since this seemed the best and most direct way to understand the logic and reasoning behind everything.

You are quite correct to say I was heaping guilt on Bamber because of the breakfast he managed to eat. However, I'm not that shallow Paul, there was much more to it than eating a breakfast, it was as if he was constantly playing games with us. To do that at such a serious time wasn't right. Everything seemed like a joke to him. Sure the tears appeared every so often, but they weren't tears of sadness, they were forced crocodile tears. I don't honestly think he cared about his family now they were gone, he wanted to get his hands on the wealth and to live the life he believed he deserved.

It's a long time ago now, I can't remember every tiny detail but what I will say is that I remain totally convinced that Jeremy Bamber was the killer, nothing I have seen, read or heard since has changed that view. He has used his time in prison cleverly. He now manipulates every detail to make it appear that a miscarriage of justice has occurred. It isn't anything of the sort. He's as cunning as they come, he likes to play the victim for his supporters, all hard done by just to gain as much mass sympathy as he can. No matter how much sympathy he receives, it will never ever prove him innocent, the reason for that is because he is the killer.

From recollection, we (the police) took a call on the morning of 7 August 1985, it was from Jeremy Bamber. The contents of this are well documented, this was the first and only notification received by us that something was dangerously wrong at White House Farm. There was not one call to us from any other source, nothing from Nevill Bamber or anyone else, the only call we received that morning about the situation came from Jeremy Bamber. A car was dispatched and the first officers at the scene were quickly accompanied by Bamber who had arranged to meet them and had driven himself there. Because of his local knowledge, they asked him to walk them round the outside of the property. As is the way, the officers privately questioned his manner and attitude. When the firearms team forced entry into the property, they found five dead bodies, two of which were children. That was the sickener for most officers. I arrived at the scene on that same morning. I attended with Detective Inspector Bob Miller, it was about 9.15am. When I got there, Jeremy Bamber was pointed out to me by another officer, he was about one hundred yards distant from me, walking across a nearby field and in conversation with Dr Ian Craig. I saw Bamber leaning forward, it looked as though he was trying to vomit.

Constable Woodcock took Bob and myself into the house, and we looked at the crime scene surrounding the bodies and throughout the house. I felt sick, it was a horrible scene. I was told that the bodies had been confirmed as being those identified by Bamber as last known to be inside the house. I was then instructed to go out and speak to Bamber and formally convey confirmation of the deaths. I said something to him like, 'All your family are dead, you have to be strong, the sooner you accept it the better.' I was stunned by his reaction, he called me a hard bastard, but the way he did it sat uncomfortably with me, it felt as though he was trying to be funny. I tried to reassure him and told him I was hard for a reason. I then instructed one of the Constables, Mick Clark, to take him home and to start taking a statement. Mick said he didn't have a car and so Bamber offered to drive them both in his car.

I remained at the scene until a time later when I was instructed by DCI Taff Jones to go to Bamber's home and to take a statement from him. Taff told me to take the softly-softly approach, I took this to mean not to upset him because he was grieving. When I got there, as well as Mick Clark a family relative, Ann Eaton, was there. Mick was talking to Bamber and taking down his statement, I remember thinking how calm Bamber appeared to be. When I spoke to him at the scene, and later at his home in Goldhanger, it just didn't feel right, he looked to me to be feigning grief and not actually feeling it. I didn't think Taff Jones could see it, he seemed satisfied that Sheila Caffell had committed four murders, then shot herself. I thought Bamber knew more than he was saying but it was too soon and inappropriate to start grilling him at that point.

It wasn't long before Julie Mugford arrived at his house, I immediately thought, poor girl she must be shell shocked by all that was happening. I went out to meet her and to explain about the murders. When we got inside the house, Julie and him hugged each other, I told them to have a few moments in private, they went into another room and I closed the door behind them. When I opened it a few minutes later I heard a sound that to me could have been a cough or even a snigger, if it was a snigger then obviously it's suspicious what he found so funny. I'm certain it was Jeremy Bamber who made the sound and, yes, I do believe it was a snigger.

I reminded Stan that some people giggle or snigger when in difficult or stressful situations, it's generally regarded as a nervous titter and this could perhaps account for the sound, if it actually was such a noise. He reminded me that Julie later confirmed that Bamber had said to her at that moment, 'I should have been an actor,' he had then laughed.

Stan reiterated that Julie was in love with the killer, she was under Bamber's influence and would not have done anything that could be construed as betraying him at the time. I asked why she waited so long to do what any reasonable person would do and report what she knew to the police the moment she became suspicious. Stan's response to this was minimal:

> She did! He (Bamber) convinced her that it was someone else who carried out the murders, but he also said that if she ever said anything about the crimes to the police, then she would be viewed as culpable too because she knew about the murders and had done nothing. The girl was frightened, she was terrified of him and that's the truth.

I then asked about Bamber's moods in court. Stan had said that Bamber became very happy, jovial throughout the day of questioning. Why did he later feel this so important?

> Well, anyone normal, anyone decent, would be devastated by such a tragedy. He wasn't, he seemed to take it all in his stride and gain confidence the longer the day went on. Yes we had a drink, I thought it would help steady him a bit, and he cracked a few funnies about whether I was concerned about being caught drink driving. It was banter, but not the sort I expected from a grieving close relative. The alcohol wasn't sufficient in quantity to make him drunk or giddy or anything like that.

I asked Stan why, and how could he know that.

> Don't be stupid, that's a ridiculous thing to insinuate. I was on duty and involved in a multiple murder investigation, I wasn't likely to get drunk on duty, or get the main witness drunk. It wasn't a session we were having! Before I left him for the evening,

I asked him whether he wanted the bloodstained carpets or any others items that were in the house that had been contaminated, destroyed. He said he did, but not anything that was valuable and could be cleaned. I got him to sign an authority for this.

Several days after this I went back to Bamber's home with DCI Taff Jones, he said he had some further questions to put to Bamber regarding his statement. I was a bit confused by it as Taff genuinely seemed focused on the rifle used in the murders and asked him if he had used the rifle that night to shoot rabbits. Taff asked him if he was sure or certain that was right because he'd told a policeman that he had. Bamber denied saying anything of the sort. Taff obviously wasn't satisfied with the answers Bamber provided and he kept pressing him with further questions about the weapon, he asked if he had made it safe. Bamber said he had put the gun in the house, removed the magazine, taking one shot out of the breach, and put it into the magazine and placed it on the settle in the scullery. He stood the rifle up against a wall – I always assumed he meant a wall in the scullery where the loaded magazine had been left.

Taff then asked him about the sights and the silencer that had been on the gun the previous weekend, and had he taken them off to shoot the rabbits. Bamber was adamant that he hadn't, and believed it may have been his father who had removed them. Looking back, I remember thinking how awful suspicious Taff was about the state of the weapon and when it had been used and handled by Bamber before it had been used in the killings. I do think he (Taff) may have held some suspicion about Bamber, but if he did he kept it close to his chest and he didn't tell me. I know he mentioned to Bob (Miller) that he felt it would be hard for Sheila to beat and kill Nevill, and he wondered how she could manage to control the household during the killings.

Taff changed the questioning of Bamber to matters of ammunition and asked him if there was any ammunition in the rifle when he handled it earlier in the evening and loaded it. Bamber said he didn't think there was. Taff then changed in his questioning technique, and for a time I thought he was behaving like he was questioning a suspect and not a witness. He asked him (Bamber) about the ammunition that was found in the kitchen. He didn't explain to him at that point, but I later learned that a total of 30 rounds were found on the kitchen work surface. He asked Bamber to account for the quantity of ammunition in the kitchen and he told us that he had taken out a box of nearly 50 rounds.

Taff told him to think carefully before he answered because what he was saying didn't tally with what had been found. Bamber avoided answering the question and was waffling on. Taff told him to answer the question. Bamber said he left the gun safe, with no ammunition left in the breach of the weapon. 25 rounds were fired during the murders, add to that the 30 found on the kitchen work surface and that came to a total of 55 rounds. He asked him to account for the additional five rounds and where they came from. Bamber looked perplexed and distinctly less confident, he couldn't answer. Taff was privately mulling something over in his mind, and I saw in his face that he wasn't convinced in his failure to explain things. I expected Taff to probe and push the matter further, but he didn't, he left it there and had a general conversation with Bamber, discussing things that he (Bamber) seemed altogether more confident and comfortable with. Taff pulled me to one side and told me to talk about Sheila's background and her general state of mind, which I did. I could tell that when I was doing this, Taff wasn't really listening, he seemed preoccupied by something. I did wonder if he felt he had let Bamber off the hook and lost the opportunity to push him further.

Suddenly Bamber came out with a question that neither of us expected, he asked if we knew what order the family had been killed in! I was shocked that such a matter should come into his consideration, so asked what he meant by order. He muttered something about having spoken to his accountant a day earlier and had been told that it would affect the wills if they didn't know. I told him we didn't know and I think Taff said something similar but wasn't so definite in his response. He followed that question up by asking us if there was any way we could tell. I told him that I didn't think there was any way we could, which seemed to satisfy his curiosity.

It seems clear from what Stan Jones says that Taff did hold doubts and suspicion about Bamber. I asked Stan if he ever wondered if DCI Jones thought Bamber played a role in the killings and that what he felt was external interference from family relatives had caused such suspicion to be diluted.

I don't honestly know. To my mind he was clarifying a few outstanding matters that's all, but he certainly wasn't satisfied by the answers Bamber provided. The investigation carried on along the four murders and a suicide route. Taff never mentioned anything different to me and the relatives were only drawing to our attention details we weren't aware of, they weren't actually interfering.

It was then that we started to piece other information into the equation. For me, it was Julie Mugford coming forward that truly altered the course of the investigation, that's when it became absolutely clear that Jeremy Bamber had a role in the killings and he hadn't been telling us the truth. I remember he took off on holiday to St Tropez, which struck me as odd, why would anyone do that when something as traumatic as this had happened? He wasn't going away because he needed to be rid of the stress or the media pressure, this was pure self indulgence. Bamber didn't see it that way, his solicitor tried to justify it by saying something along the lines that Bamber had taken the break so he could recuperate, allowing the press attention focused on him to subside. I'm not certain many people would find such behaviour acceptable, especially after such a tragedy. The press attention at the time wasn't even on him. He didn't engage with anyone beyond his small circle of friends and associates, he certainly wasn't hounded by the press like some others were.

It was always about him. He used others to support him while he played the victim, and that's precisely what he has done ever since, manipulated people for his own devices. During my interviews and conversations with him, he never once showed any remorse for his dead family, he expected everyone, police officers included, to feel sorry for him and no one else. He denied almost everything we put to him and I don't believe he ever thought he would be found guilty, or go down for the murders, he thought he was too smart for us. He wasn't smart at all, you can fool some of the people some of the time but you cannot fool all of the people all of the time. That really sums up what happened in the police investigation, we got wise to his games. The rest you can get from trial documents I think Paul.

You have asked about my professional relationship with Taff Jones. You know very well what being a policeman is all about, it's competitive, only the strongest survive, especially in the CID. I had people, colleagues, who didn't like me. There's an illogical reasoning behind such emotions. I didn't physically do anything to cause that ill feeling, it existed in their minds – envy, jealousy or personality differences – it exists not only in the police but in all walks of life. I confess my relationship with DCI Jones wasn't the best I had in my police career, we were always professional in what we did, and as in all such occupations we had our disagreements. Taff was a strong personality, a man who refused to accept that he could at times be wrong. We were two different people working for the same employer, a situation that can be found in any workplace. I wouldn't say we were chalk and cheese, but we had our professional differences, that's all. More than once he questioned my relationship with the relatives of the victims at White House Farm, he told me I should be more cynical and suspicious of everyone connected with a murder investigation. That I should view everyone as a suspect until proven otherwise. He was preaching to the converted, I knew how to handle suspects and how to handle myself in a serious investigation, no I didn't like him doing that, treating me like a rookie cop.

Granted, from a major crime perspective, nothing ever came close to those crimes throughout my career. It annoyed me that Taff would question my discretion, and I told him so. My opinion didn't seem to matter to him and he barely reacted to me. It was at times a depressing and arduous investigation, physically and mentally gruelling in the number of hours (overtime) we had to put in. I think everyone felt the pressure of the investigation, including Taff. For me, forcing a change of mindset was as tough as it gets, I didn't see it as any kind of betrayal to Taff. It's simple, to my mind his opinion was wrong, not mine. I held a sneaking suspicion about Bamber from the first time I met him, the way he was acting at the scene was odd, suspicious. He stared at me, his eyes looking directly into mine, it was as if he was trying to intimidate, or show me that he had nothing to hide. I thought to myself, 'You're hiding something lad, and I'll find out what it is.' It doesn't exactly help when someone's opening words to you include calling you a bastard! Well, you aren't going to feel much positivity towards them are you?

I didn't mention my suspicion to Taff at first, though Bob did. I was initially concerned that I had misjudged the situation and didn't want to look foolish on something so important. I later found out that I wasn't the only one with doubts about him, other officers had too. I didn't like Bamber from the moment I met him, he was full of himself, confident and asking far too many questions about the police investigation and what happens next. I thought he was a bit of a smart-arse and he showed a real lack of respect towards the entire situation.

As best as I can remember, the entire crime scene was busy, you have to understand, this was a huge incident the like of which had never before been seen in the county, or in the United Kingdom come to that. Yes, reacting to the changing detail we were in a state of confusion, some uniform officers on blockade duty were in panic mode, terrified of making a mistake or letting someone in who shouldn't be there, some hadn't a clue what their individual role was. I don't think there is a police force in the country that could have handled this crime scene, it was as horrific as they come. It didn't help that the only witness we had was an absolute liar and deliberately misguiding us with some of the detail.

I did my best to ascertain the different possibilities for a motive for the crimes. Bamber had told a number of uniform officers at the scene that his adopted sister (Sheila) was a real nutter, and she had recently received psychiatric treatment. Every few minutes a different uniform officer would come to tell me this, it was as though Bamber was reinforcing this using her mental health as the main reason for her committing the crimes.

I was always professional in my dealings with the remaining family members, careful and considerate, I tried to comfort them as best as I could. You have to listen to what people close to the victims are saying in a murder investigation, and I admit I felt a lot of sympathy for them and for their loss. It was a couple of days after the murder I think – about the time I collected the sound moderator – that Bobby Boutflour and his wife Pamela came to see me at Witham Police station. I called in Bob Miller. Bobby Boutflour told us that he believed Jeremy was the killer and that he had gained entry into the house, murdered the family, then returned to his home to call us – the police. I remember Bob Miller explaining that everything points towards Sheila being the killer. (*This recollection was accurate since Robert Boutflour recorded the following details of that meeting in his typed diary – Miller said to him: 'We have completed all the tests but one, so far they all point towards Sheila as the killer, there is one more test to be done, and that should be through soon. We have some very sophisticated equipment, and we are sure that nobody entered or left that house that night.'*). Bobby seemed to take the role of alpha male, he became the family spokesperson. It was an unusual situation. Never before have I known a family or relatives get so actively involved in an investigation, normally they are too busy grieving and supporting each other, yet in this case they took on the role of pseudo investigators. It was like something from a television movie. Taff Jones had warned them of the consequences of interfering with a crime scene and police investigation, he believed they were interfering and effectively threw them out of the police station on a number of occasions that I know of. It rubbed them up the wrong way because they believed they had evidence to prove it wasn't Sheila and that it was Jeremy. They saw it as helping build a more accurate picture of what happened.

I remember Taff telling some of the investigation team that the relatives were deliberately clouding matters, and as a result they were not helping with the investigation. I think he saw the relatives' interference as being driven by their desire to inherit as much as they could. He also believed they would get very little should Jeremy Bamber be the main benefactor from the deaths.

I never did get on that well with Taff Jones, we were at odds over many things. It was nothing personal on my behalf, just a clash of personalities, we weren't the best of friends. I once told him I didn't think they (the relatives) were clouding matters and that, to prevent any aggravation, I would act as a go between, liaising closely with them through Bobby Boutflour, and pass on any important intelligence to the investigation team. I got to know most of the family very well, they were decent people, and yes, I remained in touch with them for a long time after the trial. Nothing wrong or unfair about that.

Bobby Boutflour contacted me about his concerns over Taff Jones' bad attitude and what he felt were his unrealistic claims that Sheila was the killer. He (Bobby) didn't believe Sheila capable of such an act, none of them did apparently. I don't know why they didn't speak out about this immediately. Perhaps it was the shock of the situation, though I do know that they became more suspicious by Jeremy's behaviour and comments. The fact they didn't say anything at the time doesn't say anything about them at all.

I got to know Bobby quite well, I told him I couldn't do anything about the situation with DCI Jones, and told him he had to go above him, to go direct to Assistant Chief Constable level. Pete Simpson was in overall charge of the investigation so it was the natural chain of command I was following. I told him he should pursue a formal complaint with him. Yes, I told him how to make that contact, to call and to write, and to put the family's thoughts down in black and white. I knew Pete Simpson was the right man for him to talk to, he had been in charge of personnel matters for the force, and would know how to deal with a complaint of such a sensitive nature. I rang Pete to let him know what was coming in his direction, I briefed him in advance, and told him of my own suspicions. You ask if I think I was betraying loyalty by doing this, no, that's utter nonsense, I was doing what any good, honest police officer would do.

The murder investigation didn't need any distractions like formal complaints. Pete Simpson told me not to discuss the matter with anyone and to let him deal with it. Thereafter, I honestly don't know what was said by Bobby Boutflour to Pete Simpson, or when and where the meeting took place. I never asked because I was loyal, and it wasn't my place to know. I really don't want to discuss this aspect of the case any further, it's not relevant to what happened, I didn't betray anyone, I did my job. Ultimately what's important is that we got our man, and get him we did! There is no doubt in my mind that Jeremy Bamber was the killer, this examination of how the investigation was managed isn't really very helpful. It doesn't matter how much subterfuge, as you put it, existed between us, or what your opinion is of how unprofessional we were, the real murderer is behind bars and, thankfully, he is likely to stay there for a very long time.

I believe that any further investigations or enquiry into his claim of innocence are nothing but a waste of public money, all we as a society are achieving is pampering to his needs. Can't you see that? This book won't change anything, ask yourself why. It's because he is guilty, he did it Paul!

I was taken aback by Stan's sudden reticence to discuss the intricacies of how the investigation changed course, he refused to discuss this aspect any further because he felt it was irrelevant. I explained that I wasn't trying to catch him out or win points on behalf of Bamber. I felt it important to understand the different pressures everyone was under during the investigation, even Taff Jones.

Yes, Taff felt the pressure alright. He was so wound up that while the rest of us were busy carrying out inquiries, he went away to play golf.

It was a cutting and unnecessary remark I felt. Playing devil's advocate, I asked why such a comment was relevant since the golfing day was prearranged and he (Taff) had booked and taken annual leave which in turn would have to be authorised by a more senior officer. I told him that from all I knew and had heard, Taff had an exemplary police record, he wasn't the sort to shirk responsibility or run away, especially when it came to something as important as a murder investigation. I made mention to a comment made by DCC Ron Stone at a post trial press conference, Stone recommended pursuits such as playing golf to help officers with relaxation.

I added that the original information about Taff playing golf must have emanated from someone within the murder investigation team, that individual must have deliberately spoken out about it to the press and therefore put it in the public domain knowing it would undermine the DCI's integrity. Clearly this was a breach of confidence and cannot have been helpful to the investigation knowing that someone within the ranks was passing on private information such as this to deliberately hurt the reputation of a good officer.

> I don't know about that, it's hardly a critical detail is it? We have to use the press to our own advantage, there is a constant trade of information between the two bodies, and we always used each other. I don't know who passed on the information about Taff playing golf while the rest of us worked the investigation, a number of us felt quite aggrieved by it. I think you are getting drawn into stuff that doesn't really matter, it doesn't affect the case or the outcome. I've no doubt someone was telling the press everything, that happens in every newsworthy police investigation. All I'm saying is that some of us were surprised that he went off to play golf in the middle of a murder investigation, that's all. It didn't send a good or positive message out to anyone. I thought it was insulting and unsympathetic to the family and actually showed poor leadership, so did many others. I told Taff how I felt, and you know what? He didn't seem bothered.

I continued to ask more detail about the murders, and in particular, if he thought Jeremy acted alone, or whether there was an accomplice. This question appeared to surprise him.

> I don't know where you are coming from with that question. If there was an accomplice, it wasn't the Matthew MacDonald character if you are in fact insinuating it was him (*Macdonald was a red herring who was originally discussed by Bamber in conversation with Julie Mugford to make her falsely believe that he was the hitman who Bamber paid to execute the family, thus distancing himself from the act of murder in her eyes*). MacDonald had a cast iron alibi and wasn't involved at all. Bamber, in trying to provide himself with an alibi,

inadvertently closed down the list of suspects to two. It could only have been him or Sheila Caffell who killed the family that morning, not anyone else. The Judge said so at trial. Matthew MacDonald played no part in the killings, that was another of Jeremy Bamber's lies. Deliberately deceiving his girlfriend for his own purposes doesn't portray him in a good way really does it? MacDonald enjoyed telling a tall tale to embellish others' perception of his life. It probably made him feel important, powerful, saying such things. When we investigated him he had a perfectly good alibi for the time of the killings. He wasn't involved, and he certainly wasn't any kind of accomplice to murder.

I asked if at any time he believed Sheila could have been the killer. I pointed out that surely the initial evidence found at the crime scene indicated Sheila going berserk, and officially that's how the investigation panned out for a full 31 days.

Me personally? No, I never believed it was her. She had her problems but she could never have done that on her own. I knew from the outset that Jeremy Bamber was playing us and must have a reason for doing so. He never fooled me, and as a result of that, he never fooled all of Essex Police either. The arrangement of the bodies inside the house led some officers to believe that this was the most likely conclusion. So yes, I suppose a few were deceived into believing that Sheila had committed the crimes, but only because that is what the killer wanted us to believe.

Bamber had thought it through very carefully. He pre-planned everything, right down to what he would say to us, he even thought through how he expected us to react. Not me, as I say I was never tricked by him. I want to say that as police officers we do make mistakes, thankfully in this case the mistakes were quickly rectified and the course of the investigation was changed, mainly through my own efforts and the persistence of the family winning the faith of Peter Simpson. Ultimately we were able to successfully prove that Sheila Caffell was another victim of Jeremy Bamber. No matter what is said Paul, believe me, the killer is in prison. He knows he was responsible and he killed his family, what kind of man would shoot two sleeping children?

You have asked about how the sound moderator was missed by police during searches of the house, as it was later found in the gun cupboard by David Boutflour. The house was busy, police officers coming and going. The sound moderator that I took charge of had clearly been wiped clean by someone. I seem to recall it still felt slightly sticky and still had blood on it, there were flecks of red paint and a single grey/white hair as I remember. David came across it in the gun cupboard in the office beneath some stairs, it was during a clean-up of the house a few days after the murders. We, as in the police search team, weren't ever looking for a sound moderator. I cannot justify how or why it was so obviously missed because when you handled it you could see the blood, and if it had been seen by an officer earlier, then it would obviously have some interest to us. What must be understood is that at the time, some senior officers were convinced that it was a straightforward case of murder and a suicide, the murder weapon had been found on a suspect, so the searching police officers weren't focused on identifying anything else that might prove otherwise. It's no excuse, and it is obviously something we wished had never happened, but it did, and we cannot hide from the fact.

I questioned if he thought it suspicious, or if he could understand that the public would view it as suspicious, that based on police evidence given at court at least eight different police officers had looked in and searched the same gun cupboard, yet not one of them had spotted the sticky blood covered moderator. However, just a few days later, a relative goes to the cupboard, looks in there and immediately finds a major piece of evidence.

No, it wasn't suspicious, why should it be? It's only suspicious if you are looking for flaws in the police investigation. I don't have to justify the find to anyone, nor does David Boutflour, nor anyone else. The evidence was handed to us and accepted in court, so it's a meaningless point to be honest, not worthy of any discussion. Of course I know it's a matter of great contention to some, but that's down to Bamber's insistence. It's him all over, he is the one initiating and promulgating this sort of thing. Regarding the blood, paint and hair that were attached to the silencer, yes, all of those were obvious to the naked eye. When we put all of this evidence together we were able to prove to the court that the moderator was on the rifle used in the murder at the time of the killings. During a fight in the kitchen it had scratched the mantle – the paint flecks that were found on it matched the paint scratched from the damaged area of the mantle – and we found scratch marks to show that the moderator had been in contact with the mantle. This could only have happened during the violent confrontation with Nevill who died in the kitchen. In addition there was blood inside the baffle, again this belonged to Sheila. So ask yourself how did her blood get inside the moderator. The answer is obvious, we proved it to be back spatter caused when the blood from her own wounds from shooting entered the inside of the moderator baffle. There is no other explanation for Sheila's blood to be found where it was in the moderator unless you suggest it was planted there by someone, a forensic officer perhaps, or a police officer, or a relative. It's all nonsense, conspiracy after conspiracy. You did how many years in the police, 25, 30, how many police conspiracies did you come across or get involved in? I'll wager a bet that your answer is none!

Stan was correct, in all my years in the police I hadn't been involved in or aware of any police conspiracies. Stan continued:

So we know Sheila had been shot twice and was dead, she certainly wasn't in any physical condition or position to unscrew the moderator, attempt to wipe it clean, then wander downstairs and place it back in a box inside the gun cupboard. The only person who could have done that was the killer, and the killer was Jeremy Bamber. By his own evidence discussing the supposed telephone call from Nevill, the killer could only be Jeremy or Sheila. We proved it couldn't be Sheila, therefore it has to be Jeremy.

I agree, it was remarkably lax of Bamber not to clean the moderator properly, it's probable that he failed to see the spot of blood and the paint when he returned it to the cupboard. That was his Achilles heel in the commission of the crime. I can't remember, I think it was David (Boutflour) who described the moderator as being sticky, I imagine this was caused by the blood not being fully dried on the surface area. What I can say is that everyone who handled that piece of evidence did so with diligence. I refute suggestions that it was contrived evidence. To be honest, even if it was, which it wasn't, it was not at the suggestion of any Essex police officer. We missed it, plain and simple. David found it days later and there were witnesses to the find. I don't doubt its provenance, nor did the jury at his trial. I have no desire or reason to discuss this further with you or anyone else. There was clearly more to the conviction than the sound moderator evidence.

Stan was visibly bored by my continual probing into the sound moderator evidence. As defensive as he was, I wasn't going to let the matter drop. I apologised for any offence my questioning may be causing, the last thing I wanted to do was upset the man, especially after he had been good enough to talk so honestly with me. He understood this and was gracious in accepting my need to probe, since this, in all likelihood, would be my only opportunity to discuss the matter with him.

Don't worry Paul, I'd do exactly the same if I was in your shoes. My recollection of everything is spot on, maybe not on precise detail. Being a detective for so long indoctrinates a need for a good memory so fire away, you won't offend me, I'm too thick skinned to be offended by anything relating to this case. You say that other than Bamber, Bob and I are the only real experts. I don't like that, Bamber is no expert, he's just good at masquerading lies as the truth. Yes, it was me that collected the sound moderator from Peter Eaton. I think it was then that we both saw the grey hair attached to it. I took it from him and carefully put it in a kitchen roll tube. Before you ask, I wasn't wearing gloves at the time, nor was Peter. I don't think David Boutflour or any of the others who handled it had been wearing gloves either, but I assure you, it was carefully handled. I placed it in the boot of my car for transportation as I was leaving Peter Eaton, as it was seized as potential evidence.

With an air of trepidation I asked Stan, if, on the night he collected the moderator, he consumed a bottle of whisky?

There is no truth or mileage in stating that anything untoward happened to the moderator when I took possession of it, or the inference that I may have been drunk. It is true that both Peter and I had a couple of drinks from the bottle, and I then left.

I pointed out that a statement existed that claimed he drank a bottle of whisky then threw the moderator in the boot of his car. I disguised this assertion by asking if he had any concerns about drink driving.

None whatsoever. I was conducting a mass murder investigation, you or the rest of the world might not appreciate it, but it really was a stressful business. I was always in full control of my faculties and more than capable of driving and careful of what I was saying. I repeat, the evidence I seized was handled with the best of my care and ability. I can't remember if I drank the whole bottle or not. If I did, then we both must have needed it. It doesn't clear Jeremy

Bamber of murder does it? It doesn't make him innocent because I may or may not have drunk a bottle of whisky! You ask if I can recall what we discussed while drinking the Scotch, that is ridiculous, we probably made small talk, it's not the done thing to continually remind grieving relatives of the tragedy they have recently suffered. I may have discussed the origin of the grey hair and perhaps some of the detail surrounding the finding of the moderator.

I explained that Peter Eaton had, in a later statement, expressed concern about the quantity of whisky that was consumed by him and the illegal drink driving aspect. Something that Bamber himself was to comment upon to Jones on a different occasion.

Means nothing, just banter that's all. It's just people trying to harm my integrity or that of the investigation in any way they can. How does any of this alter Jeremy Bamber's position or is the idea to show me in a bad light? It doesn't, Bamber has no defence, he's looking for any slip up or mistake made by the police or the Crown to question the validity of his guilt. That's what he's left with, making out that I was a drunk, or the Judge was corrupt, or we made our case up against him and that everyone has conspired to convict him. It's rubbish, he did it.

I followed up my sound moderator questioning by asking why Ann Eaton hadn't mentioned finding the moderator in her statement of 14 August 1985, nor had she at that stage discussed her suspicions of Jeremy Bamber, yet she was making and keeping notes on everything he said. I told Stan that I found this behaviour odd, advising him that I could find not one statement from anyone else at the time who claimed to be present during the locating of the sound moderator in question. Surely such detail and information would be something that would need to be mentioned, especially the importance of the find. I then threw into the mix that I believed there might have been more than one sound moderator knocking about in police property.

That's your take on it, it doesn't make it right. Statements were recorded that were relevant to the facts. I've nothing else to say about sound moderators.

There was a stony silence between us as we mentally confronted each other, staring into the others mind. In this one fleeting moment I saw how seriously determined Stan could be as he used the pause in conversation to his advantage. I was first to break the silence and looked away from his stare, immediately hitting back by asking why no statement was immediately recorded from the relatives who found the moderator. The moderator was allegedly found on 10 August 1985, so why the delay in statement recording of such a vital piece of evidence? Surely detailed statements would have been necessary for the police to form the basis of their interview with Bamber after his arrest on suspicion of murder on 8 September 1985. No detailed statement about the find existed at the time of his arrest. In fact, to me it seems highly likely that the police interrogation of Bamber relied solely on the recollection of DC Stan Jones, who had taken formal possession of the moderator and, as was claimed, had consumed a full bottle of whisky during the collection. Were his recollections accurate? Hardly the ideal or most reliable evidence, that of a police officer on duty who must have been 'under the influence' after consuming such an amount of alcohol! I knew by the look on his face that Stan would have no answer for this.

> Why are you concerned about how much or what I drank during this investigation?

I reminded him that he had thought Jeremy Bamber's eating habits to be suspicious and pointed towards the actions of a guilty man. Stan laughed.

> Now I see your point, you make it well. I think you need to look at this from a police perspective and not just that of Jeremy Bamber. There was more evidence than the damn sound moderator to convict Bamber. I believe you want to prove Bamber innocent, it isn't going to happen, he's guilty of murder, he did it Paul. You making a mockery of the police investigation is achieving nothing, Bamber will remain behind bars. I've already admitted we messed up on a few things, we were heavily criticised by the Judge and in the press for this. We still got the killer.

I reminded Stan that I wasn't at all looking at the matter from Jeremy Bamber's perspective, but rather from a neutral perspective. I was merely pointing out some irregularities that in no way determined the outcome of the investigation or trial. He nodded in acceptance of this. Stan clearly wasn't prepared to discuss the sound moderator any further. I explained to him that I found the sound moderator evidence weak and felt it failed to reach an acceptable criminal justice criteria for evidence gathering and handling standards, whether that be in 1985 or in 2010. It was a complete mess. The so-called back spatter aspect was, at best, vulnerable and weak. I agreed that human DNA, potentially Sheila's, was found inside the baffle also traces of June's DNA was found inside the baffle and that of at least one male. It was also shown that animal DNA was found inside there. One has to ask how animal DNA got in there. Surely no close contact shot of an animal would be likely! A defence barrister who was on the ball might have crucified the prosecution case on this point at trial, but it didn't happen. That is simply my opinion, and at no point does it prove Jeremy Bamber innocent.

Getting back to the interview, I deliberately moved onto other areas of the investigation where Stan might feel more comfortable, and in particular the crime scene.

> I'm not enjoying this interview Paul, you are pushing me and I'm finding it very tedious.

It was at this point that I decided to reveal to Stan that, like the police, I did not believe Jeremy Bamber to be innocent, there is so much of his story that does not add up.

> As I said, it was busy when I arrived – the area around White House Farm was busy. There was an air of shock and, if I'm honest, chaos outside the house. You hope that the first police officers on the scene are sensible and experienced enough to take control and make the scene secure. I remember one senior officer commenting that it reminded him of the Amityville murders in America where Ronald DeFeo ran amok with a rifle and murdered his entire family – both parents, two sisters and two brothers, all in their beds. I thought to myself what a stupid perception.

I was surprised that Stan could not see the connection, since the case does hold similarities to the murders committed by Ronald DeFeo, he too started a killing spree at sometime around 3.00am, not too far removed from the time when Jeremy Bamber killed his own family. Immediately after the event, DeFeo didn't show much in the way of grief, nor mourning. Instead he went about his daily business as usual, outwardly showing nothing that would arouse suspicion that he had murdered his entire family a few hours earlier. There exists many more similarities between the two crimes, none of which matter here, but it does show how no crime or murder is totally unique in its conception.

I asked Stan if he was prepared to talk about Julie Mugford since she was the key prosecution witness.

Yes, not a problem, of course. As you know, Julie had for some time been Jeremy Bamber's girlfriend. When I first met her I knew she was withholding something. I wasn't certain what it was, she wasn't a suspect in my eyes and she wasn't even in Essex when the murders occurred so she had no physical role in the actual execution of the crime. It always seemed to me as though Bamber had some hold over her, she seemed to be constantly looking to him for validation. Have you ever been to a domestic when one party is bullying the other? The weak partner allows the bully to do the speaking through fear. That's what it was like with her and Bamber, she was frightened of him. It was more than a perception, but nothing really tangible, I just knew something wasn't right between them. You have asked me if I thought she was a credible witness. Of course she was, the jury knew she was telling the truth, and I'll tell you now, she was one of Bamber's victims, she suffered from the constant lies he told her and the deliberate pressure he placed upon her in keeping his secrets or else. It was a cruel way to treat someone who you are supposed to care for, to put them in such a difficult position, he abused her feelings for him. This is another example of it all being about Jeremy Bamber.

When Julie finally came to her senses and plucked up the courage to come and see me and to tell me what she knew, I realised she was telling the truth. It was the breakthrough we had wanted. Make no mistake, I put her through the ringer with my questioning of everything she claimed. I needed to be sure she was a capable and competent witness. She was terrified by the thought of giving evidence against Jeremy in open court, her mother was a rock to her, she was full of support. It took some guts to do what Julie did, but she did it and I think that speaks volumes for her. She told me that Bamber had been discussing 'the perfect murder' with her the previous summer. He discussed different plans he had, there was mention of him sedating his parents and burning the house down with them inside. His calculating scheming plan was forgotten when he realised that the insurance payout wouldn't be enough for him and some of the older more valuable antiques inside would be destroyed and weren't sufficiently covered by the policy. He told her that he had proved to himself his ability to kill by killing rats with his bare hands. He had supposedly fed them cannabis to dope them beforehand so it made them easier to catch and handle. These are not the kind of things a young girl easily makes up. Bamber must have told her what he was doing, even if some of it wasn't entirely accurate, but then the man is a good liar, he's even deceitful to those who are close to him, a calculating cheat of a man.

I asked him about Julie's deal with the *News of the World* and the article and photograph that appeared in that paper, her story in what were apparently her own words. I showed him a copy of a *News of the World* headed memo I had been sent that seemed to indicate that Julie had agreed the contract for her kiss and tell story before the trial. If this was a genuine document, then it surely put greater pressure on her to give evidence to condemn Bamber.

What you must recall is that Julie Mugford was questioned and cross-examined primarily on her witness statements alone. Most of those statements had been in our possession for some time, long before a trial date had been confirmed. Julie didn't give any evidence that we didn't already know of, or had known of for some time. To suggest that any contract she may or may not have had with the *News of the World* influenced what was already documented is inaccurate. That's another of those issues that Bamber uses to create confusion and to divert from the important facts, namely that he did it! All the *News of the World* memos on the planet wouldn't ever prove his innocence.

I asked whether he felt Julie's behaviour and support of Bamber immediately after the murders to have been suspicious. Despite her knowing that Jeremy Bamber had killed his family, including two sleeping children, she had supported him and it seems that it wasn't until Bamber ended their relationship that she came forward to admit all she knew.

I think you have to look more closely at their relationship. He was the dominant partner, a bully, not always physical but mental abuse. Someone once described him like a big kid who would sulk and lash out if he didn't get his own way. He yearned to be the centre of attention, Julie was just an object to him, another person for him to use then discard when something better for him came along. I am certain he must sit in his prison cell and regret the day he confided his intentions to Julie. I know in my own mind that he meticulously planned every deliberately false detail he was going to tell her just to maximise him showing her to be a liar or a fantasist, he would have played that scenario over and over in his mind. When you step back and look at the bigger picture, you can clearly read his scheming mind. His own arrogance made him believe that the various alibis he had put into place were solid and irrefutable.

Julie went to identify the bodies in the mortuary, that's because no one else was capable. Five people she had known were dead – two of them children – and the deaths had been apparently influenced by the actions of her boyfriend. I think there are many legitimate reasons why Julie viewed the bodies, the principle one was to show support for the remaining living family.

I asked for his thoughts on Julie's behaviour post trial, seductively posing for photographs in the *News of the World* and the kiss and tell story she sold. This, I felt, reflected badly upon her character so soon after she was portrayed as a naïve and manipulated girlfriend in the courtroom.

It's not my place to say whether it was the right or wrong thing to do, only Julie can answer that. I would have to say I don't think it would have affected the trial, but perhaps she might just consider the appropriateness of it now. There was a feeling of relief for many witnesses, including police officers, that it was over and the right result had been achieved. Justice had been done. For Julie I think she had been suffocated by him for a long time. The reality that she was free of his control and could start a fresh life without his interference or involvement was suddenly real. Though over the years since she probably finds herself frequently reminded of her past and association with Bamber. What would any of us do to rid ourselves of our nightmares? Julie moved across the globe and still her past caught up with her. It's an unfair legacy she has to endure. I see it as a punishment, an unjust legacy for someone who found the strength to publicly stand up and give evidence to help convict a vile killer. After such a period of time she should be allowed to move on with her life, yet she regularly finds herself maligned for what she has done.

Playing devil's advocate, I handed Stan a copy of a statement made by one of his ex-colleagues, Winston Norman Bernard. The statement proves that Bernard was present at a Chelsea hotel in central London along with DS Stan Jones. I had hoped it would trigger some recall and Stan could explain why this meeting, involving the Police, the press and Julie Mugford, occurred post trial, well away from Essex where both Julie and the police officers lived and worked. The relevant part of the statement relates the following: 'On a totally separate matter I have been asked if I can remember meeting Julie Mugford in a London hotel. Although I can no longer remember the specific day, I recall attending a hotel in Chelsea, Central London, with DS Stan Jones after the conclusion of Jeremy Bamber's trial, and there meeting Julie Mugford. I believe at that stage Julie was in the process of being interviewed by newspaper reporters.'

Stan looked surprised when he read the document, I asked him why the meeting had taken place, why the Police were there and why it took place in Chelsea and not in Essex. I told him that I felt it looked suspicious.

I'll give you credit, you have done your research. I cannot remember much about this, it's trivial. I'm not certain what you are suggesting. It's a long time ago and I genuinely can't recall the logistics of such a meeting. I can only think that we must have been instructed to attend. I can't remember the precise reasoning behind it. It certainly wasn't any kind of done deal with the press if that's what you think. Anything that was arranged between Julie and the press was out of my control and the control of Essex Police.

Deals and arrangements like that with the *News of the World* happen all the time in high profile cases and trials, so the press approaching Julie isn't unique and it doesn't alter what happened, it doesn't bring back those lost innocent lives. I know Bamber was trying to sell his story to the press too, along with naked modelling photographs of his dead sister, Sheila. What kind of person does that? Evil.

It was a despicable crime and an awful scene to witness. Do you think Julie Mugford, or anyone else, would have chosen to be involved in such a tragedy? They had no say in what happened. It was forced on them, a nightmare that would forever change their lives. People seem to forget that it wasn't those left behind who carried out the killings, they were innocent. It wasn't Julie Mugford who killed that family. Every day that woman has to live with the aftermath of the tragedy, she's every bit a victim of the affair.

The other police officer present at the hotel meeting was Winston Bernard, an officer who rose through the ranks and attained Chief Superintendent status. Throughout what can only be described as a splendid career, he received a Chief Constable's commendation in 2000, along with several other officers, for their part in detecting a series of armed robberies in conjunction with the Metropolitan Police. Bernard was also part of the much maligned investigation into the death of Stuart Lubbock in 2001 and 2002. In 2007 he was interviewed by the Independent Police Complaints Commission about his role in that investigation, this came as a result of a complaint that had been made to the Commission. The complaint, quite correctly in my opinion after a full investigation, was not upheld, Bernard, it was found, had acted appropriately within the original investigation. In mentioning this matter I am not inferring any wrongdoing by any individual or police officer, I am simply showing how difficult the role of police officer is when conducting an investigation that involves the loss of human life. The pressures, as Stan Jones claimed, are immense and come from all directions – bereaved relatives and friends, police hierarchy, bureaucrats, politicians and the media, and today, by armchair internet detectives who fancy themselves as a modern day Sherlock Holmes. Such persons are also armed with something no investigative detective has, time and the benefit of hindsight!

I asked Stan, with the benefit of hindsight what, if anything, he felt went wrong with the investigation. His initial answer was succinct:

Nothing, we got our man, we got the killer, that's what we aimed to do. Though maybe my relationship with Taff could have been more professional, that counts for both of us.

I followed this question by asking why Taff Jones, with all of his crime fighting and investigative experience, apparently believed that the crime scene evidence showed Sheila to be guilty, to such an extent that this claim was accepted as wholly accurate by the Coroner?

> You say that, but I'm now certain Taff had his own suspicions on what happened. If you had seen the manner in which Bamber acted, yes there was arrogance, defiance even, he had an air of superiority and confidence about him. This was a man who was cold, calculating and cruel. There was not a glimmer of sadness in how he was, he seemed extremely cool and clinical. Taff said something along the lines that people respond differently to personal tragedy, but he'd not seen anyone so clinical and calculating in their manner as Bamber. He felt it was possibly down to the psychological trauma caused through Jeremy being adopted and therefore not being a physical blood relative, whereas I put it down to him being a killer. His attendance and appearance at the funeral was insulting to every genuine person present. He portrayed sorrow to the extreme, when all the time he was playing to the camera and the press. It was all, and had to be all, about Jeremy Bamber.
>
> Look at how Colin Caffell reacted throughout. At the time the consensus of opinion was that Sheila was the killer, discounting how that must have emotionally affected him, he had also lost two beautiful children. His manner and behaviour was dignified, loyal and very supportive of the whole family. Every picture you see, Colin is there supporting Jeremy, does any image exist anywhere in the world of Jeremy supporting someone else during this tragedy? The answer to that is an unequivocal no! That's because he manipulated situations to his own advantage and managed to win feelings of sympathy for himself, that's all he's done in the years since.
>
> You do need to speak with Bob Miller about the inquest, you might be interested to hear what he's got to say about it. Bob told the truth but couldn't reveal everything we knew because we knew Bamber had manipulated the entire crime scene, and we couldn't reveal the ongoing inquiries that we were taking place into that. At the trial, the Judge called Bamber evil beyond belief. That description sums him and his involvement in this crime before, during and since, very aptly.

When I finished my meeting with Stan Jones, we shook hands

and he gave me a man hug. I confess to feeling overwhelmingly onside with him, this wasn't the man I expected for he is an individual who to most 'Bamber is innocent' supporters is viewed as their absolute nemesis. He certainly didn't come across as that, but despite having retired from the police force, he remained dedicated to the cause, professional and wholly convinced of Jeremy Bamber's guilt. He had been man enough to admit that things did go wrong, no police investigation is perfect and I confess I warmed to him as a person and understood his logic as a detective in the investigation. All importantly, I believed him.

Assistant Chief Constable Peter Simpson (Later Deputy Chief Constable)

Peter Simpson had been promoted on 11 May 1981, from a position as Chief Superintendent of traffic division in Hertfordshire, to Assistant Chief Constable, personnel department, Essex, and later in charge of the administration and finance department of Essex Police. Like most senior officers and police hierarchy, he would avoid politically dangerous situations whenever he could. Despite this he was a well respected man, but by his own admission, was hardly a seasoned thief taker or experienced detective. His outstanding leadership skills won many officers' respect and he commanded an excellent reputation as a senior officer, a position he held until 1984. It was then that he attended the Royal College of Defence Studies in London for a year. During this period he travelled extensively around the USA and Canada. He even managed to visit his old Royal Military Police company in Berlin and see the Berlin Wall for the first time. In August 1985 he was appointed the senior officer in charge of the Bamber case, a position which was viewed as little more than a figurehead. He was later promoted to the rank of Deputy Chief Constable (DCC) of the force almost immediately after the conviction of Jeremy Bamber when DCC Ron William Stone retired for domestic reasons. I interviewed him about the case in 2003.

> I've had a long and varied career and the White House Farm murders are one small part of that. I do remember how difficult and complex it was, time consuming and energy sapping for the

officers involved, who did marvellously in bringing the killer, Jeremy Bamber, to justice. There was a lot of pressure on every member of the force to get the right conviction and no, I wasn't swayed by any influences, other than from the expert opinion of fellow police officers. I refuse to discuss any kind of Masonic influence being involved in my coming to the decision that DCI Jones should be taken off the investigation. He is no longer with us, but I can assure you he knew and believed Jeremy Bamber to be the killer. He told me himself he was suspicious of Bamber and he believed he knew more than he was telling us. DCI Jones worked tirelessly on every case he dealt with, giving everything he had to an investigation at all times.

I do not feel that his removal from this case was a slight on his career and I certainly don't believe he viewed it as that either. Nor, to the best of my knowledge, did anyone else in the force. You mention subterfuge among some of the ranks affecting the professionalism of the investigation, tell me an occupation where personality clashes don't exist. Are you suggesting this 'subterfuge' affected the prosecution? If you are, then you are wrong, the prosecution was always going to be a difficult one because the killer had been so shrewd in how he manipulated everything. He framed his sister for the crimes, then we had a witness, Julie Mugford, who had acted in what could be regarded as an insensible manner and at trial she had her integrity pulled apart and she was accused of telling lies. We had to wade through the mass of deceit he had put in place. This wasn't a spontaneous crime, he had meticulously planned it, any man who can kill his parents and sister in cold blood and shoot two sleeping children is, as the trial judge asserted, evil.

Stan and Taff weren't the closest of friends, but they were both damn good cops. Taff had his own ideas of how to catch criminals, it wasn't always pretty and he didn't always endear himself to witnesses, but he got results. Stan was highly regarded and he wasn't alone in believing Bamber was the killer and not Sheila. It's wrong to suggest he stabbed his boss in the back, he didn't.

DCI Jones was not made a scapegoat, he was given support at every level. I think insinuations that he was sacrificed through Masonic or family pressures are at best, insulting. He wasn't made a scapegoat by the force, if individual officers have been negatively outspoken about him then that is their opinion only, it certainly wasn't everyone's opinion. The case isn't about the integrity of police officers, it is about the murder of five people, that is where the focus should remain.

Yes, I did speak with Robert Boutflour, this was after DS Stan Jones had requested I did so. I discussed the reason why with DS Jones, it was because Mr Boutflour wished to make a formal complaint about the police handling of the investigation, it was not because DS Jones wished to undermine anyone or cause any trouble for DCI Jones. It was in fact the opposite, he wanted matters to run smoothly and he was trying to keep all parties satisfied.

It is ridiculous to suggest that I could ever be influenced by the opinion of a member of the public. Yes, there was pressure to get the case solved quickly, no police force wants a killer at large and busy within their force boundaries, but these pressures were manageable and no knee-jerk decisions came about as a result of those. It was a team effort and I cannot praise that team sufficiently. There were administrational errors but that is all they were. In a case of this magnitude and proportion, where lies and long term deceit have deliberately been laid as traps by the killer and his allies, added to which the emotional factor that children were among the victims, it was always going to be a tough case for officers to work.

DS Jones told me that when he looked into Jeremy Bamber's eyes and spoke to him about the murders, he saw not a glimmer of any sympathetic response from him. He would often laugh and make light of the situation to the detective. I believe that DS Jones felt that Bamber was taunting him, he thought him arrogant and that he was dismissing it all as some kind of game between himself and the authorities. He's still playing games with the authorities and anyone who will listen.

Oddly enough, I recall speaking with DCI Jones not long after the murders had happened. He told me that Bamber was unnatural in his behaviour and deliberately vague in what information he conveyed to the police. He told me Bamber had a cold and clinical side to him and that he had never dealt with a suspect who was so manifestly devious and manipulative.

The death of DCI Jones was an untimely and sad incident. If he was here today to explain all of this to you, his thoughts on the case, I am certain he would tell you that he fully supported the prosecution and the right person was jailed for the crimes. I can't really comment on whether Sheila Caffell was involved since we have never investigated that. I understand DCI Jones may have mentioned that to some officers, but he did feel that Bamber was the responsible and guilty party.

6

The Girlfriend

'A man always finds it hard to realise that he may have finally lost a woman's love, however badly he may have treated her.'

Sherlock Holmes – The Adventure of the Musgrave Ritual

If Jeremy Bamber was the key orchestrator of the crimes, then the actions of his girlfriend, Julie Mugford, must be regarded with a good deal of suspicion. I tracked her down to one of Canada's major cities but sadly could not get to speak with her.

Mugford began dating Bamber in December 1983 whilst working in Colchester, she was then 19-years-old and attending Goldsmith's College at the University of London. As a result of their relationship she met Bamber's parents, his sister and her children.

She was described as an intelligent young woman which, judging by her life before and after her involvement with Jeremy Bamber, she undoubtedly she was. That does not mean she was not gullible or naïve, especially where her heart ruled her head, and she believed at the time she was in a reciprocal loving relationship with Jeremy. It is her time with Bamber – and some would say under his influence – that has created a huge amount of criticism and condemnation from supporters of Bamber. The biggest issue with her recollection of events and evidence is that the day after the murders, while still in a relationship with Bamber, she provided a statement to the police in which she said nothing adverse about him. In recounting the early morning telephone call she received from Bamber, she said he sounded disjointed and worried.

Later, after her relationship with Bamber had ended, she revealed a great deal more about him and his life. She was to state that Bamber made it clear he disliked his family and resented his parents who tried to run his life. She added that he did not get on with his sister Sheila, mainly because she lived in a nice flat in Maida Vale which was maintained by their parents. Between July and October 1984, Bamber had often commented to her that his parents were getting him down and he wished he could get rid of them all. Bamber described his father as getting old and claimed his mother and Sheila were insane, he also felt the twins were emotionally disturbed and unbalanced. He had made mention of seeing his parents' wills and she said that between October and December 1984, Bamber talked a lot about killing his family. Initially he considered being at the house at supper and drugging them before driving back to Goldhanger. He then said he would return to the farm on foot or by using a bicycle and he would burn it down. It was only when he realised that such destruction of the building would decimate valuable contents that were inside that he dropped that idea.

In the spring or summer of 1985 he had altered his plan and instead, discussed shooting his family. He could gain access to the house at night through a kitchen window with a faulty catch and leave by a different window that, through manipulation, could be latched from the outside. Because Sheila was such a soft target and was, by his claim mad, he could easily frame her and use her mental health reasons as a motive for the killings. He would make it look like she had killed everyone then shot herself!

Such revelations were volunteered by Mugford and not prompted by the police, she could not have been so aware of all the details unless she had learned them from Bamber.

On the weekend leading up to the murders, she had stayed with Bamber at his house in Goldhanger, during which time he dyed his hair black. She later returned to her London address. On the night of 6 August, Bamber rang her and during their conversation said he was 'pissed off' and had been thinking about the crime all day, chillingly he said it was going to be 'tonight or never'. In the early hours of the following morning he rang again, this time saying: 'Everything is going well. Something is wrong at the farm. I haven't had any sleep all night ... bye honey and I love you lots'. As with his earlier call, she didn't take him seriously and told him to go back to bed. Later that morning he called again, this time he said he could not speak for long, Sheila had gone mad and he told her not to go to work because a police car would come and pick her up.

She was taken to his house in Goldhanger and informed of the murders by a police officer, DS Jones. Out of earshot of detectives, Bamber told her, 'I should have been an actor'. That evening when she was alone with Bamber she asked him if he had done it. He said he hadn't, but had paid a hit man to kill the family (Matthew MacDonald) and explained how he could get in and out of the farm without being seen and leaving it apparently secure. This was key to Bamber's claim that someone within the house must have been the killer and not him, and since he made sure that he was at the scene during the discovery of the carnage, what better alibi could he have than being stood outside the farmhouse with the police as they forced entry and found the entry door locked from the inside, with the key still in the lock!

As a further fail-safe, he had told MacDonald to call him from the farmhouse once the deed was done. The last caller redial memory would show that this had occurred and support his story that his father, Nevill, had called him to say Sheila had gone beserk with a gun. He told Julie that MacDonald called and said he had done as instructed, but the old man put up a bit of a struggle and for an old man he was very strong and put up a fight. MacDonald had been angered by the struggle and fired seven shots into the man. He went on to say that Sheila Caffell had been told to lie down and shoot herself last. MacDonald had then placed a Bible on her chest to make it look like religious mania was key to the killings. He said the children were shot in their sleep so had felt nothing and there was no pain.

Julie was terrified of the repercussions should she ever reveal the truth about what had happened. Bamber reminded her that by virtue of him telling her she was implicated and would go to prison.

It is very much a classic case of criminal manipulation and bullying. I recall a situation where as a police officer I was dealing with a case of child abuse, it was a father on his children. His wife, the mother of the children, was initially frightened to report him because he had told her he would tell everyone she was involved, and when it all came out the children would be taken from her and given to social services and she would maligned for life. It took great strength and courage for her to tell me everything and despite her husband being jailed, she remained in fear of the repercussions he threatened. Julie Mugford was in very similar circumstances, a dangerous criminal had involved her in what to him was a sick game that must be played out for him to win and gain the rewards. To Bamber, life was expendable, Julie was just another toy. As David Boutflour once said, 'There are no winners in all of this.'

The following weekend she had stayed with Bamber and Colin Caffell, and during a visit to Bamber's Goldhanger home, he told her that the police had been slack because they hadn't done all the fingerprinting at White House Farm. She attended the funerals of Nevill and June on 16 August, and later on 19 August, those of Sheila and the twins. In between the funerals he had taken her to Eastbourne for a weekend and she asked him how he could behave in such a way. Throughout this period Bamber had taken her out, treating them both to meals and expensive clothing, and she described him as being very happy. On another occasion after one of the funerals they drank champagne and cocktails. A week later he treated her to a two-day break in Amsterdam.

Unable to deal or cope with the situation, on 27 August she had returned to her lodgings in London and confided in her friend, Susan Battersby, what Bamber had done. On 31 August she again spoke about the murders with Bamber and asked how he was behaving so normally and why he had to tell her what had happened since she felt guilt for them both. Bamber had coldly replied that he had done everyone a favour and there was nothing to feel guilty about.

Bamber was clearly beginning to consider the consequences of Julie breaking rank so placed another responsibility on her young shoulders. He told her that she was the best friend he had ever had and he entrusted his life to her, a truly manipulative and calculating act. The reality of the situation hit Julie as she realised she was going to have to tell the police what she knew and the probable outcome of that, so had said to him, 'I would really love to hurt you,' and at one point she put a pillow over his head. 'I took it off and he asked me why I did it, and I said if he were dead he would always be with me. I preceded it with the comment he would be better off dead.' Bamber claims she also said, 'If I can't have you, nobody can'.

On Tuesday 3 September, the couple were at the flat that had belonged to Sheila Caffell. Julie again asked Jeremy why he had implicated her in the situation and if he was telling her the truth about his part in the murders. Bamber had then received a telephone call from an ex-girlfriend. Julie heard him ask her out and she became upset at him and threw an ornament that smashed a mirror. In turn Bamber became angry and physical, he grabbed hold of Julie and twisted her arm up behind her back. She realised their relationship was over and four days later she reported what she knew to the police.

Bamber supporters maintain that Julie lied and fabricated the story, but if that is the case how could the details she described have so much accuracy? How could she know any of it if Bamber hadn't told her? Granted, some minor details such as Nevill was shot eight times and not seven, were known by a number of people. However, the information that Mugford disclosed to the police was detailed and consistent with the crime scene – facts that only someone who was personally involved in the murders could hold. Bamber said the twins felt nothing and there was no pain. Is that the kind of discussions a hit man would have with Bamber from the crime scene? It's doubtful to say the least as an intruder having just massacred a family – who could not be certain the noise hadn't been heard beyond the farm – would certainly want to get out of that place as quickly as possible, not give Bamber intimate detail of what had taken place. We now also know that the hit man, Matthew MacDonald, was totally innocent, so how did Bamber know such intimate detail to relay it to Julie. Bamber and his team of disciples believe the information came from the police and that either family members had been told everything by loose-lipped police officers or Mugford herself had been primed by DS Jones to make it all up! Once again we are at a point where we are expected to believe that everyone was in a mass conspiracy to frame Jeremy Bamber.

As a result of this information, Bamber and Matthew MacDonald were separately arrested, MacDonald was innocent and had a solid alibi, and it was proved that he had not committed or been involved in the shootings.

Julie admitted during her police interviews to a brief background of dishonesty, having fraudulently used a friend's cheque book after it had been reported stolen to obtain goods in Oxford Street to the value of £700. When discovered she said she and the friend repaid the money to the bank. She also said that in March or April 1985, she had helped Bamber steal over £900 from the offices of Osea Road Caravan site which the Bamber family owned. The caravan site had been bequeathed to Pamela Boutflour, June Bamber, Ann Eaton and Jeremy Bamber by Leslie Speakman on his death. Bamber claimed that crime had been a growing issue on the site and he had expressed much concern about it. He claimed he wanted to install CCTV since he was not convinced the site manager, Jim Carr, was doing what he should be doing. Julie had stage-managed the break-in to make it seem as though strangers had done it. She also admitted to privately using drugs and that she had once sold cannabis with a street value of £100.

Her antecedents didn't sit too well in the realms of her being regarded as a credible witness, yet the testimony of others supported what Julie had stated. Her mother claimed that Bamber had told her he hated his adoptive mother and described her as mad. A friend testified that some time around February 1985, Bamber had said that his parents kept him short of money, his mother was a religious freak and stated, 'I fucking hate my parents'. Elsewhere, a farm worker testified that he seemed not to get on with Sheila and had once said, 'I'm not going to share my money with my sister'.

On 6 September, Julie was in a conversation with her best friend, Liz Rimmington. The pair were discussing what Jeremy had done when Rimmington admitted that she had also had sex with Bamber. Bamber's supporters claim that having been dumped by Jeremy, and learning of his sexual promiscuity, she went to the police the following day and reported him. As with so many things in this case, the reality plays out rather differently to the tale concocted by Bamber.

In our meeting, Bob Miller had given more details about the calls Bamber made to Julie Mugford:

Paul, I know you question the actions of Julie Mugford and probably think her an unreliable witness, but that really wasn't the case. Yes, she had acted irresponsibly, we can all be guilty of that, but she had the conviction to hold her hands up to her past and was honest with us. You could see the fear in her eyes, every single thing in her life was, by virtue of what she was going to tell us, going to be turned upside down. It was a life changing thing she was doing, exposing her own sins and realistically losing a future life here. She was giving evidence as key witness for the Crown, and no one could assure her that the prosecution would see the man we were accusing successfully convicted. Imagine being in that situation. You are asked to give evidence against someone you know is a killer but there is no guarantee he will be imprisoned, and the credibility and value of your evidence will be questioned. Many people would not have the strength to confront a situation like that.

Julie told us in a statement that Bamber had rung her late the night previous to the murders, approximately 9.50pm, on 6 August, to say it was tonight or never. He rang her later, early in the morning of 7 August between 3.00 and 3.30am and told her that everything was going well.

She made this statement a month after the murders, and to be honest she doesn't come across as being very decent for keeping quiet about what she had known all along. It was a courageous thing for her to do, to come forward and reveal everything that Bamber had told her. She was always going to be heavily criticised by others and in the press, and likewise her testimony viewed with some cynicism, especially as she came forward 'after' he had ended their relationship. She knew that, everyone was satisfied she was telling the truth. I could see she was hurt, but that girl was terrified of the consequences, she was genuinely frightened of what Bamber would do to her once he knew she had reported him. We had to put her in a safe house to make sure he couldn't get to her.

It needs to be made clear, because it never has, that Bamber was an articulate liar, extremely cunning, and he would choose and use his words carefully, he mainly intimidated or manipulated Julie. I've said it before, she had everything to lose and nothing to gain from coming forward, and she was very brave because she knew it was likely to be her word against his. Bamber cleverly tried to cover that situation off by telling her lies about the killings, blaming a so-called hit-man, Matthew MacDonald, for the atrocity, He told her he had paid him £2,000 to do it. Bamber wasn't being honest with anyone, least of all her. Throughout the investigation there were many things revealed that she was unaware of, he was a real player.

The minute everything came out and we put the facts to him he clammed up, he couldn't provide an explanation for the calls to Julie, instead he said she was lying and being spiteful, a woman scorned. While I'm certain Julie was upset at being treated so badly by a man she had stood by, she was never a woman scorned, she had mentioned and considered splitting with him for some time and, who knows, maybe the sordid secret they shared extended that relationship forming a tenuous bond. Importantly, there is a situation where Julie put a pillow over Bamber's head, feigning suffocation. It wasn't a genuine attempt to kill him but she made the point in what she said, in her own mind it had gone too far and she had to report what she knew to the police. She knew his game was up and the relationship would be permanently over once the truth came out. She told him, 'You'd be better off dead.' If that wasn't an inference of what her intentions were, then what was?

I have to admit that Stan Jones built a good professional relationship with her, he trusted her and she trusted him. I remember him saying how she was angry with herself for being foolish and for being manipulated by Bamber for so long. When she first told us what she knew she could never have known all the detail we did, her testimony filled in a lot of gaps for us. What she said cemented our original belief that Bamber was a murderer and was involved in the crime. Really, once she came forward the game was up for Bamber and he knew it. Look at how Bamber reacted when things turned against him. He accused everyone of lying and being against him, making things up, alleging that we were conspiring to frame him. I cannot see why anyone would believe him about anything to do with this case, he's lied so often about it, then later changed his version to fit what he claims to have been previously and deliberately hidden facts.

Suspicions about Julie Mugford don't end there. Much has been made of the allegation that pre-trial she had agreed to sell the sensationalised story of her time with Jeremy Bamber to the *News of the World* newspaper for the sum of £25,000. The implication being that she had a financial reason for wanting him to be found guilty. She was questioned about this at Bamber's 2002 appeal hearing and explained that following Bamber's arrest, she was approached many times by people claiming to be reporters. They visited her house, followed her and approached her in petrol stations, bus queues and one even jumped on a bus to approach her.

She was eventually suspended from her work at a school because the headmistress felt it was detrimental to the children her being involved with an alleged murderer. Afterwards she had gone to a solicitor to seek advice on how to stop the press harassment and also to see if what the school had done was legal. The solicitor advised that it would be in her best interests to contract one press body exclusively. She claimed she probably told the solicitor that monetary offers had been made irrespective of the verdict. The use of the term 'probably' in this statement is important. For someone so sure of her testimony, and as a key witness in the murder investigation and the subsequent trial, she suddenly seemed unsure about facts which might have a detrimental impact on her. She went on to claim that the lawyer struck the deal and she had no idea who the other party was.

When asked to expand upon the matter she said she could not remember, but admitted she had a moral dilemma that this was somehow blood money! Her solicitor, she said, had got the best deal he could for her though she hadn't read the small print in the contract thoroughly. In relation to the photographs, she was unhappy with their demands but was informed that she must comply with the contract details. Surely her solicitor, whom she had relied upon to deal with contractual affairs, would have gone through that and discussed the consequences of it in lay terms with her? She recounted how she often questioned herself why she kept the money, why she didn't give it away. Instead she bought a flat, and in retaliation explained how reporters had told her Jeremy was selling his story, suggesting she should reply.

To redress the balance she said she had given a story to *She* magazine that was non-sensational. The feature article published in *She* effectively tells how gullible she had been for believing in Jeremy Bamber and ends with the most damaging comment, 'I did not want to sell my story, it was part of a process to stop the media from relentlessly harassing me and my family.' Julie Mugford had

Nevill and June Bamber outside White House Farm
© *Anglia Press Agency/ SWpix.com*

Sheila Caffell with her twin boys, Daniel (left) and Nicholas (right)
© *Anglia Press Agency/ SWpix.com*

White House Farm, the venue of the murders. The upper left
window was the master bedroom
© *Anglia Press Agency/SWpix.com*

Jeremy Bamber with his
girlfriend Julie Mugford
at his family's funeral
© *Anglia Press Agency/
SWpix.com*

Bamber in handcuffs being led to the Magistrates Court for
the pre trial hearing
© *Anglia Press Agency/SWpix.com*

Julie Mugford and DS Stan Jones on the way to the trial
© *Anglia Press Agency/SWpix.com*

A police officer holds the .22 rifle and sound moderator used
by Bamber in the murder of his family
© Anglia Press Agency/SWpix.com

Jeremy Bamber in a prison van
© *Anglia Press Agency/SWpix.com*

A plaque was placed for
Nevill and June Bamber
at St Nicholas' Church in
Tolleshunt D'arcy
*© William Metcalfe, licensed for
reuse under the Creative Commons
Attribution-Share Alike 2.0 Generic
Licence*

Despite attempts by Bamber to have his conviction overturned, the
Court of Appeal upheld the verdict
*© Rob Farrow, licensed for reuse under the Creative Commons Attribution-Share Alike 2.0
Generic Licence*

25/7/12

JEREMY BAMBER
A5352 AC
HM FULL SUTTON
YORK
...

ABLE TO PROTECT THEM — INCLUDING
SHEILA FROM HERSELF. ITS ALWAYS
THE WHYS AND THE IF ONLYS
THAT SEEM TO BREAK ME DOWN.
FOR INSTANCE: WHY DID I ALLOW
MYSELF TO BE CONTROLLED BY
THE POLICE ON OUR FIRST RECONNOITRE
OF THE HOUSE. IF ONLY I'D DONE
THINGS DIFFERENTLY AND BANGED
ON THE DOOR, AND LOOKED
THROUGH THE WINDOWS — PERHAPS
WE COULD HAVE SAVED LIVES,
WHO KNOWS WHAT WE MIGHT
HAVE BEEN ABLE TO DO.
INSTEAD OF APPROACHING THE
HOUSE PS BEWS WANTED TO
TAKE A LOOK FROM DISTANCE.
ON ARRIVAL AT PAGES LANE
CA-07 (BEWS, MYALL AND SAXBY)
WAS PARKED AT THE JUNCTION
WITH THE MAIN ROAD — AS I
PULLED UP BEHIND THEM THEY
WERE MAKING A RADIO REPORT
OF THEIR ARRIVAL TO HQ/IR.
I KNOW THIS AS IT OVERWHELMED
MY CAR RADIO — I GOT OUT AND
SO DID TWO OF THE OFFICERS
WE SPOKE FOR A MINUTE AND
I TOOK A JUMPER FROM THE
BACK SEAT OF MY CAR AND.
PUT IT ON, WE AGREED TO DRIVE
UP THE LANE AND PARK
OPPOSITE THE FARM COTTAGES.
AT THIS STAGE OUR CONVERSATION

TO
PAUL,

*Hope that Christmas
happiness and cheer,
Remain with you
all through the year.*

Christmas Wishes

'T SHOULD ALL KICK
OFF IN THE NEW YEAR

Correspondence from Bamber to the author

MASS KILLER'S THREATS TO SCOTS AUTHOR

EXCLUSIVE: Bamber 'wants to have writer destroyed' from jail

By Ben Borland

A SCOTS author writing a book about one of Britain's worst mass murders has been warned that the killer will have him "destroyed" from behind bars.

Paul Harrison received a spine-chilling letter at his remote home in Orkney from a supporter of notorious gunman Jeremy Bamber, suggesting he is being "watched".

Last night, Mr Harrison said that he believes Bamber

TURN TO PAGE 4

In 2014, the *Scottish Sunday Express* reported on the threats made by Bamber supporters to the author

Bamber lodged an appeal against whole life prison terms at the
European Court of Human Rights

At the present time,
Bamber remains
incarcerated as a
category A prisoner
in HMP Full
Sutton, a maximum
security gaol

no one else to blame for how much detail she provided. Despite the weak claim that it was contractual, she alone was responsible for posing semi-naked. In addition to such sordid images, she discussed in some detail her sex life with the child killer.

*****

There is a constant theme throughout this book that shows how Jeremy Bamber and his supporters have attempted to question the integrity of every aspect of his prosecution, including police and witness testimony. They have attempted to discredit everything and been ruthless in damning whatever or whoever they see fit in order to portray Jeremy in a good light and as an innocent victim. The puerile arguments which they contend proves his innocence are easily dismissed, and whilst I do not think it was morally acceptable for Julie Mugford to pose for newspaper photographs and sell sordid details of her intimacy with a child killer, it doesn't realistically affect the facts. I don't believe Julie Mugford was a credible witness, but that in itself does not mean she lied, or had the ability – mentally or physically – to put together such incriminating detail that incorporated matters that occurred pre-murder and its planning in police statements.

If we take the side of Bamber and consider that the police may have influenced her, that doesn't fit either since they too would have faced an impossible task in trying to fabricate evidence and make it appear like fact. If that had been the case, then surely they would have come up with more comprehensive evidence than the testimony of a witness whose credibility was likely to be questioned and therefore open to debate. The fact is, the police didn't influence or manufacture evidence or witness testimony, it existed in its own right.

It should be remembered that it was Bamber alone who created and confined the suspect list to just two people, Sheila and himself. Jeremy Bamber was convicted of the murders, yet he pleads innocence and claims that his sister did it. The evidence confirms that his sister could not have done it, at least not on her own. Every claim made by Bamber and his team that is to the contrary doesn't hold up. He knows it doesn't, he knows there is nothing that exists that can prove his innocence, simply because he's guilty. All that he is left with are procedural or administrative errors that he claims show corruption and a cover-up. Everything relating to the case points to him being the killer.

If we look at the way he has used and jettisoned people over the years he has been in prison, we can see a continuation of the way he used others, including his own family. He maligned them to suit his own needs. His efforts to destroy the integrity of those involved in his case, or anyone who dares speak out against his subsequent campaign, have been so frequent that they have become monotonous. All society is achieving in acknowledging his existence, or giving him publicity, is pampering to his needs and those of others who attach themselves to him. He isn't a good person, he isn't a normal human being. I would describe him as potentially the most cold-blooded and manipulative killer currently behind bars, and that's where he should remain.

A good example of how manipulative he can be, even whilst in prison, is the threatening letter I received, reproduced in full here for the first time. I have omitted names used in the missive because they are totally irrelevant. It's the conveying of the message which is more important. Whilst I don't think Bamber physically penned it, or even requested it, the overall influence he exerts among his disciples is clearly there, and one of those people believed they were helping him by punishing and intimidating me and my family. Anyone who says he is not a danger to the public is deluding themselves, there are countless people who live in fear of their lives should he ever be released. Julie Mugford is just one of them:

> So Mr super sleuth private detective Harrison, still think you are clever? You dodged one bullet, keep checking over your shoulder, Jeremy is still watching you and is waiting.
>
> You see how we, working with the public sector, support Jeremy Bamber. We all know he is innocent and we want him free from the hell he has had forced upon him by a corrupt system 29-years ago. You had your chance with Jeremy, he wants you out of the way.
>
> I hear you have been mouthing off about knowing what really happened at the farm that night, it's not like you are some authority on the case, you don't live in Essex, you don't know half of what

I know, I have forgotten more than you will ever know. I have known Jeremy for years, he trusts me, he has told me everything, and I trust him, I have looked deep into his eyes and yes, I believe him. I don't believe you or anything the police say.

Jeremy was framed by a corrupt system so write that in your book. Don't believe me? XXXX XXXXXX ..., he's clever, he knows it, he's very close to Jeremy too and will protect him. The police know he's innocent, the Home Secretary knows it, they are all covering it up, so you Mr super sleuth crime writer, know nothing.

Jeremy is close to getting out now and he will not allow you to harm or deny him the opportunity to gain the freedom he deserves. He may still be inside but Mr super cop he is still a powerful man, and like with XXXX he has influenced people outside who he will have destroy you and whatever pathetic claims you try to make in your book, or anyone else that obstructs his path to freedom come to that.

We will make sure he gets his way and do what it takes, so back off, Jeremy is going to get you!

It was unnerving to receive something so sinister as this at my home address, the writer clearly meant to cause distress to the household. It is a further example of why people don't come forward and speak out against Bamber, he is without any doubt passionately shielded by a frightening team of protectors, some of whom appear to be without any morals. I would think that Bamber himself would see such abhorrent behaviour as damaging to his cause. Likewise, the hacking of my computer in 2012, deleting important case related files, documents and emails, in some instances emails were sent out to third parties, such as Bamber's campaign team, these contained false content pertaining to this case only. By no means is this suffering unique to me, others with a more than passing interest in the case who have dared speak out, have confirmed to me that they too were victims of computer hacking associated with the case.

The act and crime of murder isn't a complicated one, there are basic motives behind it. From my own experience as a policeman, and later as a crime writer, I have conducted interviews with some of the world's most notorious serial killers and murderers. I have examined and investigated countless cases and can categorically state that murders, as complicated as that created at White

House Farm, complete with subterfuge, supposition and external interference, are very rare.

Killers, like all criminals, try to disguise or cover their actions, they are devious, they lie, they make false accusations and allegations, often magnifying minor and irrelevant detail and making it appear colossal in terms of importance. It's actually a very common concept among killers, and this is precisely how Jeremy Bamber has reacted.

With this in mind, over the last few years I have carried out an experiment. It's long been understood that psychological profiling of killers can help build or determine shared traits and drivers. The mind of a killer is best understood by another killer. I put the crime scene scenario and post investigative enquiries and Bamber's responses to a number of incarcerated killers across the globe. Among these was mass murderer Ronald Defeo, who, like Bamber, slaughtered his family with a firearm in the dead of night. The difference being DeFeo was strong enough afterwards to admit his guilt, and in doing so freed himself from a life of lies and torment. He remains a despised character but he clawed back a little respect by coming clean and admitting he did wrong and accepted his punishment. I asked each killer who, in their opinion, was involved. The answer was unanimous, each killer, without any provocation, believed that Jeremy, mainly through his post crime behaviour and comments, was involved. Curiously, a number believed that he probably wasn't a lone killer.

So, we not only have police detectives, a judge and jury and the majority of the United Kingdom population believing Bamber is guilty, we also have like-minded criminals convicted of their own heinous crimes who believe in his involvement too. It's not scientific by any means, however, there exists a saying, 'it takes one to know one', so who better to assess the crime than other convicted killers. As with Bamber's own claims, the experiment does not provide conclusive proof of his guilt, that has already been determined in a court of law. Anyone dismissing this as a nonsense because these are solely the views of guilty criminals, therefore their views can be deemed untrustworthy, should consider that Bamber too is a convicted criminal, a proven liar and killer, yet his views are accepted as fact by some.

7

The Friend

'You have a grand gift for silence ... It makes you quite invaluable as a companion.'

Sherlock Holmes – The Man with the Twisted Lip

I spoke earlier in this book about my attempt to locate and interview what seems to be Jeremy's only true male friend, Brett Collins. The pair had met during Jeremy's trip to New Zealand and clearly had a profound effect on each other. Both, in my opinion, had deviant personalities. Collins, by all accounts, had a dark side to his character. The way he spoke and acted wasn't acceptable, he frequently partook in immoral behaviour and was known to the authorities, leading to suggestions by some Bamber disciples that Jeremy was led astray during his time in New Zealand. It is claimed that Bamber took to the illegal drugs trade and stealing while there, fancy watches being among the stolen property he acquired. It has also been suggested, quite inappropriately because it bears no relevance to the case, that a homosexual relationship between the pair began during Bamber's stay.

Brett Collins visited and stayed with Bamber before the murders. He was out of the country in Greece when the murders occurred, so probably had no part to play in the commission of the crime. However, he was very supportive of Jeremy after the murders, so much so that he riled Jeremy's girlfriend Julie Mugford, by his 'close' behaviour with her partner, and some claim he became something of a confidante to him. The pair enjoyed holidays, fancy foods and spending sprees together, and Collins remained around Jeremy as an apparent pillar of support during the trial proceedings. Thereafter he disappeared, returning to his New Zealand home never to be heard of again.

After the murders, Bamber and Collins seemed to be drawn even closer. On one occasion Bamber asked Collins to visit his dead sister's flat with him, since he was effectively her next of kin. Inside the pair looked through her possessions and found some naked modelling shots of Sheila. Most decent people in mourning would have destroyed such images but not Jeremy Bamber. He sought to cash in on the tragedy, and Brett Collins, perhaps not the most morally correct of friends, agreed. It was Collins who approached a national newspaper and offered them for sale as an exclusive. Contact was made with journalist Michael Fielder and the group agreed to meet in the Nags Head pub in Chelmsford.

Fielder later said that he was shocked by the attitude of Collins and Bamber. They acted like naughty schoolboys, sniggering and giggling throughout. Bamber told Fielder that the images of Sheila were really, really good, with the biggest vibrator you ever saw. The reporter was stunned by the insinuations the men were making, implying that Bamber and his sister Sheila had been with each other, followed by much sniggering. Eventually the subject turned to money, with Bamber asking for £20,000 in return for 20 topless and nude colour transparencies showing every detail. According to the journalist, Bamber also offered to sell pictures of his parents and murdered nephews. For this he wanted a substantial sum and he would look at selling his own life story if the price was right. The utter callous attitude that Bamber displayed shocked the reporter, but sensing a good story in the making, he asked for a further meeting where he could see the images for himself. Jeremy Bamber arranged a further meeting at Sheila's flat.

The meeting never took place, the editor of the newspaper believed the story of the attempted sale of the pictures by Bamber was more sensational and so went to print with it. Neither Jeremy Bamber nor Brett Collins contacted the paper again but neither expressed any denial that it had happened. Needless to say, the Bamber disciples have since attempted to discredit the newspaper. In one of several bizarre attempts to question the provenance of the story, it is claimed that the editor of the newspaper partied in a pub with senior police officers in celebration of Bamber's conviction. The editor was said to have inferred that they knew that Bamber was innocent and that it was a drugs gang he was associating with at the time that had committed the crime! The inference again is one huge conspiracy to convict an innocent man, except now we have the press involved too.

I attempted to track down Brett Collins several years ago, and after several wild goose chases eventually found someone in New Zealand who knew him, but Collins didn't like or want to speak to the press, or anyone he felt suspicious of in case they were the police, he apparently held a mistrust of the law. After hours of negotiating a meeting I received a telephone call, one of a few from a person claiming to be the said Brett Collins. If it wasn't him then someone knew him well and all about his time with Jeremy Bamber. I hurriedly made notes of the calls since they were unexpected and therefore not recorded.

The caller – I will refer to him as Brett Collins since I genuinely believe it was him – started by telling me he had changed his opinion of Jeremy Bamber, he now believed him to be one hundred per cent guilty, something he claimed he didn't know before the murders. After the murders, Jeremy, he said, had seemed very excited about the inheritance and was making plans how to spend it. In hindsight he felt that Bamber didn't actually show any remorse, but was tricking everyone with his public show of tears and woeful expressions. Behind closed doors he was laughing at how foolish the police and people were. He had asked Bamber if he did it. In response Bamber had laughed at him and said, 'Come on, do you really think I could kill them? It was Sheila that killed them'. He had then winked. 'I want what's rightly mine, and that's everything they own'. I asked him what he believed the wink to mean and he told me that he felt Jeremy knew more but that was the story he was sticking to. He then claimed that Bamber, when in drink and drugs, had a loose tongue, and he would let slip things that had happened during the murders, but when asked how he knew about it he said the police had told him such things.

Collins said it came as no real surprise when Bamber was arrested and charged with the murders. He didn't speak out about it because Bamber had said things while under the influence of drugs and alcohol and he believed the police would dismiss what he said because they seemed to have issues with his sexuality and having a bit of a past. Instead, he offered support to Bamber who he thought was making himself look like a big man.

There was a point blank refusal to talk in detail about criminal offences committed by Bamber in New Zealand or elsewhere, he told me Bamber enjoyed the drugs scene, as did Julie Mugford, who he didn't like at all because she always seemed in awe of Bamber and wanted him, Collins, out of the picture.

So far as the selling of the photographs were concerned, Collins said it was all Jeremy's doing. Yes, he had acted as a front man, but that was all. He refuted suggestions that he had tipped off the press about Jeremy's arrest and the police suspicion of his involvement.

The calls were brief and on one occasion he informed me that he was ill and struggling, so he didn't wish to talk about any of it again, he wanted to be left alone to get on with his life. I was told some time later that rumours of his death had surfaced on the internet, so again this tallied with what he told me. I never heard again from the person, I am however convinced I spoke to the same Brett Collins that was involved with Jeremy Bamber.

8

The Silk

'There is nothing more deceptive than an obvious fact.'
Sherlock Holmes – The Boscombe Valley Mystery

In 2002, I was working as a clerk to a High Court Judge at the Royal Courts of Justice in London. One of my duties was to liaise with various barrister chambers involved in the cases coming before the courts. During my time working with the judiciary I made many contacts in the legal world and most, because of the nature of the role, were acquaintances. I was fortunate in that one such encounter was with a gentleman called Ed Lawson QC. I had no idea at the time, but within minutes of sharing refreshments with him I learned that he had been the junior for Geoffrey Rivlin, Bamber's defence council at the murder trial.

It wasn't something that immediately interested me since professionally I was focused on the task at hand and not on Jeremy Bamber. Eventually though, probably at my prompting, we held a discussion about the case as I sought to find out what Bamber was all about.

He was a horrible man, anything but a straightforward character, and I'm not certain anyone will ever get to the root of what Jeremy Bamber is about. There was always an air of arrogance about him, it was as if he didn't believe what was happening, not because he was clearly innocent but because I think he thought it was all a bit of a game, a game he could never lose. He thought he was superior and in control of everything that was going on around him.

I remember discussions about his initial arrest, he said the police weren't in a position to proceed or charge him because he was innocent. He was asked how we, as his public defenders, could show a jury that he was innocent, he shrugged his shoulders as though it was our responsibility to do that and not his. He was an exceedingly difficult client to represent. Wholly focused on money and how he would one day soon be able to sell his story to Fleet Street and make a small fortune for himself. It wasn't what anyone wanted or expected to hear coming from a person in that situation. He was either two steps ahead of us, or living in his own fantasy world.

For me I don't believe Sheila Caffell played any part in killing her family, there was police evidence to show that she didn't do it. However, Jeremy's actions during the entire enquiry were anything but sensible. Taking off on holiday to St Tropez, wining and dining friends and forever talking about money. Whether it was grief and the excitement and anticipation of owning so much money that caused him to lose focus on family responsibilities, I don't know. He made another comment when he was arrested a second time, I think it was at Dover. He said something along the lines that he should have come back into the country a different way! Things like that cannot sound innocent to a jury can they?

The evidence that existed to defend him was poor and we had little to work with, then he stood up to give evidence and told the prosecution QC that it was his duty to establish fact. Bloody hell, easily the most arrogant thing I ever witnessed from a defendant in a court of law.

There were times when he did seem disconcertingly composed, even when the evidence was clearly stacked against him. I wasn't really certain whether that was down to him believing he could pull it off whatever happened, or whether he was innocent. In hindsight he was guilty.

It was alarming really, I don't think I represented anyone so unaware of how they were coming across, and of their own bad attitude. I know that people worked tirelessly to prove his innocence, we searched for the evidence that showed he didn't do it but we couldn't find anything and we couldn't damage the prosecution case. Then there was the girlfriend, she wasn't a great witness but she was better than anything we had and she was able to convince the jury.

I haven't really kept up with everything that has happened since the trial. You always like to believe in a client when you represent them, especially in such a serious matter. I did at one time believe that he could be innocent but, as I say, we couldn't prove it to ourselves, let alone to a jury in a trial. That's what concerned me most. I think it's easy to look at things in this case and claim them to be wrong but it's an illusion. It comes to the stage that you have to take stock of what supporting material you have to prove your case, if there is no substance then you are going to struggle. That's what will always remain in my recollection of this case, we couldn't prove his innocence. That generally leads one to think but one thing – he was guilty.

I know it has been inferred that the police arranged some of the evidence but come on, let's look at it seriously, they were too busy fighting with each other to do that, they weren't capable of it. The police were a disorganised bunch in this case, they could never have created such a watertight cover-up that would stand the test of time.

It's all very sad because people tend to forget that a family was murdered. Because of his daft claims he keeps it live and in the public domain. I do think Jeremy knows more, perhaps he can't tell because it would implicate him further, or he won't tell because he is guilty. If he's got a spine he will tell someone, someday. There were things he said that caused me to wonder. For instance, he knew about cash that was in the house and unless he'd been searching and looking in advance, he couldn't have possibly known about how much cash and what cash was where. And anyway, why worry yourself about something like that after your entire family have been murdered? That always bothered me but the question was never asked, it was missed, but I think it could have proved most uncomfortable for us had it been raised. Then there was the telephone call from his father. Did it happen? I genuinely doubt it. I know what I would have done had I been in his father's situation. Either get out of the house or dial 999 and he did neither.

Sadly my time with Ed Lawson was all too brief, he was an extremely busy man and I felt privileged that he had spent a small amount of it speaking to me about Jeremy Bamber so candidly. I anticipated that he would be wholly convinced of Bamber's innocence, yet that clearly wasn't the case. So we now have police evidence showing his guilt, crime scene evidence showing his guilt, witness testimony showing his guilt, and one of his defence team – privately at least – believing in his guilt.

9

The Art of Deception

'What one man can invent another can discover.'
Sherlock Holmes - The Adventure of the Dancing Man

There exists a number of different aspects to this case which concern me, none of which have ever suitably been explained by the prosecution or defence at trial. According to the prosecution, it is claimed that Jeremy Bamber returned to White House Farm in the early hours of the morning in order to murder his family. He gained access to the house by climbing through a sash window he knew had a faulty catch and was therefore insecure. In doing so, he knew he was taking a huge risk since it is well documented, and was certainly known to Bamber at the time, that the family members present in the house were in a highly excitable state. According to farm secretary Barbara Wilson who had telephoned the house that night before the murders, arguments had taken place and she sensed an atmosphere in the manner of the call. It is claimed by Bamber that these related to Sheila's ability to look after and care for her children.

Bamber, if he did break in as the prosecution claim, was entering a house full of angst and a highly charged atmosphere, thereby putting himself at great risk in the commission of his crime. My concerns don't end there. Once inside he would have to systematically and painstakingly shoot three adults and two children. Even with a sound moderator on the rifle, he could not know that everyone in the house was going to be asleep, or where they were when he entered. The question remains how could Bamber – or anyone – systematically murder three adults without alerting at least one of them during the commission of the crime.

If we accept the prosecution case, Sheila did nothing to protect her children during the slaughter, and was complicit throughout the killing of her family and in the style and manner of her own death. Would she as a mother really offer no resistance whatsoever and allow Jeremy to lead her to her own death? Three adults killed in different locations within the house, and two children while they slept. Lots of noise must have been made during the execution of the murders, yet Sheila just stands by, offers no resistance and does nothing. It doesn't make sense.

I have always believed that Sheila allowed Jeremy into the house through the back (kitchen) door, which was then locked from the inside, and Bamber exited through the window with the faulty catch. This is the only explanation of how he could enter the house knowing the true extent of the domestic altercation and where everyone was. Sheila would have told him everything on letting him into the premises.

It's fair to say that over the years I have had a good deal of communication with criminals convicted of all sorts of crime types. One such instance occurred many years ago when I was a serving police officer. I was writing historical true crime in my spare time and I was surprised to receive a letter bearing a postmark, Gartree Prison, a 'Category A' prison in Market Harborough, Leicestershire. A Category A prison houses the worst type of criminal offender, those whose escape would be highly dangerous to the public or national security. Offences include murder, attempted murder, manslaughter, wounding with intent, terrorism, rape and indecent assault to name but a few. This is also a prison that once housed Jeremy Bamber. The letter I received came from one of the infamous Kray twins and it was from Reggie asking if I would be interested in writing a book on their lives. It was utterly charming and thoroughly sycophantic in its content. I was flattered to think that two of Britain's most notorious gangsters felt I was the author they wanted to pen their story. After consultation with my then Chief Constable, I opted not to have any further engagement on the book project since I felt it compromised my position in the police force. The point I am making here is how a killer, despite being jailed, attempts to manipulate matters whenever possible.

I thought Reggie and Ronnie to be utterly decent in their

communications with me as they promised me the truth and honesty, simply because that's what they wanted me to believe. Just as Jeremy Bamber would like the world to believe that he is a decent man, an unfortunate victim of the corrupt establishment and of a spiteful family, and that the people who knew him were nothing but liars because they were all co-conspirators. It sounds plausible, yet the reality is very much different. Reggie and Ronnie Kray were cold blooded killers, they wanted continued notoriety and perhaps a chance of parole. Jeremy Bamber was equally as charming in his correspondence to me, he yearns for his freedom and with that the inheritance he desperately wants. He will do or say whatever it takes to achieve this and use whoever he can to get it. He is therefore calculating and devious in all of his dealings with people outside, guiding and effectively controlling his public face.

The one thing jailed killers such as Bamber have a penchant for is getting inside your mind, to draw you in then manipulate and control your thoughts and opinions on them. When they realise it's not working, it tends to end communication. It's something I have learned to address through personal experience and via my criminal profiling research. Incarceration, for lifers especially, takes on a whole new meaning, they have little else to focus on other than themselves and, in many instances, gaining their freedom and they will attempt this by whatever means possible. So when an ex-policeman and crime writer comes along, it can be seen as an ideal situation for them to gain some leverage towards their release.

The following is the content of a letter I received from Bamber relating to the faulty window which the prosecution say was used to gain access to the property. He is answering questions previously posed by me and elaborating on some of the detail.

> I've been asked to write to you about the window catch issue – thing is it might seem like it's something that takes an hour, and I'm not complaining about this – my case papers run to millions of pages, so simply to thoroughly research an issue, it can take between 30 and 40 hours – and you have to look at everything, because if not, it's easy to miss the truth of it. The police are clever and experienced at this – they fitted people up routinely in the 70s

and 80s so they know how to cover their tracks, they also leave lots of red herrings and blind leads to confuse and loose [sic] anyone trying to track them – the other trick is that they make simple issues really, really complicated – a point in issue here. The window catch is so complex, and truly complex issues get to even baffle me so that I need to actually change your question to what we're trying to show. Once I've set that up you'll then understand.

The prosecution had to establish that I knew two things – how to break into the house undetected, and how to leave the house and make it look and be totally secure from inside and out. The prosecution concede that the house was locked up tight from inside. DCI Jones states that he checked all the windows at 09:30am. If all the windows and doors are bolted from inside, then it doesn't matter that I knew how to get into the house, I didn't know how to get out leaving the window locked on the inside.

The police suggest that Julie told them that I knew of such a window and told her that it was the kitchen window – simple timeline investigations show that Julie mentions no particular window – it's not important because DC Barlow and Ann Eaton decide that it's the kitchen window – DC Barlow climbs out and says he could bang it shut so that the catch engages a little bit. In this typed statement it's crossed out but in the hand written says '18/09/85 check kitchen window to see if theory correct – answer yes by banging when catch falls down into locked position' – except it actually doesn't fall very far – on a clock face about 8:00.

The point being that the jury were misled – it wasn't remotely possible to put the catch in the position shown in the photo. The conclusion being it's impossible for me to have broken out of the house leaving it locked and bolted – everything else re windows is to confuse and suggest someone broke in. Furthermore I had no idea about how to break out – in yes, but there would never have been a need for me to do such a thing, I'd leave by the back door (old one had a Yale lock). The new one the police smashed down had a mortice lock, it was only recently fitted some months, maybe a year earlier, but I wasn't living at Mum and Dad's and if I needed to use the house they'd leave a key in the coal shed – the relatives suggest there was always a key in the shed as if I could have used that to get in the house – but of course that's a red herring as the door key was left in the lock, we didn't always leave a key in the shed, only if someone needed to get in the house (the house keeper, me, the painters and the secretary for instance). But it's irrelevant if there was a key in the shed or not, it couldn't have been used.

Importantly after my release from five days of questioning I had to get into the house to pick up the insurance docs. Without looking it up it was 15 or 16 September I think. I used the shower room window to get in as Essex Police still had all my keys – if I'd have known how to get out, locking it all up again, then I wouldn't have left a note on Barbara Wilson's desk asking her to re-lock the shower room window 'cos I'd got in that way, and out again

What we do know is the jury heard Brian Elliott's evidence re the catch and the hacksaw blade and scratches on the window frame – what the court didn't know was that the window had been fully SOC'ed, fingerprinted and photographed on 8-12 September – the Davidson/Elliott/Cook examination was on 1 October, so why did Essex Police mislead the jury on this issue? Someone tampered with the window after the 8-12 September examination, my guess is the owner of those three fingerprints will be responsible – Essex Police obviously kept the ID of those prints secret.

Essex Police knew the house was not broken into or out of on 6 or 7/8/85. They knew after my arrest that it was forensically unbroken into or out of (tests between 8-12 September), they knew Ann Eaton and DC Barlow and Robert Boutflour had been fiddling with the house windows from mid-August to late September, they all variously refer to doing so. The game is up for them, it really is – they'll continue to tell more and more lies and give more and more excuses because that's what Essex Police do, but the truth is in these files and in the photos – and once its all put into the public arena then they will have no choice but to face up to what they've done. I know I still have all your questions to answer but this should set you on the right road.

No matter how many times I analyse this letter and its content, I find it utterly misleading and full of deliberate confusion. Bamber focuses on minor detail that is of no consequence, and yes, once again we have accusations of police keeping secrets and relatives and cops colluding to create evidence against him. Bizarrely in my opinion, Bamber admits he could break in but not out! Much of what he reiterates are little more than clerical errors contained in the police paperwork. No matter how many such errors exist, and one could suggest there are too many to detail or list, they do not prove Jeremy Bamber is innocent. Some would argue that they don't truly show his guilt either, and that's correct, but as has been shown, other evidence does prove this.

Bamber fills almost all of his time searching for weaknesses in police procedural activities and is unable, through any other means, to prove that he is innocent and that he didn't murder his family. His campaign team have periodically requested new information and for witnesses to come forward, yet in the time that has passed since, none have and it is extremely unlikely that anyone ever will.

Looking at the contents of the letters more closely, it will become distinctly obvious to the reader that Bamber doesn't always answer the questions I ask of him, he comments on this several times and promises that this will be done, it never is. On one occasion he openly states that he alters the wording of my question, this I believe is to make it more palatable for his cause and not to aid anyone else or my research. I know others who have traversed a similar route, those people also suffered frustration as Bamber's versions of accounts are inconsistent. There is always a reluctance to provide a straight answer and a level of detail in his claims that will allow matters to be more closely examined and drilled down to a level where probability would not exist, and where countless assumptions about all aspects of the case could finally be proved or dispelled.

There was a period when I thought it feasible that Bamber had suffered a miscarriage of justice. That was not through anything I was told, nor was it through manipulation by any of his supporters. My belief came about as a result of the examination of some of the police documents. It should be added that since that initial belief, I have thoroughly discussed the case with credible experts, psychologists, forensic people and scientists, and none believe him innocent.

10

The Trial

'The game is afoot.'
Sherlock Holmes – The Adventure of the Abbey Grange

The trial of Jeremy Bamber began on Thursday 2 October 1986, over a year after the murders had occurred. This chapter covers the key aspects of the trial on a day-by-day basis.

Day 1: Thursday, 2 October

The trial opened at Chelmsford Crown Court, Essex before Mr Justice Maurice Drake. Acting for the prosecution (The Crown) was Anthony Arlidge QC, and for the defence, Geoffrey Rivlin QC. After initial proceedings the jury of seven men and five women was sworn in and opening speeches delivered.

The Times newspaper reported:

Farmer Jeremy Bamber shot dead five members of his family to inherit a £400,000 fortune, a court was told yesterday. Mr Bamber, 25, had planned the 'perfect murder' the jury heard. But he was allegedly trapped when Julie Mugford, the girlfriend he had spurned, went to the Police. Mr Bamber denies all five murders, including that of his sister, ex-model Sheila 'Bambi' Caffell, 27, and her six-year old twin sons Daniel and Nicholas. The prosecution claims he also killed the adoptive parents he is said to have hated, Nevill and June Bamber, both 61.

The five bodies riddled with 25 bullets, were found at the family's £250,000 eighteenth century farmhouse in Essex in August 1985. At first Police believed Jeremy Bamber's story that Sheila – whom he claimed had thought she was the Virgin Mary and Joan of Arc – had gone crazy, shot the others, and then killed herself. But then detectives began to have doubts the court was told. If Sheila was the killer, she must have murdered her sons. But relatives agreed she loved them and wanted to keep them – she was separated from her husband. She had no aptitude for firearms, yet the shootings were 'calculated' with all 25 bullets on target. She was slightly built – yet her father, who put up a struggle, was a strong man and would easily have overpowered her. Whoever was the killer, he or she would have to reload the 10 shot rifle at least twice, said Mr Anthony Arlidge QC prosecuting. There was little lead on Sheila's hands and no oil on her nightdress – impossible had she handled the rifle.

Then 22 year old student Julie Mugford went to the Police on 7 September. Mr Bamber allegedly told Miss Mugford he wanted to kill them, 'the perfect murder, a murder that would not be discovered.' She said, 'If you hate them that much, why not clear out?' He told her he had too much to lose, she alleged. Mr Arlidge told the jury that Mr and Mrs Bamber had an estate valued at about £436,000. Jeremy was the main benefactor of Nevill's will and Sheila of June's, with a proviso that if either died before their own parents, their own children would inherit.

Many questions were asked in court of Police Constable West and Malcolm Bonnett. West had been the first officer to speak with Jeremy Bamber and record details of his call. Generally the police do not suddenly happen across crimes, they learn of them from a third party, a witness or perhaps a victim, and in some cases from the offender. From the outset it's imperative that as much detail is extracted from the person reporting the crime or incident, this dictates the appropriate and immediate police and emergency service response.

One of the first things one is taught as part of police procedure is to note time, date and place. The content of all police reports contain such information from the outset and it's not exactly rocket science why such detail is important in the timeline of evidence – obviously timing is critical throughout. It's a highly responsible position that requires supreme confidence and a need for expert listening skills and precise articulation of the facts. There is little room for error, but in police circles it isn't generally regarded as an overtly taxing role, more of a comfortable one since the information room staff have no direct dealings with confrontation or grotesque crime scenes, they are merely there to record detail.

Operational police officers act upon, visit, and deal with crime scenes as a result of the detail provided from the information room. The attending officer's actions are based upon the original information received and recorded by such staff. At the crime scene itself, the first officer to arrive has a duty to ascertain the facts and convey updates for the communication and incident log. No matter what the crime, the actions, perceptions and messages of the first officer at the scene determine how the investigation subsequently proceeds. It is their call as to what resources are required. Uniform police back up, dog handlers, CID, firearms, scenes of crime teams and other emergency services are but a radio call away. This is why the initial communication and crime scene assessment has to be precise. If human life is at risk then there is no room for error or mistake.

To assess the trial details correctly we must look at the evidence provided in the manner it was presented to the jury. The chronological order of events offered by the prosecution is laid out factually beginning with the original police notification of something being wrong at White House Farm that morning.

Police Constable 1990 Michael James West was on night duty and working in the control room at Chelmsford Police Station on the morning of 7 August 1985. He had begun his duties several hours earlier. Part of his control room duty included the answering of and dealing with telephone calls from members of the public, assisting with their enquiries and ensuring that details reported were accurately recorded for any further crime investigations. Regarding the Bamber trial, West officially recorded the following statement he took in a telephone call and his subsequent response. The signed statement is dated 9 August 1985:

> About 03.26 hours, Wednesday, 7 August 1985, I was on duty on the control desk at Chelmsford Police Station when I received an exchange phone call from a person I now know to be Mr Jeremy Bamber of 9 Head Street, Goldhanger.
>
> Mr Bamber said to me, 'You've got to help me, my father has just phoned me saying, "Please come over, your sister has gone crazy and has the gun," then the phone went dead. My father sounded terrified, I don't think he was kidding.'
>
> I then said to Mr Bamber, 'Where does your father live?'

He replied, 'White House Farm, Tolleshunt D'Arcy.'

I then said, 'Does your sister have access to any guns?'

He said, 'Yes, my father has a collection of 12 bores and .410s (shotguns) and .22 rifles. Look my sister has a history of mental illness, you've got help me.'

I said to Mr Bamber, 'Hold the line please, I'll contact our information room and find out where the nearest unit is.'

I then contacted the information room and relayed the preceding conversation to them.

They informed me that the Witham area car had just arrived at Witham Police Station and to contact them. This conversation with the information room lasted approximately three minutes.

I then contacted Witham Police Station via our radio link and requested that their area car attend White House Farm and related my conversation with Mr Bamber.

This conversation also lasted approximately three minutes.

I then spoke again to Mr Bamber and told him that a police unit was attending his father's address from Witham. I also asked him to attend and liaise with the police officers on his arrival, this he agreed to do.

I then completed an Essex Police Form C1 and commenced a log of events. Log produced Ref

MJW/1.

Signed MJ West PC 1990

The Essex Police form (C1) to which West refers is what was known as a telephone message report or telephone log or event log, it is hand written and signed. However, on examining the form C1 completed by Police Constable West, it becomes clear that discrepancies exist within its content, including the time written down which is 03.36 hours, 10 minutes later than West put in his statement above. It is obvious that West regarded the call as coming from a distressed member of the public, Jeremy Bamber, as he officially refers to it as such. West then adds the caller's details as Mr Bamber of 9 Head Street, Goldhanger. Telephone: 88645. The message details are then recorded as thus:

FATHER PHONED AGE 62 'PLEASE COME OVER YOUR SISTER HAS GONE CRAZY HAS THE GUN' PHONE WENT DEAD.

FATHER – MR BAMBER

H/A WHITE HOUSE FARM, TOLLESHUNT D'ARCY

SISTER – SHEILA BAMBER AGE 27 HAS HISTORY OF MENTAL

Constable West was asked to make a further additional statement, this time an altogether more detailed and opinionated statement about the telephone call and conversation he had with Jeremy Bamber:

On Tuesday, 6 August 1985 I commenced duty at Chelmsford Police Station and my duty for that night tour until 6am the following morning was in the Control Room at Chelmsford Police Station.

At 3.36am Wednesday, 7 August 1985, I was in the Control Room when I answered an in-coming telephone call on the external GPO line. I answered by saying, 'Police, Chelmsford. Good morning.'

A youngish male voice of a man possibly in his middle to late twenties said, 'I am Jeremy Bamber of 9 Head Street, Goldhanger. You've got to help me. My father has just rung me and said, "Please come over. Your sister has gone crazy and has got the gun. The line went dead."'

I said, 'Who is your sister?'

He replied, 'Sheila. I can't remember her surname. Sheila Bamber.'

I said, 'How old is she?'

He replied, 'About 27. She's had a history of psychiatry. She's been depressed before.' He then said words to the effect, 'She could go mad at anything, she's done it before,' although I cannot recall those exact words.

I said, 'Has she got access to any guns?'

He replied, 'Yes. My father's got a collection of .410s, 12 bores and .22s.'

I said, 'What's your father's name and where does he live?'

He either replied, 'Mr Bamber, or Nevill Bamber,' I cannot remember which and continued, 'White House Farm, Tolleshunt D'Arcy.'

As far as I can recall he then said, 'I tried ringing Witham but there was nobody in so I rang you.' He definitely said that, although I cannot remember if it was at that stage or when I later spoke to him.

I then asked him to hold the line and put the call on hold. I contacted Headquarters Information Room but cannot remember if it was by internal telephone or via the radio channel. My call was answered by a male operator whose details I do not know and I related to him the details of my conversation with Mr Jeremy Bamber.

I was informed that police officers had just returned to Witham and then spoke with, I think, PC Saxby at Witham Police Station via the personal radio link between Chelmsford Police Station and Witham Police Station. I again related the details of my conversation and the officer told me that he would go direct to White House Farm with his sergeant.

I spent about three minutes maximum speaking to Information Room and Witham Police Station and then returned to Mr Jeremy Bamber who was still on the line.

I said, 'Hello.'

He replied, 'Christ. You took a long time.'

I told him that I had contacted my Information Room and Witham Police Station and a car was on its way to his father's address at Tolleshunt.

I then said, 'What's your father's telephone number?'

He replied, 'Maldon 860209.'

I said, 'How old is your father?'

He replied either, '62,' or 'About 62.'

I said, 'Do you know who's in the house?'

He replied, 'My father obviously. My mother and Sheila.'

During the course of this second conversation his voice had become progressively more urgent and excitable [sic] and was beginning to speak quicker and quicker and at a higher pitch.

After his last reply he continued in an even more excitable [sic] vein, as though he thought I was not taking the matter as urgently as I should, by saying, 'Look, when my father rang me he sounded terrified. I don't think he's kidding about. He sounded really frightened.' I think I asked him if he had tried ringing his father back and I recall him saying, 'I tried ringing him back and I can't get any reply.'

I said, 'Will you go to the house and wait for the police officers and liaise with them there?'

He replied, 'Shall I go now?'

I said, 'Yes, the car from Witham won't take long.'

I asked him for his telephone number which he gave me as Goldhanger 88645 and he then rang off.

I informed Acting Inspector Targrass of the situation and immediately afterwards dialled Maldon 860209 and received an intermittent tone showing the line to be engaged. I can only say that I made this call prior to 3.42am. After dialling Maldon 860209

I telephoned the GPO operator and asked her to check the Maldon number as we needed to know if the telephone was off the hook or whether someone was speaking on the line. I timed her reply to me at 3.42am when she told me that the phone had been left off the hook.

As a result of a negative reply from Information Room to my request as to whether Mr Jeremy Bamber had arrived at the scene at about 4.12am, I telephoned his number at Goldhanger 88645 but received no reply. During the course of my first conversation with Mr Jeremy Bamber I found him to be speaking throughout in a cool, calm and collected manner. His voice was not raised at any stage and I did not get the impression that he was in any way excited. Neither was he speaking quickly thereby indicating great urgency. I would describe his voice at that time as deep and laconic.

I noted all the above times by reference to the control room digital clock beside me about seven feet away. As far as I am aware this clock is normally accurate although it is possible that when I noted the time of the original call from Mr Jeremy Bamber at 3.36am I may have misread it for 3.26am. However, I cannot be sure of that.

Since 7 August 1985 I have made no written records of the above information and the conversation shown above is made from my memory of the occasion.

Signed M J West PC1990

It should be noted that there exists an unwritten rule that is indoctrinated into the minds of all police officers that when giving detailed evidence in court they should ask, in order to recount to the court succinctly and accurately, to refer relevant documents such as statements, official records or notes, or pocket book notes made by them. The magistrate or judge will always ask when such records and notes were completed and the police officer should state along the lines of, 'they were made and completed independently from their own recollection of events while the facts were fresh in the memory.'

So, we are asked to believe that West was so proficient in his accurate recall of events, that he could remember telephone numbers, voice intonation and suspicious statements made by a caller over five weeks earlier, yet when questioned about other more basic facts during trial, he wasn't even certain what time he took the call, nor could he remember who he spoke to about it, or even how he contacted his colleagues in the Police Information Room! To leave it five weeks before committing it in full into statement form is both unprofessional and highly irregular, particularly as he was the first contact police officer.

Interestingly, the day following PC West giving evidence at the Chelmsford Crown Court trial, an internal police memorandum, titled 'Police Constable 1990 West' was submitted to Chief Superintendent Harris, Chelmsford, by Detective Superintendent Mike Ainsley, it read:

> This officer was required to give evidence in the case of R v Bamber on 2 October 1986.
>
> While he presented a smart appearance and spoke firmly and directly to the court, not once did he refer to the judge as 'My Lord' and in fact not once did he complete his evidence or cross examination with 'Sir'.
>
> In addition he gave the appearance of not knowing his evidence and had to be reminded by defence counsel of the contents of his statements. Overall his outward appearance was spoiled by his lack of respect for the court and obvious lack of preparation for the occasion.

There can be no doubt when reading the trial extracts that Constable West came across as an unconvincing witness, his testimony lacked the conviction and confidence one would have expected from someone whose role demanded total accuracy. It was an uninspiring start to the prosecution case, hence Ainsley condemning in writing the officer's performance and demeanour in the witness box. So what was the 'preparation' that Ainsley alluded to? When giving evidence there is never any doubt that a police officer is going to be able to see and refer to his/her original statement(s), that evidence will be questioned since it is the officer's sworn testimony. The preparation alluded to by Ainsley is little more than a pre-read of the statement before a trial. West clearly hadn't done so. The knee jerk memorandum to a more senior officer was covering Ainsley's own back. Supportive he was not! Defensive he most certainly was.

The cross examination should have probed the witness much deeper, certainly about the time span between the incident and the second statement where the additional detail and perceptions were added. Today the question has to be if West was solely conveying fact and held such an incredible accurate memory recall, why did he get so confused by the most basic questions? As far as cross examinations go, this one was insipid, it didn't at all reflect the astute ability that Geoffrey Rivlin QC became renowned for. Although I do believe that West was recollecting matters as accurately as he could, and to my mind no deliberate intent to confuse or alter the course of a criminal investigation was intended.

Police Sergeant Chris Bews was next in the witness box to give evidence

Bews went on to tell the court how at the scene at 4.02am, he and Constable Myall left Bamber and Constable Saxby at the police car, which was parked in Pages Lane. It had been their intention to carry out a reconnaissance of the farm, however it made more sense to have someone with them who had expert knowledge of the layout. Sensibly they asked Jeremy Bamber to go with them. As they did so, Bews questioned Bamber about the persons who would be within the house, the threat those persons posed, and any other detail that may be of use. So at 4.09am, the occupants of police vehicle CA7 (radio identification call sign) contacted the Information Room and confirmed: 'No sign of life in house ...'

Day 2: Friday, 3 October

Day two of the trial saw more police witnesses called to give evidence and other important expert testimony was heard.

Police Constable Stephen Myall who was one of the first officers at the scene told the jury, 'He described his sister, Sheila Caffell, as a depressive psychopath who had been receiving treatment from a Harley Street doctor. He said she had been committed to psychiatric hospitals and had last left hospital six weeks previously.' He claimed he spoke to Bamber to offer sympathetic support while officers of the tactical firearms unit approached the family home. Myall described Bamber as remarkably calm when he met police at the scene only hours after the murders. Bamber told him that he hoped his father's caravan park, where he worked, would be able to 'Stand him a Porsche' later in the year. None of which shed Bamber in a very positive light and no matter how one tries to justify talk of buying a car, it comes across as crass and unsympathetic.

Another officer, Police Constable Robin Norcup, said he heard Bamber mutter, 'Oh God, I hope she hasn't done anything silly.'

Police surgeon Dr Ian Craig told the jury that Bamber broke down and cried when told his father had been killed. Dr Craig said he believed that Bamber was in a state of shock after hearing about the murders, he went on to say how he was involuntarily told by him that his family had considered having Mrs Caffell's twin boys adopted because she had caused them injury. Every opportunity was seized by Bamber to ensure Sheila and her episodes were the focus of attention.

As the waiting continued, Inspector Douglas Adams said that Bamber grew agitated and had asked him, 'What's happening in there? They are all the family I have got.'

Police Constable Lawrence Collins was the first policeman to enter the farmhouse. He claimed the only sign of life was a small dog cowering under a bed in the main bedroom where Sheila Caffell and June Bamber lay dead.

Miss Julie Foakes, the daughter of one of the farm labourers, said how she saw Mrs Caffell with her sons and dog walking towards the farmhouse on the day before the massacre. 'She seemed happy. She was jumping, skipping about with the children and the dog. She always seemed a very loving mother.'

Miss Foakes' mother, Dorothy Foakes, recalled a conversation with the farmer Jeremy Bamber the previous Autumn. 'He said he didn't get on with his sister and he wouldn't share his money with her,' she said.

Day 3: Monday, 6 October

Detective Inspector Ron Cook was recalled to the court to find himself sternly rebuked by the trial judge when he admitted that a grey hair attached to the bloodstained sound moderator that the prosecution claimed was used in the murders, had gone missing on its way to the forensic laboratory. He admitted that forensic experts had not been warned of the hair's existence. The Judge told Cook 'They should have been told – you know they should have been told.' Cook, a fingerprint expert with 19-years experience was forced to admit that he had touched the .22 semi automatic weapon used in the killings without wearing gloves. He said it was a few weeks before the rifle and a Bible were examined for prints. Other evidence, including the sound moderator, were not found until Mr Bamber's cousin, Mr David Boutflour, went to the house. Boutflour and his sister noticed blood on the sound moderator as well as traces of red paint which came from the mantelpiece in the kitchen where Nevill had put up a fight. When Boutflour had told police about the silencer it had taken them several days to collect it! Cook admitted that, despite obvious signs of a struggle in the kitchen, he had not examined score marks on the mantelpiece.

White House Farm Secretary Barbara Wilson told the court that Bamber had become arrogant and nasty since the murders, and he had awarded himself £75 a week pay rise because of his new responsibilities. He complained that the funerals for his family were expensive and told her to get rid of everything belonging to his father from the farm office. She said that a week after the murders he came into the office, sat down and put his feet on the desk. He told me to get rid of all his father's things. When I said I wanted to sort through them in case there were one or two things of sentimental value he said, 'I don't want any of it.' He said he didn't want anything which would remind him of his father, adding that he knew his father had money and he wanted to know where it was. He was also concerned that valuable antique furniture in the house was under insured and ordered her to get better insurance cover for these items.

Day 4: Tuesday, 7 October

Colin Caffell recalled his ex-wife Sheila as, 'A naïve and frightened child, she had been through a difficult confusing time. The world frightened her. She had tried to cover this up and only those closest to her knew how lonely and vulnerable she was.'

Day 5: Wednesday, 8 October

Julie Mugford was the key prosecution witness and she claimed that Jeremy Bamber had been plotting the crime for some time. He had told her he had hired a hit man to carry out the killings and paid him £2,000. Matthew MacDonald was named as the individual who killed the family.

When Matthew MacDonald was called to give evidence a somewhat different story transpired. MacDonald gave his occupation as a plumber. Furthermore, he denied the accusation made against him by previous witness Julie Mugford, claiming that he had been with a woman friend on the night of the murder. The police had checked out his alibi and it was proved to be accurate. He admitted that he did know Jeremy Bamber having met him in a Colchester wine bar five years earlier, but the pair were hardly friends, more acquaintances. He told the court that he had previously worked in Libya in 1982, and in Penang, but never in the army. 'I've never been a mercenary. It was bandied about a bit apparently and became a rumour.'

A friend of Julie Mugford, Susan Battersby, explained to the court how she had been awakened by two telephone calls on the morning of 7 August, one at 3.12am, the other around 6.00am. These calls had come from Jeremy Bamber. She told how on 26 August 1985 she had gone for a meal with Julie Mugford, and as a result of a conversation they had she had said to Julie, 'Jeremy did it, didn't he?' Julie replied, 'No, Jeremy didn't do it,' but said that Jeremy had told her a mercenary had killed them and Jeremy had paid him £2,000 for doing so.

Day 6: Thursday, 9 October

Julie Mugford gave further evidence and claimed that Jeremy Bamber grew marijuana and killed rats by strangling them with his bare hands to test he had the will to kill. Asked how he managed this she said, 'I was aware at the time that the rats on the farm ate a lot of marijuana grown by him. Jeremy was laughing that the rats had slowed down because of eating the marijuana and I imagine that's how he caught them.' She said Jeremy Bamber frequently smoked the drug and she did occasionally. She denied getting all her information on the killings from newspaper reports, 'I'm only telling you what he told me. I don't like it, I hate it.' She left the courtroom after being stood down by the judge in tears and was clearly upset at the end of her evidence.

Another friend of Mugford, Elizabeth Rimmington, said she was part of a group who regularly went out with Bamber and Mugford for meals at a restaurant and had done so the night before the family's funeral. Rimmington claimed that Bamber, 'Was in a good mood, he was quite cheerful,' and was discussing what type of car he was going to buy with his inheritance money. He had also said it would be a good idea if he bought a restaurant or a wine bar. More damningly was her statement that quoted Bamber as saying, 'I believe I should have been an actor because I could convince anyone of anything.'

Day 9: Tuesday, 14 October

Malcolm Fletcher, a Home Office ballistics expert, claimed in court that all but one shot of the 25 fired to murder the Bamber family was fired at point-blank range. The only shot fired from more than three feet was the one which struck June in the forearm. According to one newspaper report of the time (*Glasgow Herald* 15 October 1986) 'He (Fletcher) has told the court he believed a silencer was fitted to the rifle when Sheila was killed because blood from her grouping was found inside the mechanism. He said the most likely reason for blood getting into the silencer was back-spattering from the contact wound to Ms Caffell's chin. Failing that the only other possibility is that it was put there deliberately.'

Day 10: Wednesday, 15 October

One of the first police officers to enter White House Farm told the court how he did not think of searching for any sound moderator. Detective Constable Peter Woodcock said he went into the White House Farm murder scene four times on the morning after the killings, but it did not occur to him that a sound moderator might have been used in the crime. Woodcock was, at the time of the killings, a senior instructor in the Essex Police tactical firearms unit having 10-years experience. Nearly three and a half hours after first going into the house, he re-entered the property and removed the rifle from Sheila Caffell's body to make it safe. He was wearing special gloves to protect existing fingerprints. In addition to the rifle that lay across Sheila Caffell's body, he made safe a shotgun which he found in a downstairs gun cupboard. It was in the same gun cupboard that the relatives later found the incriminating silencer.

Woodcock testified that after making the murder weapon safe he handed it to Detective Inspector Ron Cook. He claimed he could not recall whether Cook was wearing protective gloves but added: 'Knowing him as an experienced scenes of crime officer I would imagine he was.' Cook had already admitted he wasn't wearing any such protection! Woodcock told how he never saw a silencer resting against any boxes and added that as well as him, another six officers might have looked in the gun cupboard. 'There were in the region of 20 firearms officers at the farm on the morning after the shooting and perhaps another 20 officers altogether.'

Home Office Forensic Scientist Alexander Allen told the court that blood samples had been collected from each of the victims, and a slight trace of cannabis compound was found in Sheila Caffell's urine.

Detective Constable Michael Clark explained how on the morning after the crime Bamber appeared very calm and later enjoyed a breakfast of fried bacon, toast and coffee. 'He seemed more concerned with getting the harvest in than what had happened at the farm house.'

He told the court how Bamber drove him from White House Farm to his home in Head Street, Goldhanger in his Vauxhall Astra, and that during the journey they discussed the car's performance. Bamber had said that he was hoping to get a new Porsche as a little present from the caravan business, but feared that it might not now materialise because of the circumstances.

Day 11: Thursday, 16 October (Defence)

Jeremy Bamber was called to give evidence for first time. He told the jury that his jilted ex-girlfriend was lying outright. His sister 'Bambi' had told him she wanted to be in heaven and wished to take people with her. That he had never used the word 'hate' about his parents, or said he could easily kill his parents. He did enjoy the good things in life and stayed in St Tropez during the time police were interviewing him. He stated, 'I had a very loving relationship with my father and with my mother,' and said he found it difficult to understand his sister's illness, 'She used to come out with some bizarre things.' He also said how he and Mugford had talked of marriage. He said he had rung her on 6 August but had not said, 'Tonight is the night. There was nothing remotely which could be thought of that way.' he said. He denied telling Mugford that 'things are going well' and said that as he drove to the farm, not too fast because he wanted the Police to arrive first, that he was frightened.

At the farm, he recalled a senior officer telling him his family had been killed and he remembered calling him 'a hard bastard'. He mentioned his pet way of entering the house through windows and said he used that method to collect his car keys, even after his arrest. He denied using it to get back into the house on the night of the killings. He described the only time he saw Sheila use physical violence against her children stating, 'As we were driving along, one of the twins interrupted Sheila. She turned round and she punched him with a full fist in the face twice.'

Day 12: Friday, 17 October

Bamber returned to the dock to be cross-examined on his evidence. At one point his voice dropped and he seemed to be choking back tears as he told Anthony Arlidge QC in relation to leaving the rifle unsecured, 'With Daniel and Nicholas in the house, more care should have been taken. I wish I hadn't done it. I was in a hurry. I didn't know what was going to happen, did I?' He then muttered inaudibly and was asked by the Judge to speak up. Bamber then agreed with Arlidge, 'I was being lackadaisical. I was saying that to myself.'

Arlidge responded, 'You are not telling the truth, that you didn't do it, are you?'

Bamber's voice rose an octave when he replied, 'That's what you have to try and establish.' There was an audible gasp in court on hearing this comment, and several seconds silence ensued as nobody could quite believe what Bamber had said. Arlidge adjusted his gown and composure and continued to question Bamber, this time about the rifle which, he had claimed, had been used to shoot rabbits and foxes. Bamber was asked what noise it made with and without the sound moderator, and how the telescopic sight that was generally affixed to the rifle, but wasn't when it was found by the police, affected accuracy. Bamber replied, 'I can't say it did. I never really had a lot of luck with that gun.'

Bamber went on to accuse his former girlfriend of making up stories that he was responsible for the killings and claimed that other witnesses who had given evidence against him were 'mistaken' and influenced by media publicity.

Day 13: Monday, 20 October

On Monday 20 October 1986, the jury was taken to Fingringhoe army gun range, near Colchester, to hear rifle shots from the murder weapon. In a 10 minute demonstration, Malcolm Fletcher fired the rifle five times, minus its sound moderator, into a block of soap to absorb the impact. He then fired four times with the sound moderator in place. There was very little difference in the noise. The Judge, Mr Justice Drake, was also in attendance and asked Fletcher if the weapon would sound louder in a room. 'In a normal room it is bound to be a bit louder. You are bound to get sound reflected about the room.' Fletcher said.

As the rifle was being carried to the range, the wooden butt, allegedly broken during the battering about the head of Nevill Bamber before he was fatally shot, fell off! It was fired without its broken end.

The jury had earlier been told that Sheila was in an acutely disturbed state and claimed to have seen the devil just months before the massacre. Consultant Psychiatrist Dr Hugh Ferguson said Sheila was 'almost incoherent' when she was admitted to hospital at her father's request in March 1985. In August 1983, when she had first been admitted to hospital, she said she had to have some kind of exorcism and that if there was no hope of that she would want to die.

Sheila Caffell's life was discussed in more detail. She was born in 1957 and was, at the time of her death, 28-years old. Having received a private education she later went on to attend a secretarial college in London and then worked as a model. During her time in London she had met Colin Caffell and they married in May 1977. Just over two-years later, on 22 June 1979, their twin sons Daniel and Nicholas Caffell were born. The children were six when they were killed.

Shortly after her marriage, Sheila began to develop mental health problems, ultimately the couple divorced in May 1982. After the break-down of the marriage, she fell into a state of depression and began to suffer prolonged periods of acute paranoid schizophrenia. Having been admitted to St Andrew's Hospital, Northampton in 1983 she was, it was claimed by some, a danger to herself and others.

Schizophrenia is regarded as a brain disorder that affects the way an individual acts, thinks, and sees the world. People who suffer from schizophrenia tend to have an altered perception of reality, they might see or hear things that don't actually exist, or speak in a strange or confusing way, many believe that other people, family members included, are trying to harm them. The schizophrenic will act out in confusion and fear. It is known from research that people suffering from schizophrenia very often develop alcohol and drug abuse issues, some may be heavy smokers. Smoking further complicates any medical aid provided as the cigarette smoke can affect the effectiveness of prescribed medication. There is also evidence that shows a high level of attempting suicide, especially when the sufferer is enduring a psychotic episode.

According to Walsh and Fahy, *Violence and Schizophrenia, British Journal of Psychiatry,* June 2002, people with schizophrenia are not generally violent, however some symptoms are associated with violence such as delusions of persecution. Meanwhile, Swanson, Swartz, Van Dorn, Elbogen, Wager, Rosenheck, Stroup, McEvoy and Lieberman, *Archives of General Psychiatry,* May 2006, claim that substance abuse may increase the chance that a person will become violent. If a person suffering does become violent then it is usually directed towards family members and tends to take place at home. The symptoms of schizophrenia are many and it affects every individual differently. In Sheila's case we know she was a heavy smoker and a drug abuser, thus the chance of further mental health complications was duly increased.

In March 1985, Sheila was re-admitted to St Andrew's Hospital and was discharged shortly under four weeks later. In the months leading up to their deaths the twins, Daniel and Nicholas, had been living with their father Colin, but regularly saw their mother during this time. On 4 August 1985, three days before the killings, Colin Caffell had taken his ex-wife and their two children to White House Farm so they could enjoy a break and spend a few days with their grandparents in the countryside.

Sheila was first referred for treatment by her doctor, Dr Angeloglou. She referred her to Dr Hugh Ferguson who initially saw her at his private consulting rooms in London on 2 August 1983. Ferguson had also provided treatment to June Bamber in 1982, in fact June had a previous history of mental health issues dating back to the late 1950s.

Ferguson stated that Sheila had suicidal thoughts, and for about two years prior to that first examination she had become more liable to misinterpreting the world around her, to draw the wrong conclusions, to feel threatened in some way, particularly with the concept of good and evil. She had been struggling for two years with these concepts, especially that of her being evil and at risk of being affected by evil in some way. Over a short period of time she had become completely overwhelmed in the themes of good and evil, more specifically her ability to project evil onto others. She believed the devil had taken her over, giving her the power to project the devil's evil onto other people, and particularly her twin sons. She began to perceive in the twins other malign adult intelligence, as if they had their own source of effect on her. Particularly, and very disturbingly, she was at risk of having to have sex with them or to join with them in some violence to something or someone else.

Sheila felt that her son Nicholas was capable in adult life

of becoming a woman hater or even a murderer. She felt that people could read her thoughts and be shocked by them. At one point she felt she was capable of murdering her twin sons, or communicating some ability for them to become evil or murderers at a later date. Sheila held an extremely strong belief that she had evil in her mind and that her mother June also had evil in her mind, and that both would need this evil cleansed. Ferguson believed this emanated from her being caught in a sexually provoking position by her mother with a farm hand when she was 17. As a result of this, June had often called her 'Devil's Child.'

By 1985 her thinking was more directly associated with excessive religious ideas of being in touch with God and wanting to be by his and Jesus' side. She also wanted to join the Campaign for Nuclear Disarmament (CND) movement and believed that the Central Intelligence Agency (CIA) were following her. She said that a friend of hers, Freddie, was the devil himself, and that she had direct connections with God and was being monitored and watched by everyone around her. Sheila said that the devil was attempting to take away her Godliness and that many people were involved in this conspiracy including the nursing staff. Sheila's close friend was restaurant manager Freddie Emami. He told the court he feared she would 'do something nasty.' He said she had a quick and violent temper and he had seen her suddenly become hysterical when he called at her flat in March 1985. On another occasion he was present in her apartment when she took a telephone call and described the scene:

> During the call the phone went dead. Sheila suddenly became hysterical, mumbling about the phone being bugged. She became like someone possessed, ranting and raving. She was striking herself and beating the wall with her fists. I tried to calm her but she did not seem to hear me. I became extremely frightened not only for her, but for myself. She kept talking about the devil and God, and stated that God was sitting opposite her and unlike what her step mother said he in fact loved her. I contacted her ex mother-in-law and asked her to come round. This aggravated the situation and Sheila became even more violent and abusive. Her mother-in-law called and found a prescription for Sheila's drugs and asked

me to get them for her. I went to the chemist and when I returned I was met at the front door by the mother-in-law who was leaving. She told me Sheila had kicked her out. I went in and tried to pacify Sheila but was unable to do so.

I became extremely concerned for my own safety. I telephoned Sheila's doctor and a short time later one of her partners arrived. Sheila refused to let him examine her shouting that he was trying to poison her. By this time she had become completely irrational. The doctor eventually left without being able to do anything. Being unable to do anything I contacted another doctor who arrived shortly afterwards. Again he was unable to do anything because Sheila would not allow him near her.

He wrote a short note which he handed to me and asked me to hand it to Sheila's GP and gave her a stronger drug ... I was extremely scared for everyone's safety. At that time I felt that Sheila may use violence towards someone.

Emami also stated that after she was released from hospital he discussed this episode with her, but she could remember none of it and accused him of making it up. He also stated that during the psychotic episode he witnessed, Sheila could not recognise anyone who came to the flat and believed that 'everyone was trying to hurt or kill her.'

In the days prior to the murders, according to Bamber, she had been looking vacant and acting very quietly, withdrawn almost. Yet at lunchtime on 6 August she appeared happy and was playing with the twins, while much later that afternoon she was again recorded as being very quiet and more vacant. Ferguson claimed to the court that Sheila often looked quite distracted, vague, somewhat distanced and somewhat withdrawn. He said he could conceptualise Sheila, acting under some delusion or belief, harming her mother, but could not envisage that happening about her father or her children.

Ferguson was asked how he felt Sheila would respond to a suggestion that her children should be taken away from her care. 'I would have expected, were this to be put to her suddenly, to be a very substantial threat, and I would have expected her to react very strongly to what to her would be the loss of her children. I would not have expected her to be passive about that.'

When he had been advised on 8 August 1985 that Sheila Caffell had killed her parents and her children then herself, Dr Ferguson said that he felt this did not fit 'his concept' of Sheila as his patient. He personally did not feel she was someone who would be violent to her children or towards her father, although she was a highly disturbed woman and had expressed disturbed feelings towards her mother.

Also called to give evidence was Miss Helen Grimster who had seen Sheila Caffell on 30 March 1985. Grimster claimed that Sheila saw herself as a white witch and had told her that she had once contemplated suicide. Meanwhile, Sandra Elston saw Sheila Caffell on 31 July 1985 and said she appeared quite well and her only concern was about a poor haircut she had been given recently.

Day 14: Tuesday, 21 October

QC Anthony Arlidge gave his closing speech. He reminded the court how Bamber had said to the police that his father had telephoned him from his farmhouse home, asking him to come quickly because his sister Sheila Caffell had gone beserk with a gun saying, 'If the telephone call occurred, it meant Sheila was running amok with a gun. If he didn't get the call and he was lying, it meant it was Jeremy Bamber who did it and was trying to cover it up.'

He said the fact that Sheila's palms and feet were clean suggested it was unlikely she had gone around the house shooting people. 'Realistically, only two people could have carried out the killings, Mr Bamber or his sister. But Mr Bamber's explanation of why he had not made a 999 call to police after receiving his father's telephone call, and why he had left a rifle with ammunition in the house before the killings, was not credible.'

Day 15: Wednesday, 22 October

QC Geoffrey Rivlin in his closing speech claimed Bamber had no motive to slaughter his family. He was unaware of the value of his wealthy parents' estate, and allegations that he hated them did 'not get off the ground'.

'The case of financial motive is pathetically weak,' Rivlin claimed. Some witnesses had also testified that Jeremy Bamber had a good relationship with his adoptive father and had 'no problems' with his adoptive mother, his sister and her twin sons. Rivlin said, 'There was not one scrap of evidence to support the claim that Mr Bamber knew his family's estate amounted to £436,000.' He stated that a number of items which were listed as part of the estate on a schedule shown to the jury were unknown to him. 'Mr Bamber was living independently, which contradicted the evidence given by his former girlfriend that he wanted his family all dead so he could live his own life. He had his house, car, friends, freedom, he was doing well and he had good money. The evidence of the ex-girlfriend, Mugford, had been unreliable, untruthful and poisonous'

Rivlin said, 'Mr Bamber himself has been painted as an actor by the prosecution,' and added that when he had cross-examined Mugford, 'she had cried almost immediately, and let slip droplets of poison throughout her evidence. When being re-examined by the prosecution however, her tears had dried up as if by magic and she had been able to answer questions.'

Rivlin told the jury they must consider the question, 'Who are we dealing with in this case? A consummate actor or a consummate actress?' He said evidence had shown that Mr Bamber was a friendly, outgoing, non-violent young man who worked hard and was settling down well at his parent's farm. Whereas Miss Mugford had lied on oath, she had gone to the police originally with the story that Mr Bamber had hired Matthew MacDonald to carry out the killings because she wanted to do the maximum harm to the defendant without destroying him – a story that could easily be disproved. Rivlin claimed that what Mugford had told the court about Mr Bamber's alleged account of the massacre could have been taken from talking to relatives and from newspaper reports. Rivlin pointed out to the jury that witnesses had also testified that after the killings Mr Bamber was stunned, deeply shocked and unable to communicate. 'If he had taken drink or bought a new suit for the funeral and gone to Amsterdam and France, this was his way of trying to cope with the tragedy. If Mr Bamber had shown emotion in the witness box he would have been accused of shedding crocodile tears, if he did not, he ran the risk of being called calculating.'

Day 16: Thursday, 23 October

Geoffrey Rivlin delivered his final summing up. He stated that the evidence about the sound moderator was, 'An absolute hopeless mess ... What we say is that the whole circumstances surrounding the finding of this silencer are thoroughly, if not hopelessly, unsatisfactory. The prosecution claims that Mrs Caffell could not have killed herself as she could not have fired the murder weapon with the silencer on. The silencer was off the gun when the bodies of Mrs Caffell, her parents and twin sons were found, but was discovered by relatives three days later in a gun cupboard at the home. Blood on the silencer matched Mrs Caffell's group, said the prosecution.'

Rivlin said that the members of the jury had to ask themselves two questions: 'Where had the silencer been between the deaths and its discovery?' And, 'How, if it was in the gun cupboard, had so many police officers failed to find it on the morning after the shootings?'

He then referred to the evidence of firearms expert Malcolm Fletcher saying it lacked the objectivity expected from an expert witness. 'If Mr Bamber's evidence was right, and that the silencer was not on the gun when he left it on the night before the shootings, then it was Mrs Caffell who would have put the silencer onto it. Only someone with as little experience of guns as Mrs Caffell would be worried about the sound the gun would make. It would be Mrs Caffell who would have been much more likely to have put on the silencer than the defendant. If you think that's far-fetched, don't believe that anything can be far-fetched when one is dealing with someone like Mrs Caffell.'

Rivlin described how DI Cook had recalled how he had put his fingers all over the vital parts of the gun. 'How do we know if Mrs Caffell's fingerprints are not on those vital parts?' Rivlin also claimed that the entire silencer evidence produced by the prosecution did not disprove that Mrs Caffell may have killed everyone with the silencer on, and then taken it off to kill herself. He also told the jury that Jeremy's ex-girlfriend, Julie Mugford, had a convoluted mind and was jealous and had got her information about the shootings from the police, newspapers and others. 'There is not one single thing that Mr Bamber ever told her that she could only have got from him. In all that time they were together after the dreadful incident, you could expect that she would have heard one thing that only the murderer could have told her, but she didn't.

'Police arrested Bamber after Mugford went to them claiming he had told her he had hired a mercenary, Matthew MacDonald, to carry out the killings for £2,000. The prosecution said Miss Mugford would have needed a convoluted mind to have made all this up. We say that she has. That Matthew (MacDonald) story is not only wrong in itself, but contains in it a number of details which can be proved to be untrue and which she can only have got from the police or Ann Eaton.'

Day 17: Friday, 24 October

Mr Justice Drake addressed the jury in his final summing up of the case, asking them the following questions:

> Do you believe Julie Mugford – Mr Bamber's former girlfriend who told police he had hired a mercenary to kill his family – or do you believe Jeremy Bamber? Are you sure Sheila Caffell did not kill her family and then commit suicide? Was there ever any telephone call in the middle of the night to the defendant?
>
> The answers to each of these can independently of each other lead you to the decision to find the defendant guilty or not guilty. The evidence of Mr Bamber and Miss Mugford has flatly contradicted each other. The evidence of Miss Mugford has to be treated with a great degree of caution because of her possible motives for what she has said. There is a possibility that the person feeling jilted may, in order to hurt the other, tell lies.

The Judge proceeded to warn the jury that the initial police belief in Mr Bamber's story, that Sheila had carried out the killings before committing suicide, was wholly irrelevant. He referred to evidence given by the prosecution witnesses that Mr Bamber had said to his uncle, 'I could easily kill my parents,' and to a friend of Julie Mugford's, 'I hate my parents.' If they accepted these remarks they showed that, 'on occasions he revealed something of an evil intent.'

Day 18: Monday, 27 October

With the summing up complete, the jury retired for five hours and 10 minutes, and being unable to reach a verdict, they had to spend the night in a hotel. Before they retired, the judge told them: 'If the crime had been committed by Sheila Caffell, who had no experience of firearms, it would have meant she would have had to reload three times.' He also reminded them there had been a violent struggle between the killer and Mr Nevill Bamber. 'He was a six foot, four inches tall farmer. She was small and fairly slight.'

He further told the jury, 'There were no bloodstains on the soles of Sheila Caffell's feet when her body was discovered. Neither were there lead marks from the firearm. If, as the defence suggested she had been the killer, it would have meant she must have washed herself before committing suicide – using two bullets.' He also pointed out that it was suggested a silencer had been removed from the gun by Sheila Caffell. 'If this was the case she just didn't throw it to one side before committing suicide. According to evidence she had gone from her bedroom, through the house, placed the silencer in a box, and then put it in a cupboard. Having done that she made the long journey back to her bedroom where, it was suggested, she committed suicide. All this – the violent struggle with the father, the murder, washing herself, hiding the silencer, and then the suicide – had to be completed within 20 minutes. This was the period between Mr Bamber's telephone call to the police and the time the first officer arrived.'

Day 19: Tuesday, 28 October

The jury returned to court and delivered a majority verdict of 10-2, finding Jeremy Bamber guilty of the murder of his family. The court gasped and there was clearly some satisfaction with the verdict. The judge, in his statement to Bamber said:

> In March 1985, you stole nearly £1,000 from the caravan site owned by your parents and family. Then you told your girlfriend Julie Mugford: 'I shall be the prime suspect, but they will never be

able to prove it against me.' When you planned the killing of five members of your family, you went one better. You used the mental illness of your sister and planned matters so she became the prime suspect. I don't doubt that you thought that your sister's illness would be such that it would be difficult for people to be aware of your guilt should you become a suspect. For one so young, you have a warped, callous and evil mind, concealed behind an outwardly presentable appearance.

Having passed five terms of life imprisonment, with recommendation that Bamber serve a minimum of 25 years, Bamber, seemingly unmoved, was led to the cells by two prison officers.

11

A Sound Conviction?

'There is nothing like first hand evidence.'
Sherlock Holmes – A Study In Scarlet

The verdict given, Bamber was incarcerated and the case concluded, and this should have been the end of the matter but it wasn't. It was the beginning of a horrible never-ending nightmare for the living relatives and family left behind as Bamber began a process of appealing against everything he saw as an injustice. Countless formal complaints were made against Essex Police Force as he began to abuse the appeal system for his own devices.

The firearms officers who were first to view the body gave evidence that stated Sheila's hands and feet were perfectly clean. All her fingertips were clean and free from any blood, dirt or powder. Detective Constable Hammersley, the scenes of crime officer, placed plastic bags on Sheila's hands and feet before her body was removed from the farmhouse. He saw some blood staining to the back of the right hand but to his eye, apart from that, the hands were clean. The deceased's feet were also free from blood staining.

If we then look at the handwritten notes of Dr Peter Vanezis who examined Sheila's body at the scene. He states:

> Bloodstained palm print on nightdress. Bloodstains appear to have transferred from right hand, also bloodstain R side of nightdress. Yellow metal ring on ring finger L hand, nicotine stains R hand, both hands not contaminated apart from bloodstains.

Now that is very clear in what it states, that there was a bloodstained palm print on Sheila's nightdress and the bloodstain had been transferred from her right hand – as it's a palm print it must have been from her bloodied palm. This is contrary to what the police officers state, and in particular Detective Constable Hammersley.

In his later typed report Vanezis states:

> There was blood staining of her nightdress where her right wrist had been lying. This blood appeared to have been transferred from her wrist ... The palms and the fingers were not contaminated with blood.

Constable Hammersley was later interviewed in April 1991 as part of the City of London Police investigation into allegations made by Jeremy Bamber, he was then a Sergeant. Hammersley was agitated during the interview and made some irrational comments to the most basic of questions put to him. On one occasion he said: 'I did not find it, I want to make a statement on tape today.' Despite this curious statement, no one appears to have asked what he was referring to and there exists nothing in the public domain that accounts for it. This has led to unsupported assumptions that it could have been the so-called sound moderator evidence, or perhaps something more sinister. Some claim this as evidence of a police set up and subsequent cover-up. His frame of mind at the time has never been taken into consideration as Hammersley was an officer under severe stress, suffering from serious domestic and marital issues as well as being subject of an internal police investigation. He clearly blamed the force for his sad circumstances.

In another report about the same interview it is recorded that Superintendent Noakes of Essex Police complaints department was spoken to immediately afterwards and alerted to Hammersley's emotional state. Noakes stated that he, Hammersley, was in Scenes of Crime in August 1985 and that he was a good SOCO, albeit a loner.

In 2013, Andrew Hunter MP released to the press a photograph of what is claimed to be the soles of Sheila Caffell's feet. The image appears to show a few minor red marks on the soles of her feet. There is nothing that denotes blood, it looks more like graining of the image, however, there is nothing definitive which confirms it is Sheila's feet in the photograph. In conjunction with the aforementioned comments about blood being found on Sheila

Caffell's hands by Dr Vanezis, and the subsequent altering of the statement, we can now see that when Mr Justice Drake told the jury that Sheila's hands and feet were spotlessly clean he was wrong, blood seemingly existed on her hands and possibly on her feet. Would this have made a difference to the verdict? Possibly yes it would. Does it mean Jeremy Bamber is innocent? No it doesn't.

Also found on Sheila's body was an open Bible, an item that has led to much deliberation. Researcher Caroline Rowland has investigated the evidence regarding the Bible since it seems key to identify why it was there. The Bible was face down and is believed to have been open at pages 656 and 657. These pages were heavily bloodstained, the largest of which covered the upper corner of page 657. In 2002 the Court of Appeal considered the significance of the Bible in respect to non disclosure aspects at trial and whether the police had tampered or moved the Bible before the scene was photographed. The court concluded that the largest area of blood seemed to have got onto the Bible when it came into contact with a pool of blood beside the body.

As already observed, the Bible must have been shut whilst the blood was wet. It does not seem very likely that it was still wet hours after the event when the Police might have handled it. If this is so, it was shut by someone and then reopened to lie beside the body after Sheila Caffell had been shot. However, the crime scene photographs show the Bible placed face down so that page 656 and not page 657 is positioned over the pool of blood next to Sheila's body. The blood stain existed on the wrong page, it could not have been transferred from the carpet onto that page. The Court of Appeal made a schoolboy error by not taking that into account.

Given that it is impossible for the Bible blood staining to have come from the carpet, it suggests that the carpet blood stain was dry when the Bible was placed there as there is no staining on the page that was in contact with the blood. The large stain itself is interesting because it resembles the shape of a palm print. There is heavier staining on the area that resembles the ball of the thumb which would be consistent with pressure from that area. There is also patterning consistent with palm lines. Clearly the

Bible still has some significance as a piece of evidence with many unanswered questions surrounding its presence at the crime scene, because if the stain didn't come from the carpet, where did it come from? Is it a palm print or just a shape containing a similar pattern? If the former, who does it belong to and whose blood preserves it? It is crucial to note that the dimensions of the Bible are 14cm x 20cm which would rule out Jeremy Bamber's hand, and if the print belonged to Sheila why did the pathologist's statement claim that Sheila's hands were clean (even though his written autopsy notes claimed her palms were bloodstained)? This also has implications for the swabs taken from Sheila's hands, initially rejected they were resubmitted under a different reference where analysis found no trace of blood or gun residue.

Since the trial, much has been made of the evidence relating to the sound moderator that the prosecution claim was attached to the Anschutz rifle (murder weapon) at the time of the murders.

If we look at this evidence – and make no mistake about it, the moderator was produced as one of the key instruments in proving Jeremy Bamber's guilt – then we can assess its provenance and see how relevant it is.

The first time in any context that the sound moderator was officially mentioned by the police came in a press release dated 11.30 hours 17 September 1985. The statement itself was authorised by Superintendent Mike Ainsley and is attributable to ACC Peter Simpson. The official document reads:

> In the course of enquiries into the deaths of the Bamber family at Tolleshunt D'Arcy, a detailed search of the surrounding area was of course made. Two torches were found in a hedge at some distance from the house. These are believed to have been abandoned by poachers and not to be connected in any way with the incident.
>
> At an early stage of the investigation a silencer was taken away from White House Farm for forensic examination. The Police do not consider it unusual to have found a silencer in this house but until results of the scientific tests are to hand, it will not be possible to confirm whether or not it was used in connection with the deaths. Information in this report will not be made public until such times as it is appropriate to do so in the context of the enquiries.

The reference to two torches being found is curious, since not only do the police concede they found such items hidden close to a murder scene, they then dismissively disregard these items as having no connection with the murders.

The sound moderator and silencer are one and the same item. According to statements recorded by the police, we know for certain that David Boutflour, on Saturday 10 August 1985, found the sound moderator inside the gun cupboard in a box. Also found in the cupboard was a telescopic sight for the murder weapon. There were other people present at the find, these were Robert Boutflour, Ann Eaton, the Estate Executer Basil Cock, and Barbara Wilson. According to excerpts taken from Robert Boutflour's typed diary, David Boutflour was rummaging about near the floor of the cupboard and emerged with a box containing the silencer. Robert Boutflour told his son David to, 'Put it in the bag of ammo (that David had removed from the top of the box) and take it for safekeeping to Ann's house for the police to collect from there.' David later produced the telescopic sight and that was put with the silencer. All of these items were then removed from White House Farm in a plastic bag and the all important sound moderator was given a police exhibit number (ref DRB1). According to David Boutflour's statement, he took the moderator and a number of guns to Oak Farm, Loany Hill Road, Tolleshunt Major and in his own words handed the sound moderator, gun and ammunition to, 'Ann and Peter Eaton living at that address, the items I handed to Mr and Mrs Eaton included the telescopic sight.'

The same evening 10 August 1985, family members examined the sound moderator and they noticed that the surface of moderator had been damaged and there appeared to be red paint and blood on it.

Robert Boutflour's recollection of this is, 'David's curiosity got the better of him and he tried to take the end off to examine inside, but immediately he spotted a drop of what looked like blood the size of a match head near the exit hole.' The Witham police were informed of the silencer that evening.

On the evening of Monday 12 August 1985, the sound moderator was collected by DS Stan Jones from Peter Eaton at Oak Farm. He too examined the item and noticed a grey hair about an inch long attached to it. Jones then consumed the best part of a bottle of whisky before putting the moderator in the boot of his car and driving off. This fact is confirmed by Peter Eaton in a later statement made to a police inquiry.

On 8 September 1985, Ann Eaton, Jeremy's Bamber's cousin, made a statement to the police. In this she refers to the sound moderator.

> I cannot be precise of when it was and if it was by the police or Jeremy but during the taking of the statement questions were raised about the silencer and telescopic sights of the gun. Jeremy made replies to the effect that the silencer and telescopic sights had to be removed from the gun before it could be stored in the cupboard.

The date to which she refers that this discussion took place was 7 August 1985. A look at every related police statement prior to the Ainsley press release of 17 September 1985, dictates that they were apparently unaware of any silencer or of its relevance in the crime!

In the same statement a few paragraphs later, Ann Eaton explains that on Friday 9 August 1985, David Boutflour, Anthony Pargeter (a nephew of Nevill Bamber) and herself visited DS Jones at Witham Police Station. She had started to make notes but had been asked to refrain from doing so by Jones. It was then that DCI Jones told her that the rifle (murder weapon) did not have telescopic sights fitted:

> A conversation took place of our concerns about discrepancies. One was relative to the silencer and telescopic sight not being on the gun ... (*Something they had only just discovered a few moments earlier!*) ... This was because Jeremy had told the Police on the morning of the 7 August 1985 that the gun would not fit into the gun cupboard if the silencer and telescopic sight was attached. This was untrue and Anthony Pargeter confirmed that it would go into the cupboard with the attachments on.

Ann Eaton at this point became certain that it was Jeremy who initially raised the issue of the silencer and telescopic sight with the Police! She continues:

Anthony Pargeter, my brother David and I asked questions about the silencer and the noise that the gun would have made being fired without it on. Anthony Pargeter and David had a fairly long conversation with the two police officers.

It is clear from each of the relevant statements that it was the relatives who drew attention to the silencer evidence. One can understand Taff Jones' reluctance to readily accept their involvement in the investigation as there does seem to be a keenness to cast doubt on Jeremy Bamber without knowing all the facts. I say this because at this point, 48 hours into the investigation, the police were not in possession of all the facts and enquiries were still being made, so no one else, not even the relatives, could be certain.

Much later in her statement Ann Eaton tells a slightly different story from that told by her father, Robert Boutflour, about the finding of the silencer and how it was handled:

My father, my brother David and I started to look around the house. David collected all the guns from around the house so that we could take possession of them for safe keeping. This was on the authority of Mr Cock.

David then went into the downstairs office and I stood in the doorway and saw David open the gun cupboard. He got onto his knees and he then checked the cupboard. David then took out a silencer and a telescopic sight and a carrier bag of ammunition. David said to me that the silencer and telescopic sight belonged to the rifle which had killed the Bambers and the Caffell twins. The items were put into the kitchen with other guns and ammunition ready to be conveyed to my house for safe keeping.

Shortly before we left, my father had a conversation with me about the windows of the house. He was indicating that somebody could have entered or exited from the house through a window without having to use the door and nobody would be aware of it.

My father also told me that the kitchen door forced by the police was in the garage near the back door.

Shortly after this my father, brother and I loaded my car with the guns and ammunition. I then drove my father to Vaulty Manor Farm, Maldon Road, Goldhanger. I returned to my house and the guns and ammunition, including the silencer and telescopic sight, were unloaded and taken into the house. In the kitchen the various items were put onto the table and my brother then exclaimed that there was something on the silencer. I was going to pick it up but my brother told me not to. My brother then carefully picked it up and I could see what appeared to me to be coagulated blood around the exit hole of the silencer. There was also a fleck of red paint on the end of the silencer.

The colour of this paint immediately reminded me of the red paintwork around the surround of the kitchen at White House Farm.

My brother David decided to put the blood and paint-stained silencer in a secure cupboard at my house. The telescopic sights and the carrier bag of .22 ammunition was also secured similarly.

We discussed the implications of how this silencer could be in the gun cupboard with blood and paint on it. Obviously if it was being alleged that somebody had had a brainstorm and shot dead four people, they would surely not have stopped to remove the silencer, put it back in the gun cupboard, go back upstairs and shoot herself dead.

Robert Boutflour claimed that he was present when David Boutflour tried to dismantle the sound moderator, yet we have Ann Eaton stating that he wasn't! Nor does she mention that her brother, David, tried to dismantle the object to look inside the baffle. When those present looked more closely at the silencer there is no mention of a grey coloured hair being present. Yet both DS Jones and Peter Eaton clearly see it on the evening of 12 August 1985. Stan himself told me it was visible to the naked eye. The fleck of red paint must have been so visibly prominent that it immediately reminded them of the colour of the surround of the kitchen mantle. How did it remain secured to the end of the sound moderator – through coagulated blood perhaps? Within a few sentences the fleck of red paint changes into 'the blood and paint-stained silencer'.

The entire evidence surrounding the locating and handling of the sound moderator thereafter is questionable to say the least. None of the relatives or others present who may have picked it up, and we don't officially know who did handle it, were wearing protective clothing or gloves. There is a huge possibility of cross contamination through the accidental mishandling. Forensic science was nowhere near as capable in 1985 as it is now, so handling of evidence too was less stringent, however, the importance of mishandling a piece of evidence was still commonly known at the time.

I have serious doubts whether the sound moderator would stand up to scrutiny as evidence today. It has to be said that even by 1980s standards, as far as criminal evidence was concerned, the sound moderator was handled in a remarkably lackadaisical manner. Each piece of evidence that was seized by the police should have been labelled and logged in a property register/book and stored in a secure cupboard. Any movement or handling of the exhibit thereafter should have been recorded in that register. In this instance, the sound moderator was given a unique exhibit reference that related to the initials of the person finding it. For some reason the moderator was assigned SBJ/1 (Stanley Brian Jones), it was then ascertained that the moderator was found by David Boutflour, so the reference was altered to DB/1 and that identification should have remained with the exhibit throughout the case. In this instance, the exhibit reference relating to the sound moderator changed yet again as Essex Police already had exhibit references using the initials DB (David Bird). Ultimately the reference changed to DRB (David Robert Boutflour) and the entire scenario caused huge confusion. The police stated these changes, alterations, amendments – whatever terminology they wish to use – were created solely for administrational purposes. The same exhibit wasn't officially handed to the police by the finder of the evidence, but by his brother-in-law Peter Eaton. I did say it was poor!

If we look a level deeper and examine the secure holding records relating to Exhibit DRB/1, these show that no written record of the storage of the sound moderator between the dates 13 August 1985 and 30 August 1985 – when it was resubmitted to the Forensic Science Laboratory – exists other than a pocket book entry that claims it was retained at an unknown location in the Scenes of Crime Department at Essex Police Headquarters. It simply doesn't appear in the Police property register! Its integrity and provenance is yet again compromised.

This location failure has led to scurrilous and unfounded suggestions that DCI Jones was so dismissive of the moderator as a piece of evidence that he used it as a paperweight on his desk. This it is claimed resulted in his removal from the case! The sound moderator was then supposedly rescued by DS Jones and re-submitted as forensic evidence. Such speculation is pure nonsense. The chain of evidence relating to the sound moderator shows that it was submitted to the Forensic Science Laboratory on 30 August 1985 by Detective Constable Wolton who, when later interviewed about it, could not recall from whom or from where he collected it!

Piecing all this information together it shows how fragile this evidence really was. We have the sound moderator evidence first introduced by relatives – not the police – which isn't good. These are the relatives who first mooted the suggestion of a sound moderator being used, then physically produce such an item from a gun cupboard that had previously been searched by a number of police officers, none of whom spot the relevance of what was described by another witness as a 'blood and paint-stained silencer.'

Then we have the evidence relating to the grey hair that was allegedly attached to the item. DS Jones states it was clearly visible to the naked eye, yet it isn't mentioned at all in the original statements of those who actually found the moderator. Then before anyone else can corroborate the presence of the hair it disappears altogether, lost en-route to the Forensic Science Laboratory. If we then throw into the mix Detective Sergeant Stan Jones' over indulgence in whisky when formally collecting the exhibit, it doesn't take the guile of Sherlock Holmes to realise that the moderator evidence is suspect.

To add further damage to the credibility of the sound moderator evidence, the prosecution firearms expert, Malcolm Fletcher, testified at trial, 'I have been unable to establish whether any of the bullets or bullet fragments have been fired through a sound moderator.' A forensic expert, John Hayward, stated that the blood found inside the sound moderator was group A1, he concluded it was Sheila Caffell's. Hayward also noted that the blood group A1 belonged to Robert Boutflour, the same Robert Boutflour who had been present when the sound moderator was found. More surprisingly Hayward said at trial that in all his experience, he had never seen back spatter before.

Fletcher meanwhile accepted that a .22 calibre weapon was the least likely weapon to produce back spatter and that a sound moderator made it less likely still.

It's unfortunate that Mr Justice Drake in his summing to the jury at the trial once again misguided them. 'The sound moderator is clearly of very great importance and the evidence relating to the sound moderator could, on its own, lead you to the conclusion that the defendant is guilty.' Firearms experts have subsequently stated that, 'There are no grounds to believe a silencer was involved, apart from that the silencer was found.'

Witnesses called to give evidence at trial were questioned about the locating of the sound moderator and its handling thereafter. Some seemingly found it difficult to convincingly recall basic details, such as which box the sound moderator was in, who moved it where within the Eaton family home. Even the identity of the person who initially notified the police was never properly established, with Ann Eaton telling the court, 'probably me.'

As with all instances in this case, none of this proves Jeremy Bamber is innocent, however, based on the sound moderator evidence alone, nor should it be viewed as concrete evidence of his guilt.

Then we have the mysterious figure reportedly seen at an upstairs bedroom window. There is nothing in the official logs that discusses this, however, the following is the official entries recorded in the lead up to the alleged sighting.

At 04.02 am, 'Duty Sergeant, one Police Constable and Mr Bamber junior, left vehicle and approaching house on foot, vehicle parked out of sight.'

At 04.09 am, 'No sign of life in house, all lights on in premises and 2 dogs going berserk. Son says dogs are normally quiet. Son, PC and Sergeant backing off from premises.'

This is the point where mass confusion reigns, as all three persons mentioned in the last log entry believed they saw movement in an upper bedroom window. Sergeant Bews has over the years, and understandably as time often dulls the memory, changed his recollection of such events, first claiming that PC Myall saw movement. Indeed in another police document Myall confirms this as an unidentified male. Then it was Bamber who he claimed saw movement, finally he confirmed it as nothing more than a trick of light. This is something Bamber continues to argue, he believes there was a person inside the house in the master bedroom stood by the door. The police refuse to be drawn any further on the matter and Bews himself dismisses it outright, maintaining it was a trick of light.

As if sufficient anomalies did not already exist, it was later confirmed in various police statements that not all the lights were on in the premises as was originally reported and claimed by Sergeant Bews. Constable Collins, who was one of the firearms officers who entered the farm house, arrived at the scene after Bews' communication about all the lights in the house being on. In his statement Collins states, 'We looked around the farm house and saw that on the kitchen side of the house the following lights were switched on - kitchen with no curtains at window, and two upstairs rooms directly above kitchen, one room had pink curtains drawn closed and one room with blue curtains drawn closed. There was only one other light switched on in the house which was situated directly over the main door.'

So why did Bews earlier claim all the lights were on? There is no doubt that everyone inside the house at the time of Bews' arrival was dead, so it's not remotely feasible to imagine someone wandering around switching lights on and off. The only answer is that in attempting to absorb all the information he mistakenly believed all the lights to be on. Clearly PC Collins confirmed that all the lights were not on, though PC Collins himself could be criticised because he was the firearms officer who briefly looked into the kitchen through a window moments before the firearms team entered the house and mistakenly believed the corpse of Nevill Bamber was that of a woman, and so called in one dead female in the kitchen. The officers recording this data in the control room, as discussed by Bob Miller, are clearly at fault for the manner in which the radio transmissions were documented.

Another log entry timed at 05.25 states, 'Firearms team are in conversation with a person inside the farm.' In 2004, after further claims of his innocence by Bamber using the wording of the logs, Chris Bews, who had been at the murder scene from the outset and remained there until around 8.00am, dismissed the phraseology of this log as an administrational error:

> At first I was not sure whether there was anybody still in the house. The firearms team did shout in, as they always do. You always try and establish a dialogue in a situation like that, even if you do not know if there is anybody there. They were shouting into the house but they definitely were not talking to anybody. There was no-one there. The person who would have made that log would have been 15 miles away at force headquarters in Chelmsford. My guess is whoever wrote that down substituted the word 'conversation' for 'talking' or something similar. There is absolutely no way they were ever talking to anybody in that house. I am 100 per cent certain of it. It sounds like Bamber is going a bit stir crazy. It is absolute rubbish and nonsense.

Perhaps one of the most baffling inconsistencies in the police recording of the incident is when the firearms unit first entered White House Farm. A door was smashed down and entry established through the kitchen area of the house. At 07.37 a Police incident log records a message from the scene, it states, 'One dead male and one dead female in the kitchen.'

One would imagine that of all people, police firearms officers would have to possess some sensitive skills when it comes to risk assessment of a scene, maintaining a calm, level head, clarity of vision, and in communication and listening. So when the afore-stated message was conveyed, one could be forgiven for believing it be wholly accurate. It wasn't!

At 08.10 the log records, *'three* bodies upstairs'.

I have looked and looked at this situation, one simply cannot find any cogent argument that could explain how the logs were so wrong. It can only be complete incompetence on behalf of the staff completing the log. It is an ascertained fact, that is also accepted by Bamber, that four bodies were found upstairs not three, so how this number can become three is quite unbelievable and alarming. What is also baffling is why, when the police reported a two-body find in the kitchen, it seemingly took them a further 33 minutes to locate the other bodies, and then only three of them! No matter how much police radio traffic there may have been, important communications and facts such as this should never be so poorly recorded. It's impossible to believe that it took a further 33 minutes for the shout to be made that further bodies were found upstairs.

The body count inside White House Farm was five, the corpses were located as follows:

Nevill Bamber (male) – Kitchen
June Bamber (female) – Main bedroom
Sheila Caffell (female) – Main bedroom
Nicholas and Daniel Caffell – Bedroom

As can be seen, and there is no doubt about this, just one body was found in the kitchen of White House Farm, that of Nevill Bamber.

Supporters of Jeremy Bamber would be ecstatic if the police had genuinely found two bodies in the kitchen, and that one of those, Sheila, wasn't dead at all but only stunned by the failed first shot in attempting to kill herself. Accordingly the noise of the police entering had somehow awoken her, and she then ran upstairs to apparently shoot herself again! Forensic Scientist Professor John Glaister told me of a case concerning an elderly man shot in the head with a much more powerful weapon than a .22, this was a Colt .45 pistol. 'The bullet entered under the chin and passed through both the frontal and temporal lobes of the brain. Death, or at least unconsciousness, should have been instantaneous but the wounded man could still walk a short distance to his hotel where he not only spoke to a servant but also hung up his brolly, took off his overcoat, and walked down a flight of stairs to the bathroom where he finally collapsed and died.'

At the trial of Jeremy Bamber, Dr Vanezis was asked a similar question about the probability of whether Sheila could have wandered around after sustaining such an injury:

> 'Well, a wound like that, as I said, has not hit a vital organ as such although it has caused haemorrhage ... some people, in fact, do get up and walk around with such injuries, but quite clearly if one walks around with such injuries, then one would see quite a lot of blood distributed or coming from that wound, unless the person held the hand to the actual entry wound itself and tried to stop the blood coming out.'

Sheila showed no such signs.

If Sheila had been sighted on the floor in the kitchen, and was mistaken for dead by the police, why would she feel the need to rush upstairs then shoot herself again? Surely she could have achieved this downstairs and it would have made no difference to the outcome. Indeed, why would she shoot herself in the kitchen at all? If her body had been found in the same room as her children, then perhaps it could be more understandable and believable.

As critical as I am of the erroneous entries made in the police logs, I am also aware that we are all human and therefore prone to mistakes, especially when confronted by a crisis. The incompetence – and it cannot be described as anything else – does sadly bring into question the professional credibility of certain aspects of Essex Police.

Indeed, by 8.50am the same morning, the press were on site before the Senior Investigating Officer – it was entered onto the log 'member of press on board!' What a ridiculous and unprofessional message, what does 'on board' actually mean? Could it be that CA05 who called it in had a member of press in his police vehicle? I can only assume this is so. This was a serious incident, five lives had been lost, it was not the time to make misleading quotes over the police radio system. It begs the question why were the press 'on board' with police vehicle CA05? Little wonder that by the time DCI Jones arrived at shortly after 09.00am, the area was in a state of confusion.

The logs and communication documentation are certainly found wanting. One can only assume this was because the crime was the biggest, most gruesome and high profile incident these officers were likely to have dealt with, causing panic and misinterpretation of messages. Others would prefer to allege a cover-up. I have not gone into every intricate detail of the numerous errors in the prosecution paperwork, they are legion but largely inconsequential in proving or disproving Jeremy Bamber's guilt. However, since I have pointed out the obvious failures in Bamber's defence and claims, it is fair to be equally as critical of the police. I take no satisfaction in doing so, it pains me to see such incompetence.

It's important to focus on real matters that are of genuine concern, not the failure of the authorities to dot the i's and cross the t's. The incident and communication logs should, in my opinion, have been more thoroughly dissected and questioned by the defence team during the trial. I believe they failed Jeremy Bamber in this respect. It would never have shown him innocent but it would have perhaps lead to more prudent cross examination of prosecution witnesses.

12

He Did It – But He Wasn't Alone

'Nothing clears up a case so much as stating it to another person.'
Sherlock Holmes – Silver Blaze

In late 2013, I received an anonymous letter that was to change my way of thinking about the case against Jeremy Bamber. Because the letter was unsigned, its provenance is questionable. I am not proposing it as cast-iron fact but I am simply putting it in the public domain as an alternative. It was sent to me by someone who claimed to know Bamber during a term of imprisonment. In the letter, the author claims that Bamber had made what amounts to a confession of sorts to him.

Over the years I have received over 50 anonymous letters relating to this case, some good, some bad and some downright ridiculous. What makes the writer of this particular letter different is that he provides a reasoned overview without seeking anything from me. It's clear from what he says that he felt the knowledge he had acquired to be a burden. The level of detail contained within it shows that someone had a better than good knowledge of the case. It isn't so much the damning content that has caused me to rethink and review many of my own beliefs of what happened, but I confess to being somewhat surprised that no one else has arrived at such an obvious conclusion that the writer has.

When I read it and later returned to my interviews with police officers involved, something jumped out from what each of them had said to me. If the letter is fake, then someone has carefully constructed it around the known facts and the personal opinions of police officers who, prior to speaking with me, had not previously divulged so much detail to any writer.

Few people beyond friends and family know my personal

details, yet the author of the letter did! Normally reader's letters or communications of enquiry come to me via a publisher, not this one. However, one of the few people who did know my address is Jeremy Bamber – as the writer of the letter states!

I believe that acting together, Sheila Caffell and Jeremy Bamber killed their family. However, from my own research and experiences, and looking at all the evidence in the public domain, I believe that DCI Jones also held similar suspicions. It is my opinion that he hadn't concluded his investigation into Jeremy Bamber. His private comments to some of his colleagues and his questioning of Bamber about the number of rounds of ammunition that were found in the kitchen, displays a level of inquisitiveness that goes beyond witness testimony. The interference of the relatives affected his investigations and he was then told what action to take with his inquiries before being entirely removed from the case and placed on gardening leave.

It also explains why Sheila's actions were never correctly explained within the prosecution or defence case. It's remained one of the most popular questions of researchers: 'What was Sheila doing whilst Jeremy Bamber walked through the house killing people?' Furthermore, it explains how Jeremy Bamber entered the house before the murder. Sheila would have let him in through the kitchen door which was then locked with a key, the key remained in the lock and was there when entry was effected by the police. He exited the house, post-murder, via the faulty window. It would explain how one of Sheila's fingerprints was found on a shotgun, and how the rifle was reloaded during the executions. The order of the shootings becomes understandable, and why Sheila was complicit in her own death and made no struggle, and – important to the entire case – why no gun residue was found on her hands.

If the letter is correct then it shows that Essex Police did get it right. It may not have been co-ordinated correctly however, as DCI Jones was prevented from assessing a sterile crime scene because Sheila's arm had been moved by officials ensuring that she was dead. The police never saw her final death pose. Bamber moved her and staged her body long before the police found her. The murder weapon had been moved by him and by the police on finding the body, and placed back on her torso.

It's explosive and mind-blowing stuff not only because it provides some closure to many of the anomalies that exist, but also because it casts doubt on the entire sound moderator evidence. I don't doubt David Boutflour's, or Ann Eaton's, or her husband's testimony, or integrity. They claim they found the sound moderator in the manner documented and genuinely believed it to be key evidence. However, how it got there in its blood and paint-stained state has been the subject of debate for many years. I've never been convinced by the sound moderator evidence.

The contents of the letter do pose many serious questions. As I said earlier in this book, I have made every effort to communicate this letter to Essex Police. A copy was posted to them, but several months later I have yet to receive any kind of response. If the letter is a hoax then it is indeed a cruel one. The following is part of that letter reproduced here for the first time:

Dear Mr Harrison,

I know you are writing a book about Jeremy Bamber. I am writing as someone who has served time with him, I did some time with him at Full Sutton. He isn't well liked inside and he has something of a lonely existence partly through choice. He doesn't trust anyone and everything he does has an agenda. Most inmates don't believe a word he spouts, he is full of bullshit and always harping on how hard done by he has been by everyone. Everyone he has any sort of contact with at some point he'll say they are part of a conspiracy to keep him banged up. Believe me, he repeats this rubbish all the time. I would say that most prisoners inside get a feeling for who's guilty and who's innocent, you won't find many that believe he is innocent.

I became involved with him in a physical and emotional way. I am one of the few people who have got inside his head and he confided in. He didn't see me as a threat to what he's after to be free and rich. His attitude gets the better of him and he reckoned he was better and cleverer than I could ever be. He got that wrong, he underestimated me and I was a lot cleverer than he could ever have thought. Since I got out it has taken me such a time to put this together. I don't want to offend you or make you think I am a crackpot. I want to make sure everything he said to me is here for you to see and read. I think there is a lot that people don't know about him.

You might be thinking how I got your address? Jeremy gave it to me. He is so full of who his supporters on the outside are, he thinks it gives him some power to boast about the people who he has influence over. He showed me letters with your detail on, that's how and where I got it. I hear that some killers and cons see an association with you as a cop turned crime writer as something to brag about, you probably get letters off prison inmates all the time. I hope you don't dismiss this as one of those types.

Jeremy had a plan to use your address and give it to other prisoners as a bartering tool for them to write to you, he could get better privileges from them for that. Nobody was really interested and they didn't believe an ex-cop would be on his side. In prison he is known as a liar.

I don't want anything from you for me giving this information to you, I want to let you know about the real him, not the guy he portrays to the outside. He has what he calls his 'lackies' (this is what he calls his team that campaign for him). He would say these people act on his every command. He says jump, they say, how high? Then he has what he calls 'Jeremy's Desperate and Lonely Housewives Club', almost all are women (there are some men) between 30 – 60 years old. Some send him photographs of themselves, it's really strange how women are drawn to murderers don't you think? I would say that most declare their love for him, they belief [sic] in him, and are loyal, they all promise to expose the truth and fly the 'Jeremy is innocent' flag. It's like he's a celebrity or something. I doubt if these people would be so supportive if they knew what he called them, or knew that they meant nothing to him. He would tell me that they all wanted to 'tame the beast, but the beast cannot be tamed!'

Don't think you have escaped his manipulation either. He thinks that he has you in his pocket. He is using you, you are what he calls his latest pet project. He revels in the fact that you are a retired copper and you believe him innocent. 'Mad fool risking his reputation on me.' I don't think he is innocent Mr Harrison. I know you probably know this already but be very careful in your dealings with him and them that support him. I'm not certain that anyone in civvy street understand what they are dealing with, he isn't the victim he plays. He isn't a good person and his word in prison isn't trustworthy, that's why he is in prison, he is a chameleon. He puts on a show whenever he feels like it. Knowing him like I do, his whole life is a big act, he loves to be centre of attention in everything.

Behind his mask he is bitter and driven by genuine hate. He will stop at nothing to get his own way and he doesn't mind who he upsets to get that. What you are dealing with is a sly trickster, a man who will do anything and say anything to get what he wants. He makes up accusations about other prisoners to get them in trouble. What you need to remember is he has spent 28 years of his life banged up in a prison cell, there is no real social life like we have in the free world. I've been there, it gives a man time to think, in his case it gives him time to plot and scheme about his predicament.

This isn't a normal human being, you are discussing a lifer, he is dangerous, he has no respect for others and has no emotions for anybody outside his own circle. He doesn't cry or show any emotion unless he's in danger, then he blubbers like a brat.

Inside a few of us knew the truth, he has confided in parts to a couple of inmates, me more than others I think. Since the time when he scrawled in his own shit 'Bamber is innocent' and it got out into the papers what they had done, and it wasn't very good, he tries to do things out of eyesight of the screws, so that no bad reports come out that affect people's thoughts on him. He believes there are thousands of people who back him and think he didn't kill his family, how misguided and dangerous.

As a person I thought he was unresponsive and cold, it's like everything is one big game, he told me he wished he wasn't the most infamous prisoner in the whole of the prison system. And he complained to the screws that the system puts unnecessary pressure on him and he cannot relax, he said it was unfair and he wanted to make a complaint about it. The screws didn't know how to deal with it, anything for a quiet life.

Every so often he deliberately plays up, and that's when he can be a bit of a loose cannon. If he's got something on someone else, or he needs to get an advantage over somebody, especially one of the screws, he'll blab. If anyone tries to have a go back, he threatens to mouth off and tell what he knows to the Governor, it's controlling mind games. He knows the system and that's why people inside are wary of him, he's regarded as dodgy and very much a liar. All the time his mind seems to be scheming about one thing, getting his own way.

I didn't try to position myself as someone he could trust or tell things to, he came to me and told me he had been watching me and he felt sorry for me coming from of a lower social class and he felt the need to act as my mentor. I almost laughed out loud when he said it, I didn't want any grief from anyone, inside or outside, I wanted to hide myself and not bother with anyone else. At first I felt repulsed by him because I knew he was a double child killer. I didn't want to make friends with him, then I thought I needed to do what I had to just to survive! It's never been an issue for me people talking down to me, I don't care and to be honest at times he was easier to listen to than some of the other prisoners because he told a good story. His waffle kept my mind going and instead of having a conversation with him, I listened and stored what he was saying away in my head. He did get more intimate towards me and through the odd hug and one sided conversations I gave him the support I think he needed.

One of the things I disliked about him was the stupid grin he had on his face, it became more obvious when he was lying, it's like he thought himself clever and smarter for being able to fool people. I remember once talking to the screw psychologists about him, they wanted to know what he was like as they said he spent more time talking to me than anyone. I said that I thought Jeremy wore a mask that he hid behind. Not many get to see what's behind the mask, I did but it's not something I'm proud of or want to boast about, but I really got inside his head and into his mind. Some of the screws treated him like someone special, and he would sign autographs for them for their friends or relatives. It's sick, why would anyone want anything like that from someone who had killed two children? I believe that some of the screws are scared of him, not by his physical presence but because he has a dangerous mouth and is capable of any accusation against anyone!

Every so often, and this was rare because his life is one big lie, all the pretence would wear him down and he would hit a low, it was then that he'd often ask me for a hug, a cuddle, and that's when I knew when he was likely to talk. I know he tested me with information, at first he would tell me things that were all rubbish, he wanted to see if I would leak anything to the screws or other prisoners. I never did. Then things got more serious and he started to talk about the family and the murders. It was weird because he would call them 'the' family, like they were not 'his' family, it was in the third person I think. I never questioned or probed about anything, I would let him ramble on, sometimes it made sense, other times it seemed like ridiculous drivel. It was powered by guilt I would guess. I think I would make a good undercover copper because I have a photographic memory and do remember trivial things, especially in conversations. When you are inside and banged up you get to hear stuff about what other cons got up to or where the loot is stashed, but mainly they all say they had dealings with dodgy cops, some of it is clearly bullshit, other things have a ring of truth about them. Just about every con thinks they have been fitted up by a dodgy cop!

So when Bamber first talked about the murders, I thought he was talking his usual rubbish but it came from nowhere really, he just blurted it out, most was in the third person. He would tell me what happened as though he was an impartial observer and it wasn't him or his actions or his family he was talking about. He would stare at the ground like he was watching the re-enactment on a screen and repeating what he saw to me. I never showed any emotion, every so often he would stop, look up and take a good look at me, he was checking if I was taking it in or making any notes, I think he was looking for the shock value of what he was saying too. If I showed it made me sick I don't think he would have said anything more. I just stayed calm and didn't respond.

At first I didn't believe him, then over a period of weeks he would repeat things and added more information. He would ask my thoughts on situations, like did I think it wrong to steal from family if it didn't hurt anyone, especially it was money that no one really needed? Another thing he asked was if I thought drugs made good people bad? I would never comment or pass my opinion on anything, I didn't commit to agreeing or disagreeing with him on anything as I was trying to show that I wasn't that fussed about what he was saying. He was so selfish and self obsessed that not once did he ever ask anything about me or my life, he wasn't even bothered about what I had done to be inside, he wasn't interested in anyone else, it was always Jeremy Bamber, Jeremy Bamber, Jeremy Bamber.

I once heard him mention you when he was writing a letter. He was planning what to write down He would sometimes speak out loud what he wanted to write, it was as if he said the words to double-check that he wasn't giving anything away that he didn't want you to know. I remember him saying, 'Another gullible glory hunter, I could make him very rich and very famous if I wanted to, but I won't because he was a cop and I don't like them, he'll have lots of money I think, so he doesn't need any of mine, he doesn't serve my purpose. That's the power I hold. They all want a piece of the Jeremy Bamber empire.'

I was shocked because I had heard him say before this that you were highly thought of as both a copper and a crime writer. I casually asked him what he meant. He told me that he had got someone on the outside to check you out in case you were working undercover for the law or someone else using your professional name. He said he was easily able to do this, pull strings outside of the prison walls. I asked him why he thought you were a glory hunter when you were well known. He was certain that you would be desperate and so pleased to hear from him because he was regarded as killer number one, notorious, and top of the killing tree. He said that you were likely to believe anything he said for your 15 minutes of fame, and you were nothing but another lemming hanging onto his shirt tails to find glory.

It was during one time when he was writing to you that he seemed to forget himself. He was talking out loud, he was reliving something bad because he was agitated and excited. He turned to me and said he wanted me to consider some things that he had never told a living soul. For the first time I saw a look on his face that was really serious and he started to tell me things.

Before the murders happened, there had been a lot of fall outs between Sheila and her Mum, June. Lots of angry words between them because June said Sheila was an unfit mother, a drug addict and in need of constant mental care. June had said that if something didn't change then Colin, Sheila's ex-husband, would get custody of the twins or they would have to be put up for fostering. Sheila had got to the stage where she could no longer stand her mother and she told Jeremy she wished that both her and her father (Nevill) weren't part of her life because they interfered with everything and it was affecting her and the children.

Jeremy said he had been out shooting, he didn't say where, and that Sheila had gone with him. He told her shooting was good for getting rid of tension and let her fire off some shots. He said Sheila was a nut job and was always high as a kite, but he had the measure of her and he wasn't worried about her having a rifle in her hands because he was controlling everything she did. Sheila had really enjoyed it and laughed when Jeremy told her to think of Mum and Dad's face on the target she was firing at. Sheila wasn't confident with how the rifle worked but she knew how to point and shoot and hit what she aimed for. He said that Sheila had wished that life could be so simple.

Jeremy had then put into her mind that life could be that simple if she trusted him and if she really wanted it to happen. Sheila had said that something had to change in her life to let her be who she wanted to be, and to stop her parents making her feel like she was crazy. He agreed that the whole religious side of things was overwhelming, and he thought Sheila was stupid and made problems for herself by putting up with it and allowing their mother to preach to her and the twins and dictate to her. When they were walking back to the farm, Sheila had gone to feeling angry again and didn't want to go back. Jeremy told her she had to go back inside and not mention she had been shooting or to talk about what they had chatted about.

On the night of the murders there had been a bad atmosphere at the farm, his sister, Sheila, had been okay with Jeremy, but arguments happened between their mother and father and her for most of the afternoon and into the evening. Jeremy said he had been out in the fields working when he saw Sheila and the twins out walking. He told her that he was sick of farming and how their parents stopped them from leading good lives. Sheila had said that she hated them and was really upset that Nevill always supported June against them. A little later he went to the farm himself and an argument was taking place. Sheila had called one of the twins a name that offended June and she had hit him. There was a slanging match between them and ended with Sheila threatening to run away and out of their lives with the children, and she would never allow them to see the children again. She said she would turn the children against them and make sure they hated them. The father had jumped in and started to shout at Sheila, he told her she needed medical help and he was going to call the doctor first thing the next morning and have her put away, it was her who would be saying goodbye to her children, not them, and that's the way it would stay until she was fully better and could prove she was able to take care of them. In Jeremy's own words, it had all kicked off.

The parents went upstairs in anger and upset, the mother was in floods of tears and the father was clearly angry with Sheila and how she was behaving. Jeremy and Sheila remained downstairs in the kitchen. Sheila was acting weirdly, he said her eyes were staring wildly and darting around the kitchen without stopping to look at anything. Jeremy said he knew she had lost it, she was weak and needed no encouragement to let her feelings explode. Sheila was repeatedly saying, 'I hate them, I hate this place.' He had sat her down at the kitchen table and told her to wait there while he went upstairs to speak with the parents, he said he needed to keep everyone calm because it was out of control and it wasn't giving him any time to think.

He told his parents he would calm Sheila down and said to leave them downstairs for an hour or so, he was tricking his parents into thinking he cared as he didn't want to alert them to anything that he was discussing with Sheila. I don't know what time any of this happened, I think it may have been early evening.

Apparently this wasn't the first time anything of this type had happened, there had been arguments before, most of them to do with Sheila not being a good mother and acting immaturely. The mother was always calling her an embarrassment to the Bamber name. Jeremy said both of the parents were religious freaks, their mother often told them she was ashamed of their behaviour. Depending upon Sheila's mind, she would bite back by telling the mother that she and Jeremy did not have her blood in their bodies, they were not her offspring and the Bamber name had been forced on both of them.

According to what Jeremy said, Sheila despised June, and at one time she had met her real mother but that meeting hadn't worked well. Jeremy would say that the family was fucked up because June had serious mental issues and at one time had been in a mental institution. He believed Sheila was messed up because of the mother and because she had been through a lot of failed relationships, he said his parents were not the most stable to raise two adopted children. Jeremy believed he was the only normal one among them!

On the night of the huge row Sheila had talked with Jeremy about her hatred for everyone in her life. She had said to him before that she wished she had the money to go and do what she wanted without being criticised or called a harlot, she wanted to leave her Bamber life behind and move on. Jeremy said he had the same thoughts, he knew it was the time and that both of them were ready and wanted out. He reckoned he wasn't cut out to be a working farmer, more gentry, and that Sheila hated having religion rammed down her throat day and night. He said it was Sheila who first mentioned faking an 'accident' to get rid of the parents, a house fire or something like that. Jeremy didn't think she was being serious at the time and never mentioned it again.

When they were in the kitchen, Sheila had said to Jeremy that as far as she was concerned it was over, she hated her mother and wished she was dead, and that her father was nothing but a weak religious zealot. She was sick of him preaching good parenting to her. 'It's them or us Jeremy,' she said. Jeremy had taken hold of Sheila and looked her in the face and asked if she could really go through with it. Sheila's state changed and she became excited whispering to him that she wanted to do it right away, she felt that no matter what she did she would never be the daughter they wanted. Jeremy agreed and told her how they could get away with it, but it would have to happen quickly and that night. Jeremy said that to win her over he reminded her he was the only one who really knew the pain they both suffered. He said it felt like a eureka moment for both of them.

Jeremy told Sheila that she had to sort the twins out and get them to bed while he went home. He told Sheila he would be back as soon as Nevill and June had gone to bed. He drove home then used a bicycle to get back to the farm later. He arranged for Sheila to let him into the house by the kitchen door and got her to lock it up after he was inside, so her fingerprints would be on it. He had planned how to get rid of the family, and said he had thought of nothing else since talking with Sheila earlier that afternoon.

Sheila was easy to control and to get wound up, he got her so excited that she even wanted to shoot the parents as long as Jeremy was with her and helped her. He went to fetch a rifle and Sheila had followed him into the office, he was looking in a cupboard and heard a muffled noise like someone snorting, when he turned round he saw that Sheila had picked up a shotgun. He said it looked like an elephant gun she was holding because it looked so big in her hands. He took it off her because it wasn't right for the job, too much time reloading and too noisy and messy. Instead he gave her another rifle that she had used before and reminded her how to fire it. He said that there was no silencer or sight attached to the rifle. He would be with her and reload if it was needed but she would have to make sure her shots were good. He asked her if she could still do it, and told her to think about how Nevill and June had talked about her going into a mental hospital and her never seeing the twins again and how they were enemies of the devil. The devil loved her and cared for her, she had to get rid of them.

Apparently Sheila would go on about how the devil visited and talked to her, it really pissed Nevill and June off because they were so religious, they didn't like to mention evil or the devil in their home. About 10 minutes later, the two of them went upstairs to shoot and kill their parents when they were asleep. Jeremy said this is where they would offer least resistance. By this stage he said Sheila wasn't with it, she was hyped up, full of passion and hatred for their parents and was making ranting and snorting noises like a mad woman out of control.

He guided her and told her to shoot the mother first and then Nevill quickly after, the idea was to sneak into the bedroom to a good position beside the bed. He lied to her and said he would arrange it to look like an intruder had broken into the house, been disturbed and had murdered them both. Sheila was then to call the police. Sheila really believed me, he said.

Everything went wrong because June woke up and saw Sheila and him stood in the bedroom. Before he could do anything Sheila was shooting and hit her mother first, the shot didn't kill her. The noise woke Nevill and he sat up in bed next to June, Sheila fired again and Nevill leapt out of bed to try to defend his wife. Jeremy said he was urging Sheila to shoot Nevill again as he wasn't far from her, he managed to get past her before she fired another shot into him, again the shot didn't kill. Nevill had run downstairs and he had followed him. In the main bedroom, he could hear that Sheila was still letting off shots, she told him later it was until her mother stopped moving. Nevill was already badly wounded and Jeremy manhandled him into a chair, Sheila came down into the kitchen and was ready to shoot her father. He said it was madness, Sheila was shouting angry things. Jeremy said he didn't think Sheila could see him, she was that angry. She fired the rifle at their father, but nothing happened, it was empty of ammo. So Sheila ran at him and attacked him, hitting him with rifle. Nevill was apparently so weak at that time that all he could do was raise his arms and cower. Jeremy fought with her to get the rifle out of her grip, he reloaded it and handed it back to her and told her to shoot again and again. Sheila was poking Nevill with the gun telling him to get up, he wasn't moving, he was already dead.

Sheila was pumped up and Jeremy said he had to calm her down. He told her to leave him alone while he sorted things out. He told her to go and thoroughly cleanse herself and to get changed while he cleaned himself up. He said Sheila she was screaming and crying so he went upstairs after her and the way she was acting frightened him, she was talking about the twins being little devils and evil, she was like something possessed. She told him she was going to call the police but he asked her who would look after the twins because it was her who had shot their parents, not him. She said she couldn't bear the thought of anyone else having them. She was screaming that they needed to get out of the house because the devil had taken her over.

Jeremy stopped her from ringing anybody but he was messing

with her mind. There was a discussion about the children being killed. I don't believe he was telling the truth about this because he seemed to dismiss it. All he would say was Sheila had gone mad and he didn't reveal detail about the children being killed, he seemed to be ignoring it. She had told him that she wanted to be with the twins in death and she pleaded, begged him to kill her, so I think that is what he did. He said he told her she must look presentable to the twins in heaven so she had to make sure she was clean and tidy, she did this. She asked to read something from a bible before she died. She sat down in their parent's bedroom, she couldn't bear to think her children might see her die so that's apparently why it happened in that room. He said he was trembling and terrified as he pulled the trigger, the first shot didn't kill her, she flopped backwards and she was staring at him, she tried to speak but it sounded like an animal gurgling and snarling at him. He got into position and then fired a second shot, everything went quiet. He cleaned up and made it look like a murder and suicide, wiping the rifle to get rid of prints with an old pair of socks. He took Sheila's clothes with him and went downstairs, climbed out through a window and left. He told me this version a few times and it didn't vary that much. He was clever because he would make it sound like he was giving an alternative version of events and he never actually said this is what happened, it was always, what if, or, this could be how it happened, and I might have said this, that or the other. It was sort of vague but complete.

Another time when I was talking about why the support of my family had been important to me Jeremy got angry, he blurted out that his so-called family had lied about him. I don't know the full story but he was convinced some of them had concocted evidence that helped convict him. He always said there was never a silencer on the rifle used in the killings. He was shocked to hear the lies they made up about him and that the police must have been in on it too. He was angry with the Judge at his trial because he had called him evil, but he said that his family were much more evil. He told me that all the silencer evidence is made up.

There was a girlfriend of sorts, Julie, who he says double-crossed him because he dumped her and had cut her out of the money. On the night of the murders he rang Julie to tell her Sheila had completely lost it and was threatening to hurt the family. He said when he spoke to her Julie was fucked up with drugs, she was like that most of the time, off her head, and when he called she laughed at him and told him to go back to bed.

I think that's about it. I think he had always intended to kill Sheila, so if that was the case then he must have intended to kill her children as well. That's why I think he wouldn't mention how they died.

Some lifers play the reformed character just to get their own way inside, Jeremy has bigger ambitions, when he talks about his innocence he lies and his lies sound reasonable. It's when you see him when he is at his most vulnerable that you appreciate how devious and cunning he is.

It's not anything new, but for hours on end he sits and go's [sic] through every statement and document in his case, he is obsessed in looking for flaws that he can use to show he was fitted up. He isn't right in his own mind. He thinks that if he finds an overwhelming amount of faults it will show that the police got it wrong and he'll get out. It's unhealthy, unbalanced behaviour.

You have to ask yourself why he never used a lot of this stuff at his trial. It's only when he comes across something in those documents that he blows it out of all proportion and says it shows his innocence. It isn't the real world he lives in, it's a prison. You are dealing with a complex character.

I don't wish to jeopardise my own safety or my family's so I can't reveal my identity, I'm sure Jeremy will know who I am and that worries me. I know that you probably won't believe me because I'm an ex-con, and it doesn't matter to me what anyone thinks because I know I am telling the truth and I've told you now, so it's not my secret anymore. At least I can die without having this shit on my conscience.

*****

Jeremy Bamber has spent almost 30 years in prison for a crime he claims he did not carry out. Only Jeremy Bamber truly knows if any of the above is true or accurate. My own thoughts do not sit kindly with Bamber or his disciples. I genuinely believe he killed Sheila Caffell and the twins, and was clearly more than instrumental in the deaths of the family that morning.

When I first read the statements and case documents and talked to the people involved, I considered whether Bamber could be innocent. The fact is I could never honestly see how Sheila Caffell could commit the crime alone, likewise as has already been discussed, it would have been difficult for Bamber or anyone else, to have killed that family without an accomplice or at least one of them being complicit. If one looks more closely at the case it can seen that Bamber never operated as a solitary individual. Throughout there is a record of him using 'friends' and 'family' as a defence by getting Julie Mugford involved in his murderous plans, Brett Collins to try to sell his story and nude images to a national newspaper, and so on. This, I believe, is because he could ultimately betray those people, blame them for everything in order to protect and save himself. So when it comes to the physical act of murder, it is more likely that he would continue in that vein, manipulating someone else who he could blame, in this instance Sheila.

When one looks at the investigation objectively, there appears more evidence that both he and Sheila could well have been involved together, than either of them acting alone.

It is obvious that Sheila Caffell was struggling mentally and had been for some considerable time. In 2006 I was contacted by a woman who claimed that she had attended college with Sheila and had known her quite well and they had often gone out for a drink. The woman, who referred to herself as Alison, told me that Sheila often acted crazy and could get very angry about things, especially her family. Alison also told me:

> There was clearly some ill feeling in that family because Sheila rarely spoke fondly of any of them, she didn't seem to have time for them, she always seemed so mentally mixed up and confused about her life, I think she felt the parents were pushing in one direction and she wanted to go in a totally different direction. I do remember her saying that her brother was moody and selfish and they weren't really close in a trusting way. All I think she wanted was to be loved, and because she was adopted she never really felt that she was part of that family. I know they provided for her but that wasn't love or affection, you can't buy that and she didn't get it. I'm no psychiatrist but I know when something isn't right and when someone is sad inside, Sheila was sad, she seemed to feel that she wasn't ever good enough or wanted. I think she needed to be needed.

A neighbour in the Maida Vale flats where Sheila lived described her as 'the woman with mad scary eyes.' Others referred to her as vacant, almost angry looking much of the time. She seemed to have highs and lows, there was no in-between or grey areas. Some claimed to hear her shouting abuse and slamming doors, this they felt was down to her being a drug addict. There is no doubt in my mind that underlying everything Sheila suffered from serious mental health problems and this made her both vulnerable and susceptible to external manipulation, a situation that Jeremy Bamber used to his own advantage – how many times did he disparagingly refer to her as a nutter? He knew only too well what buttons to press to wind his sister up or to get her in an emotional state.

There have been claims that Sheila would not know or recognise one end of a gun from another but, as will be seen, this is not a wholly accurate statement. David Boutflour originally denied that Sheila had any knowledge of guns and she had never been seen firing one. Yet in court and during the trial, when questioned by Geoffrey Rivlin QC, he was forced to reassess that belief, and after denying all knowledge that Sheila had been on a shooting holiday to Scotland with him he said:

> I have a feeling now you have brought back the grey matter a little, Sheila may have come up with me on one occasion. It's such a long time ago I cannot recollect but she certainly did not carry a gun. She may have fired a gun off in the party perhaps.

We are also aware from paperwork contained within the City of London Police investigation report of 1991, that both David Boutflour and Anthony Pargeter initially agreed in front of DCI Jones, that Sheila could have been capable of using a gun to kill the family! It is a further known fact that Colin Caffell, when first informed of Sheila's death and the murders, said, 'Oh no then she finally did it.'

It's evident from information available at the time that there were people who believed her capable of killing. One friend, Freddie Emami, described a horrific incident about one of Sheila's psychotic episodes in which he was frightened by her violence. During this, Sheila had not recognised anyone visiting her and later had a complete memory loss about the matter.

If she was sufficiently distressed and had been ably co-erced into such a state by the situation with Nevill and June with the threat of losing her children, the misguided belief that people wanted to hurt her and that the devil loved her, and through the constant encouragement and manipulation of Jeremy Bamber, could it not be that she lost control and with her brother by her side had killed her parents? She may not have been aware who she was killing, but unfortunately we can never truly know.

The evidence of the sound moderator does sit most uncomfortably, not only forensically but also its provenance can be questioned. Then we have the evidence of farm secretary Barbara Wilson whose recollection of events has altered dramatically. When interviewed pre-trial by Chief Inspector Dickinson she said that she found Jeremy 'very pleasant, always okay with her. Probably got on better with him than my own son.' She said she never heard him say anything bad at all. However, in a television documentary screened in November 2013, Wilson recalls being frightened of Bamber and provides instances of how he deliberately tried to annoy June.

Elsewhere, DS Stan Jones noted on the police Home Office Large Major Enquiry System (HOLMES) programme (45/22) that Ann Eaton had told him in confidence that Barbara Wilson had said that Sheila had said words to the effect 'all people are bad and should be killed.' No statement to this effect was ever recorded, it has been alleged that it was part of the investigation never actively pursued.

In the twins bedroom, scrawled inside a wardrobe/cupboard door were the words, 'I HATE THIS PLACE.' No one knows who the author of the inscription was or when it happened. It's for certain that Bamber would like us to believe that it was a final chilling message to the world from Sheila, scratched during a psychotic episode. Realistically, it tells us nothing about the murders and does not materially affect the trial or outcome.

The police did make mistakes in this case, but none that could genuinely change the course of the trial. The sound moderator evidence was weak and is, in my opinion, suspect by virtue of the procedural inefficiency of some of the police officers concerned. Some witnesses have in more recent times altered parts of their recollections when speaking with the media, I put that down to the passage of time and media pressure and unless we were there, we cannot know how the question being answered was originally phrased. Documentary makers are effectively journalists, they seek sensational claims, it helps sell the product, so an impartial review of the evidence is unlikely, certainly it could never be proposed as serious evidence to prove innocence or guilt. One needs only to look at internet footage produced by some Bamber disciples to see how sensational and compelling they make their evidence seem when in fact it isn't, all that is produced is a regurgitation of arguments that hold no legal credibility, which is why Jeremy Bamber remains in prison.

Having committed to an in-depth and long term study of this case, I don't believe Jeremy Bamber to be innocent, the evidence shows that he didn't have an unfair trial, and I certainly don't believe he was framed by anyone. I am of the opinion that it was both he and Sheila who were responsible for the killing of their parents and that he murdered both the twins and Sheila. I further believe he orchestrated the entire crime, abusing Sheila's mental vulnerability, showing if anything an increased degree of culpability!

It is clear that throughout his life he has cunningly manipulated and used people for his own needs, and in my view is without emotional balance and compassion. The words he uses now are carefully phrased to portray him as a kind, considerate son/brother/uncle who has suffered. They are meant to tug on emotional strings causing society to have some sympathy for him, and clearly a minority have fallen into this engineered trap and do believe everything he utters.

Finally, do I believe Jeremy Bamber deserves to be released? He must surely now be institutionalised, and it would undoubtedly be problematic for him should he ever gain any sort of release. However, that is but an observation, and it should not be used against him in any way. His release is something for the courts and judicial system to decide, but I do consider that he could present a danger to the public if released, and furthermore, I think it fundamentally wrong that a life-serving child killer has access to all manner of media where he can freely roll out his own propaganda. Finally, we should remember that innocent lives were lost during the commission of this crime, a loss that affected many and continues to do so. My sympathy lies with the living relatives, particularly Colin Caffell who lost his children, and with the Boutflour family relatives for the unsupported suffering and vile accusations they have had to endure from faceless, nameless cyber-bullies. That is a crime that should be investigated, prosecuted and stopped immediately. Only then might Jeremy Bamber and his disciples understand the hurt they have caused to those involved and some closure brought to this sad affair.

Appendix

For the first time in print, below is the official Summary of Judgment document produced for the 2002 Appeal.

Case No: 20011745 S1

IN THE SUPREME COURT OF JUDICATURE

COURT OF APPEAL (CRIMINAL DIVISION)

REFERENCE BY THE CRIMINAL CASE REVIEW
COMMISSION

UNDER SECTION 9 OF THE CRIMINAL APPEAL ACT 1995

Royal Courts of Justice

Strand, London, WC2A 2LL

Date: 12th December 2002

Before:

LORD JUSTICE KAY

MR JUSTICE Wright

and

MR JUSTICE HENRIQUES

Mr M Turner QC and Mr M Duck instructed for the Appellant

Mr V Temple QC and Mr J Laidlaw and Ms A Darlow instructed
for the Respondent

Hearing dates : 17 October 2002 to 1 November 2002

SUMMARY OF CONCLUSIONS
CONTAINED IN THE JUDGMENT

1.   This summary is not intended to replace or explain anything contained within our judgment in this case. Its purpose is simply to enable the basis of our decision to be assimilated more quickly than would be possible if the judgment had to be studied in full.

2.   Jeremy Nevill Bamber was convicted on 28 October 1986 of the murder of five members of his family, his mother and father, his sister and his sister's twin sons. He then renewed his application to the full court and the full court presided over by the Lord Chief Justice, Lord Land, refused his renewed application.

3.   The case was unusual in that it was common ground that only two explanations for the five killings were possible. The first was the prosecution case that Jeremy Bamber entered the farmhouse owned by his mother and father at night and shot the five members of his family with a rifle that was lawfully in the farmhouse. The second, the defence case, was that Sheila Caffell, the appellant's sister who had a history of psychiatric (sic) evidence, had shot the other four members of her family with the rifle and then turned the gun upon herself committing suicide.

4.   In the initial stages the Police thought it likely that the second explanation was correct. Some officers, however, thought that some of the findings were inconsistent with this explanation and members of the Bambers' extended family did not believe that it was consistent with their knowledge of Sheila Caffell. Approximately one month after the killings, the appellant's girl friend, Julie Mugford, came forward and gave the Police a statement describing how the appellant admitted involvement in the killings. This led to the arrest of the appellant and to more extensive inquiries into what had occurred. As a result of that inquiry the appellant was charged with the murders and in due course convicted.

5.   Since the date of trial, two further Police inquires (sic) have been held into the case. The first, an internal inquiry conducted by Essex Police, focused on the Police inquiries in the early stages and was no doubt a response to criticisms made at trial of the Police for assuming that they were dealing with a case of murder by, and suicide of, Sheila Caffell without investigating as carefully and thoroughly the available facts as they should have done.

6.   The second inquiry followed a complaint made by the appellant about the conduct of the Essex Police which resulted in the matter being examined by the City of London Police on the instructions of the Home Office.

7.   These two inquiries gathered a vast amount of documentary material and generated further statements from witnesses and reports. This material has, so far as possible, been made available to the legal representatives of the appellant.

8.   In due course application was made to the Home Office for the case to be referred back to the Court of Appeal. That application was transferred to the Criminal Cases Review Commission (the CCRC) when that body was formed.

9.   Having studied the papers and made such inquiries of its own as it deemed appropriate, the CCRC referred the case back to the Court of Appeal as a result of fresh scientific evidence. Once a case has been referred back to the Court of Appeal, under the legislation as it presently stands, it is open to an appellant to raise any grounds of appeal that he wishes without any prior assessment of the merit of the ground [sic] by either the court or the CCRC. Those advising the appellant raised 16 grounds of appeal, one of which was abandoned before the hearing.

10.   In opening the case to the court, Mr Michael Turner QC, on behalf of the appellant made wide ranging allegations of serious misconduct by the Police ranging from fabrication of evidence to the deliberate concealment of documents which it was appreciated would be of assistance to the defence.

11.   The court has examined with care all these allegations and

where there seemed any possibility that they might be justified, and heard oral evidence.

12.   As a result of the evidence given by those involved, Mr Turner himself recognised that many of the allegations made in his opening speech, including the most serious of fabrication of evidence, simply could not be sustained and by the conclusion of the appeal he did not suggest to the court that they were right.

13.   He has, however, maintained that documents have come to light as a result of the two inquiries that show that some important information was deliberately concealed from the defence by the Police. We have examined with care each of the documents to which he has referred and we have found no evidence at all to suggest that there was any deliberate concealment of any documentation by the Police or by anyone else connected with the prosecution.

14.   We have also considered whether any documents were not disclosed to the defence which should have been so disclosed. The regime of disclosure in 1986 was very different from that which operates now and it may be that under the new regime, some of the documents would have been made available to the defence even though they were not at that date. Our conclusion is that the disclosure that was given to the defence at the time was comparable to disclosure in most major cases in 1986 and that there was no evidence of impropriety or want of care in this regard. In so far as we have identified documents that under the modern regime, or even under the regime operating in 1986, should have been made available to the defence, we have considered whether any of these documents might have had an impact upon the jury's verdicts. For the reasons which we have given in detail in our judgment we conclude that they would not.

15.   Thus we have concluded that there was no conduct on the part of the Police or the prosecution which would adversely affect the safety of the jury's verdicts. Equally we are satisfied that despite the extent of the material revealed by the inquiries, no fresh information has come to light which could have impacted

upon the jury's conclusions.

16.	We have anxiously scrutinised the fresh scientific evidence, which caused the CCRC to refer the case back to this court and we deal with this aspect of the matter in paragraphs 452-508 of our judgment.

17.	At trial an important part of the prosecution case was that at the time when the shots which resulted in the death of Sheila Caffell were fired, the rifle must have had fixed to it a sound moderator (a silencer). If this was so, Sheila Caffell could not have fired these shots and hence could not have committed suicide because it would have been physically impossible for her to have reached and pulled the trigger. The contention that the sound moderator was on the rifle at this time was based in large measure, although not entirely, on the finding of human blood within the sound moderator which when subjected to blood grouping tests was consistent with being the blood of Sheila Caffell but not of any of the other four who were shot. At trial it was accepted by the prosecution scientist that there was a 'remote possibility' that the blood could have been a mixture of blood from Mr and Mrs Bamber.

18.	Evidence, which the jury might have accepted as showing that the scientist's evidence about the origin of this blood could not properly be relied upon, might have had any impact upon the jury's ultimate conclusion and thus would call into question the safety of their verdicts.

19.	At the time of the trial the science of DNA comparison had not been developed and it was clearly right that the CCRC should have explored whether DNA evidence, which could now be obtained, cast doubt upon the scientific evidence at trial.

20.	Initial tests suggested that there was no trace of any DNA that could have originated from Sheila Caffell now to be found in the sound moderator and that there were traces of DNA which could well have come from the blood of Mrs Bamber and of a male person, who could not be identified and therefore could have been Mr Bamber. This evidence seemed to support the defence

o

case on this point at trial and point away from the prosecution case. The case was, therefore, referred to the court by the CRRC.

21.   Since the date of referral further DNA testing has taken place. This provides evidence of the presence of DNA within the moderator that could have originated from Sheila Caffell although there is nothing, or at best, very, very limited evidence, that it did in fact do so.

22.   Over and above the further testing, we have been provided with evidence which we consider highly material on this aspect of the matter. The first is detailed evidence as to what it was that was tested for blood grouping. It was a flake of blood removed from a point where it was lodged against one of the baffle plates and the wall of the moderator. That flake was removed and in order to carry out the blood grouping tests, was necessarily used up in the process. Therefore it has not been possible to subject the material which was used for blood grouping testing to DNA testing. No direct comparison between the blood grouping tests and the DNA findings was, therefore possible.

23.   The other evidence which we have had before us in this regard related to the possibility of contamination. The form of DNA testing used to produce the results in this case is highly sensitive and even a few cells may be detected. Thus contamination is a very real possibility. If the moderator were to be the subject of DNA testing today, very extensive precautions would be taken to avoid contamination. Because there was no such testing in 1986 no remotely comparable precautions were taken and in any event the moderator and other exhibits were handled at trial without the possibility of later testing ever being considered. As a result a scientist instructed on behalf of the appellant to consider the blood evidence, who carefully reviewed all the available evidence, concluded that there were 'specific feature of this case that render the results completely meaningless'.

24.   In the circumstances, we concluded that the available evidence did not suggest that the evidence given by the forensic scientists about blood grouping, which in any event

acknowledged the possibility, albeit as a remote one, that the blood was a mixture of blood from Mr and Mrs Bamber, could be thought to be unreliable.

25.   One other aspect of the blood grouping evidence was raised and this was evidence critical of the forensic scientist's evidence at trial that the possibility of the blood being a mixture of blood from Mr and Mrs Bamber was a remote one. We heard evidence from a scientist called on behalf of the appellant but concluded that since his evidence was based upon a theory unsupported by either any experimentation or any material contained in scientific literature and which had no apparent support from other scientists, it would not have had any significant impact upon the jury causing them to form a different view of the prosecution scientist's evidence.

26.   For these reasons, explained in full in our judgment, we have concluded that the jury's verdicts were safe. It should be understood that it is not the function of this court to decide whether or not the appellant committed these murders. Under our system of justice that is entrusted to the jury, drawn from ordinary members of the public. The Court of Appeal does not hear the evidence and does not see the witnesses and thus cannot reach any fully informed view on the matter. The court only interferes with the jury's findings of fact if they are ones which could not properly be reached on the evidence or if material is now available to suggest either that the jury were misled by the evidence or that they were not provided with a proper opportunity to reach a fair conclusion because evidence that would have assisted them was not made available to them. We can see no reason on the information before us to think that any of these situations have arisen in this case. Thus we do not doubt the safety of the verdicts and we have recorded in our judgment the fact that the more we examined the detail of the case the more likely we thought it to be that the jury were right although as explained we can never go further than that.

27.   We finally draw attention to paragraphs 514-520 of our judgment in which we deal with an application to call fresh

evidence made by the prosecution. The prosecution had shortly before the appeal caused a study to be made of the distribution of bloodstaining associated with the body of Sheila Caffell. This study resulted in a conclusion that Sheila Caffell could not have killed herself. On its face, this fresh evidence was further powerful evidence that pointed to the guilt of the appellant. However we concluded that evidence of this kind was available at the date of trial and should therefore have been called at trial if the prosecution were to rely upon it. In any event, we did not see how the evidence could properly be tested without reference to all the other evidence at trial which, of course, we had not heard or seen. It was therefore impossible to assess what effect it might have had on the jury if called at trial even though it may well have represented another formidable string to the prosecution's bow in a case which has to be seen as a very strong prosecution case. For these reason we did not admit this evidence and it was not tested before us.